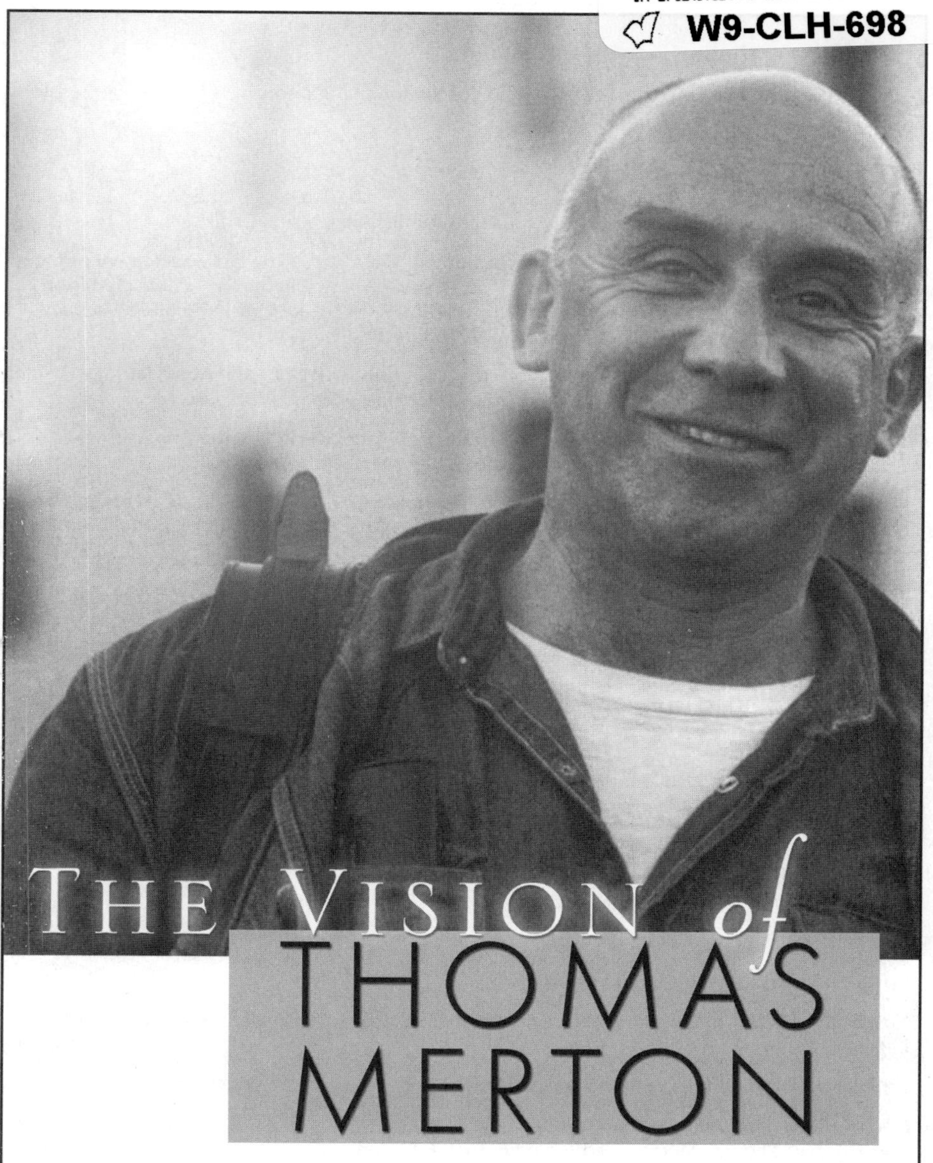

THE VISION *of* THOMAS MERTON

PATRICK O'CONNELL

ave maria press Notre Dame, Indiana

Ave Maria Press acknowledges the permission of the following publishers for use of excerpts the following books:

The copyright page continues on page 255.

www.avemariapress.com

International Standard Book Number: 0-87793-991-8

Cover and text design by Brian C. Conley

Cover photograph of Thomas Merton by John Lyons. Used with permission of the Merton Legacy Trust

Printed and bound in the United States of America.

Library of Congress Cataloging-in-Publication Data
The vision of Thomas Merton / edited by Patrick F. O'Connell.
p. cm.
Includes bibliographical references.
ISBN 0-87793-991-8 (pbk.)
1. Merton, Thomas, 1915-1968. I. O'Connell, Patrick F.
BX4705.M542V57 2003
271'.12502--dc21

2003007335
CIP

Contents

FOREWORD

PATRICK HART, OCSO

It seems appropriate to be writing a foreword to this volume honoring the late Robert E. Daggy. We had cooperated on many Merton projects during the years when he was director of the Thomas Merton Studies Center at Bellarmine College (now University). One stands out as especially significant for both of us: the facsimile edition of *Monks Pond: Thomas Merton's Little Magazine*[1] by the University Press of Kentucky at Lexington. We gathered all the original artwork from the Abbey Archives, with Bob doing the introduction ("Beyond Cheese and Liturgy") while I provided an afterword. It turned out to be one of the most enjoyable projects we were involved in over the past twenty-five years, although the royalties were negligible.

Robert Daggy was "discovered" by Tommie O'Callaghan at a time when the Merton Collection in the former library at Bellarmine really needed someone with Bob's training to move in and bring order out of chaos. Bob did just that, sorting out manuscripts, some of which were still unpublished, identifying correspondents of Merton, as well as organizing the enormous collection of art work and photographs that were crying out for acid-free containers before it was too late. I first became acquainted with Bob Daggy during these early years in an effort to assist him in his work of identifying the correspondents. Our friendship continued for a quarter of a century.

Of course, Daggy was over-qualified for the job. In addition to his undergraduate work at Yale on manuscript collections and memorabilia, he did graduate studies at Columbia on the religions of the Far East and earned a doctorate in history from the University of Wisconsin, Madison. Although he knew very little of Merton when he arrived at Bellarmine, a quarter of a century later he had grown and developed into one of the great authorities on the life and writings of Thomas Merton.

The friends and colleagues of Robert Daggy represented in this volume all tell us something of their relationship to Bob, or expatiate on an aspect of Thomas Merton that was often inspired by Daggy. It is a fitting memorial for someone who became very important to all of us, without ever losing his marvelous sense of humor. It has been said that he did not "suffer fools gladly," but I can testify to the fact that he often overlooked protocol and became just one of the Merton aficionados, joining in the general dance. No one can doubt his academic qualifications or his uncanny ability to get to the heart of Merton's thought; yet he was also aware of the larger number of members of the International Thomas Merton Society, of which he was second president, who discovered in Merton's writings something that changed their lives. Although always helpful to scholars in their research, he had a sympathetic ear for the simple lovers of Merton whose words had meant so much to them over the years.

Daggy really began to excel in Merton studies with his editorship of the second volume of Merton letters, *The Road to Joy: Letters to New and Old Friends*,[2] which brought us into an even greater collaboration, since I was asked by William Shannon, the general editor, to edit the third volume on monastic renewal and spiritual direction, *The School of Charity*. We also began at this time giving panels at the various meetings of the ITMS concerning Merton's letters.

One of the last projects we worked on together was the private journals of Thomas Merton. Bob agreed to edit the fifth volume, and fortunately, his health was sufficiently strong for him to complete this last work. He mailed off the proofs to the publisher just prior to the final collapse of his health. For this reason, I am happy to see in this volume Victor Kramer's article "'Crisis and Mystery': The Changing Quality of Thomas Merton's Later Journals," and Jonathan Montaldo's "Loving Winter When the Plant Says Nothing: Thomas Merton's Spirituality in His Private Journals." They articulate so well what all the editors were striving to achieve in this long-range project.

Lawrence Cunningham's preamble to his "Interiorizing Monasticism," which appears in these pages, speaks for all of us who worked closely with Bob Daggy over the years: "He did his job so well that he served as a conduit for all those folks, serious and not, who trudged to the Center to commune with the works of Thomas

Merton. In writing about how Merton interiorized monastic life and made it available to others I am, in a sense, attempting to explain why so many people came and still come to the Merton Center—a center forever marked by the love and energy that Bob lavished on it." Well said, and I know many of us can readily say "Amen" to those words of tribute.

Robert Daggy's introduction to the fifth volume of the Merton journals, *Dancing in the Water of Life*,[3] is probably his best writing on Thomas Merton, and happily it appeared shortly before Bob's death on December 15, 1997. He was buried in the Abbey of Gethsemani's secular cemetery on December 17, following a special ecumenical liturgy presided over by Abbot Timothy Kelly and joined by members of the Gethsemani Community who had known him. The burial, coincidentally, was on the twenty-ninth anniversary of Thomas Merton's own funeral liturgy on a bleak afternoon in 1968. May his ever-expanding spirit now join in the eternal dance of life.

Introduction

Patrick F. O'Connell

In the summer of 1998, when I came across some unpublished poems of Thomas Merton in the Columbia University Library archives, my spontaneous response was to think, "Won't Bob Daggy be interested in this!" Of course I knew that the former director of the Bellarmine College (now University) Thomas Merton Center had died the previous December, but he had been so much a part of my own study of Merton, as he had been for so many others, that it was difficult to realize that he was no longer there to offer insight and encouragement.

For twenty-three years, Robert E. Daggy served as the nerve center for the field of Merton studies. First as archivist and associate director, and then from 1980 through early 1997 as director of the official repository of Merton's papers and the largest collection of Merton materials in the world, Bob Daggy had an unrivalled knowledge of the vast trove of published and unpublished writings that Thomas Merton left behind as his legacy. He served as both guardian and as guide, allowing access only to those materials made available to the public by the Merton Legacy Trust, and directing researchers to those sources most pertinent and most valuable for their own areas of study. Through the pages of *The Merton Seasonal*, which he edited for almost his entire time at the Merton Center, he not only provided scholars with an outlet for their research, but also kept readers of Merton at various levels of expertise informed and involved. As one of the principal founders of the International Thomas Merton Society, as the main organizer of its first General Meeting, held at Bellarmine in 1989, and as the society's first vice president and second president,

Bob Daggy was instrumental in spreading knowledge of and interest in Thomas Merton throughout the U.S. and indeed the rest of the world. Along with his friends Brother Patrick Hart and Monsignor William Shannon, Bob Daggy was one of the trio of giants in the first generation of Merton scholars.

When the Publications Committee of the ITMS convened shortly after Bob's death, it was decided that a collection of essays on Merton by Bob's friends and colleagues would be a fitting tribute to his memory. And so the idea of this volume was born. The committee decided to invite as contributors Bob's fellow editors of the two great Merton publication projects, the five volumes of selected letters, and the seven volumes of the complete journals, as well as those who worked closely with Bob in the Merton Society itself either as presidents or General Meeting program chairs. Merton Legacy Trustee Tommie O'Callaghan, a close friend both of Thomas Merton and of Bob Daggy, was invited to open the volume with a short memoir of Bob, which she has done in a way that is both informative and moving. In her essay, she mentions Bob's particular interest in Merton's artist father, Owen, an interest reflected in the opening essay (an article by Bob himself that was previously unavailable in this country) on Merton's "search" for his father, which continued throughout the younger Merton's life and which has spurred further research on Owen Merton. Not the least of this research was by Bob Daggy himself and might well have resulted in a full-scale biography of Owen had Bob lived.

The two essays that follow look at themes that run throughout the entire range of Merton's writings. Christine M. Bochen examines Merton's understanding and articulation of the basic Christian theme of faith, and demonstrates that while it may not initially seem particularly prominent in Merton's writings, it is nevertheless fundamental to a proper appreciation of his thought. In his essay on "Interiorizing Monasticism," Lawrence Cunningham examines the initially puzzling question of how a cloistered monk could have such a continuing influence on Christians, and even on nonbelievers, living lives far different from that inside monastery walls, and demonstrates that Merton touches the solitary dimension that exists as an integral part of even the busiest activist.

The next pair of essays considers from two quite different perspectives the massive legacy of Merton's private journals, now completely published. Victor Kramer looks at the journals through a literary lens, examining both the shape of the published sequence and how this version affects the perceptions of the reader, along with the evolving purpose and use of the journal for Merton himself, with a concentration on what Kramer sees as a critical turning point early in the 1960s. Jonathan Montaldo approaches the same material from a more psychological and spiritual perspective, seeing the radical honesty of the journal project as exposing a kind of spiritual poverty that by the paradoxical reversal of the Gospel is evidence of abundant grace and mercy.

Thomas Del Prete examines a relatively neglected but fascinating and significant aspect of the later Merton's wide-ranging synthesis of knowledge and religious experience, his investigation of the spiritual implications of new discoveries about the physical nature of the universe. This focus is connected with Merton's more long-term interest in the world of nature, evident particularly in his journal observations, which Monica Weis shows to be related both to the traditional Christian belief in the sacramentality of the created world and to the just emerging ecological consciousness of which Merton was an early proponent.

The next two essays delve into the corpus of Merton's poetry. My own piece considers the eucharistic focus and the more general awareness of the sacramentality of the created world in some poems from Merton's first volume of verse, *Thirty Poems*. Bonnie Thurston turns her attention to the contemplative awareness expressed in a number of Merton's later poems, in which he was able to convey deep religious experience without using the explicitly religious language of his earlier verse.

The final set of essays explores Merton's relationship to Eastern thought. Erlinda Paguio examines Merton's interest in the work of Indian art historian and philosopher Ananda Coomaraswamy, who continued to fascinate and influence Merton from the time of his Columbia Master's thesis through the last years of his life. William Shannon provides a more general overview of Merton's deepening dialogue with Eastern wisdom and its crucial importance for our own time, focusing on five insights Merton drew from Western spiritual classics that were fundamental in finding resonances with the spiritual traditions of the East.

The title *The Vision of Thomas Merton* was chosen for this volume to reflect a continuity with two previous collections of essays, *The Message of Thomas Merton* and *The Legacy of Thomas Merton*, both edited by Brother Patrick Hart, whose gracious tribute to his friend Bob Daggy in the foreword provides another element of continuity. But it also reflects the fact that each of the contributors to this book was enabled to see Thomas Merton and his work more clearly and more broadly because of the writings and the personal assistance of Robert E. Daggy. For this we will always be grateful, and we hope that these essays will contribute to sharpening that vision for the readers of this collection as well.

Robert E. Daggy

Courtesy of Thomas Merton Center, Bellarmine University.

Remembering Bob Daggy

Thomasine (Tommie) O'Callaghan

Though it may sound strange, I've always felt that Thomas Merton sent us Bob Daggy. Certainly we couldn't have found anyone better qualified or better suited to oversee the Merton Center for the twenty-three years that Bob was there. Providence must have had something to do with it.

The process that led to Bob's arrival began, of course, with Tom's death. My husband, Frank, was out of the country when I heard the news through Dan Walsh, who had been my teacher as well as Tom's. The next day, I made the trip out to the monastery alone, which I had never done before, since usually I was picking up or dropping off Dan, who was teaching philosophy to the young monks, or coming with the family for an occasional picnic with Tom on the monastery grounds. When I got there, I met Brother Patrick Hart for the first time; he had returned from a period in Rome earlier that year and was serving as Tom's secretary, taking care of all his correspondence and other business while he was away on his trip to Asia. Now it was Brother Pat who took me up to the hermitage, where we loaded up the car with three or four file cabinets filled with Tom's correspondence and other papers. According to Tom's directives, if anything happened to him I was to take charge of the papers, since I was the local member of the Trust he had set up a few years earlier.

These file cabinets sat in my dining room for three or four years, maybe longer. I gradually went through the hundreds of folders of Tom's correspondence, pulling out all letters written to Tom that were private or sensitive, "conscience matter," as they were called by the Trappists, and putting them away in a safe-deposit box, along with the "restricted journals" that were not to be published for twenty-five years after Tom's death.

Finally Naomi Burton Stone and J. Laughlin, the other two members of the Merton Legacy Trust, came to Louisville for a meeting, and we decided that it was time to move the papers to the "Merton Room" at Bellarmine College, which Tom had designated as the repository for his papers about five years before he died. But we knew we needed someone who would be responsible for overseeing the collection, cataloguing it, getting and keeping it in order, and making it available to scholars, who were already beginning to come to do research on Tom and his work.

I got in touch with Dr. George McWhorter, who was, and still is, an archivist at the University of Louisville, and who lived nearby. He came and looked at the materials and said we needed someone who was a combination of an archivist, a historian, and a philosopher to take charge of a collection like this. Quite a tall order! He said he'd keep his eye out for likely prospects. I wasn't sure what to expect, but in a very short time he got back in touch with me and said he might have just the person for the job. Dr. Robert Daggy, originally from Indiana, had graduated from Yale, had later returned there to work for two years as an archival assistant, had earned a Ph.D. in history and educational policy studies at the University of Wisconsin, and between Yale and Wisconsin had even done graduate work in Chinese and Japanese at Columbia, Tom's old school. He fit the requirements perfectly—that's what I mean about feeling like Tom had sent him to us. At the time, he was living in Louisville and painting houses while looking for a more permanent job. We went out to lunch, and I liked him very much. I recommended to the other trustees that we hire him, they agreed, and so Bob Daggy began the work that he would continue almost to the end of his life.

One of the other "qualifications" Bob had for the job was that he wasn't Catholic. At that time, he knew nothing about Merton; I'm not even sure that he had heard of Tom, though I suppose he must have. We were very concerned that no "cult" develop around Tom, and so we preferred a professional who had no previous attachment to Merton, rather than someone inclined to put Merton on some sort of pedestal. But of course, Bob immersed himself in Merton and his work over the years and became a first-rate Merton scholar; he gave himself the educational experience of his life, and Merton obviously became very important to him personally as well as professionally.

Initially the Trust planned to pay Bob's salary, but Bellarmine volunteered to pay half of it, which we readily agreed to. Within a fairly short time, he became a full-time Bellarmine employee. From 1974 to 1980, Bob's title was curator of the Thomas Merton Collection and associate director of the Thomas Merton Studies Center of Bellarmine College. Msgr. Raymond Treece, who was the official director of the Merton Center for most of that period, retired from the position in 1980, and Bob became the director of the Thomas Merton Studies Center, the chief of research of the Merton Legacy Trust, and also the curator of special collections and the college archivist at Bellarmine, positions he held through the spring of 1997, when his illness would force him to resign. He was also a lecturer, first in the Bellarmine education department, where he taught courses on "Personal Health and Safety," and then in the humanities department, where he taught a variety of courses in film, which he loved, as well as courses on Merton. He developed various adult education courses on Merton, and beginning in the mid-1980s, coordinated a summer Elderhostel program on Merton that was wildly popular.

Bob showed the same passion for organization in many areas of his personal life as he did in his work as archivist. He loved clothes, and he had the process of coordinating his outfits down to a science. He was a great cook and was famous for decorating his dinner table to fit in with the appropriate season. He was an avid collector of ceramics, particularly fruits and vegetables; he was very much a collector—of books, of films—and everything was always in its proper place. He was very interested in the genealogy and memorabilia of his own family; this probably explains his particular interest in Merton's family background, especially in Owen and Ruth, Tom's father and mother.

When Bob began at Bellarmine, the "Merton Room" was still in the library, but it quickly outgrew the space available and moved up the hill to the basement of Bonaventure Hall, the building that formerly housed the Franciscans who used to teach at the college and the place where Tom Merton spent his last night before beginning his Asian pilgrimage. It was the Center in its Bonaventure location that was really associated with the "Daggy era." It was tucked away in a far corner of the campus, and most of the students probably didn't even know it was there, although people from all over the country and even the world came to Bellarmine to visit and work there. The end of Bob's time at the Center coincided almost exactly with the end of the Merton Center's stay in Bonaventure Hall. With the building of the new Brown Library on campus, the Merton Center moved back into the library after about twenty years away, but by this time, Bob had given up the directorship. I'm not sure how he would have settled in at the new Center—for one thing, he wouldn't have been able to smoke there! I took him around the new quarters after Erlinda Paguio and I had supervised the transferal of all the archives—and of course he had some "constructive criticism" to make of the new arrangements! He was able to come to the dedication of the Center in October of 1997, including the official naming of the central room of the Center the Robert E. Daggy Reading Room, but by that time, he was in a wheelchair, and he had only two months left to live.

During those twenty-three years of curatorship, Bob provided tremendous assistance to me and the other trustees. He took many of the headaches involved in watching over the archives on himself and so relieved us of the burden. He came to know the collection inside and out, knew exactly where to find everything that was there, and was able to guide both established scholars and younger students writing dissertations to exactly the sources that would be of greatest benefit to them. Together we built up the correspondence files by getting in touch with those we knew Tom had written to and asking them to donate any letters they had, which most of them did. Bob also worked very closely with Brother Patrick Hart in transferring materials from the monastery archives to the Center.

Bob also served as a kind of gatekeeper for me personally, keeping away the merely curious, who might want to "shake the hand that shook the hand of Merton," as it were, but putting me in contact with friends of Merton, like Canon Donald Allchin from England, for example, or Merton scholars like Victor Kramer and Anthony Padovano, many of whom would stay at our house. Bob made possible a growing circle of friends connected through Merton and the Center.

Over the years, Bob became a very close personal friend himself. He lived for most of that time just down the street from us, and we saw him often. Perhaps surprisingly, though, we spent very little time talking about Merton, other than in the course of business concerning the Center and the Trust. Memories of Bob that stand out are of very ordinary things, such as watching *Jeopardy!* after dinner, when between them, Frank and Bob would answer virtually every question correctly. As a team they would have been unbeatable. Bob was especially good at any questions on the movies; Frank and I finally decided that we had to take one of Bob's film courses, but by that time, unfortunately, he was starting to get sick, and never taught the course again.

Bridge was perhaps just as important as film in Bob's life. For a while, he was the editor not only of *The Merton Seasonal* but of *The Kibitzer*, the newsletter of the Louisville Bridge Association. He was successively historian, parliamentarian, and president of the Association; in fact, his term as president of the Louisville Bridge Association almost overlapped his term as president of the International Thomas Merton Society! During the last year or two of his life, when he was able to do progressively less and less, he was still able to play bridge at the top of his form, so we spent a good deal of time together at the card table.

It was about the time that the Merton Center Foundation was forming, to provide a stable financial base for the Center, that Bob's illness started to become evident. One of the people attending an early organizational meeting asked me what was the matter with Bob. Seeing him regularly as I did, I hadn't noticed any change, but as I looked more carefully, I could see that he was getting thin and worn-looking, and before long, it was obvious to others as well as to himself that he wasn't well. He had taken a trip the summer before to China with his friend Dr. Cyrus Lee, and for a while we thought he might have picked up some sort of parasite there. But the local doctors weren't able to figure out what was wrong. Finally I asked Abbot Timothy Kelly of Gethsemani if he would underwrite a trip to the Mayo Clinic for Bob. He immediately agreed, so I took him up to Minnesota for about a week, and the doctors there finally diagnosed his illness as systemic mastocytosis, a rare blood disease. The doctors were hopeful that treatment could arrest the progress of the disease, and Frank or I would regularly go down the street to Bob's house to give him his shots. But it soon became evident that he was continuing to become weaker, that the medicine wasn't working.

I last saw Bob in mid-December 1997. Frank and I were going away on a trip to New Zealand a couple of days later, and we and Bob both knew that he probably would not be there when we returned. We had a wonderful visit, which included talking about the plans for his funeral—we had arranged with the abbot for it to take place at Gethsemani. As we flew above the Pacific, I said a rosary for Bob—something I hadn't done for quite some time—and just as we were walking into our hotel room in Auckland the phone was ringing with the news from our son-in-law that Bob had died at just about that same time. And so once again, we lost a friend half a world away, though this time it was we who were in the East, and of course this time we had known what was coming. Bob was buried in the secular cemetery at Gethsemani, right in front of the abbey church, on December 17, 1997, two days after his death and twenty-nine years to the day after Thomas Merton was laid to rest in the monks' graveyard to the side of the same church. It was certainly not someplace that he could ever have imagined as his place of burial when he came to that luncheon interview more than twenty years before, but everyone who knew him would agree that this is where he belongs. Frank was the executor of Bob's will, and so in time, Bob's papers also came to our house, and in turn were passed on to the Merton Center, which is where they belong. Bob's legacy and Merton's have become inextricably connected.

Many, many people came to know and love Thomas Merton through Bob Daggy, people who came to the Center, who read books of Merton's that Bob edited, who read Bob's articles in *The Merton Seasonal* and elsewhere, who heard Bob's talks on Merton, or attended his retreats on Merton. But for many of us, it is just as true, and just as truly a gift, that through Thomas Merton, we came to know and love Bob Daggy.

Owen Merton with infant Tom

Courtesy of Thomas Merton Center, Bellarmine University.

Thomas Merton and the Search for Owen Merton

Robert E. Daggy

> *"Death ends a life, but it does not end a relationship, which struggles on in the survivor's mind toward some resolution which it never finds. . . . But, still, when I hear the word 'father'!"*
>
> – Gene Garrison
>
> in Robert Anderson's *I Never Sang for My Father*

"I realized today after Mass what a desperate, despairing childhood I had. Around the age of 7–9–10, when Mother was dead and Father was in France and Algeria."[1] Thomas Merton wrote these plangent words in his journal on January 24, 1966, one week before his fifty-first birthday. Merton, a monk of the Cistercian (Trappist) Abbey of Gethsemani near Bardstown, Kentucky, has emerged at the end of the twentieth century as a significant figure in outlining human and spiritual values for our confused and troubled world. Writing from his monastery on the fringes of society, he engaged issue after issue, seeing them with a clarity—at times a frightening clarity for one supposedly removed from the mainstream—which enables us to grasp the root and cause of many problems even if we, like him, cannot always find solution and resolution.

Merton has become a guide for us about so many questions that it is not surprising to find him involved in a conundrum which pervades our twentieth-century literature—the search for the father. He captures for us, once again, as he relates his own story, the *zeitgeist* of our time. He mirrors the disquietude, the restlessness, even the rootlessness of the century. Like William Faulkner, Chaim Potok, Tennessee Williams, Eudora Welty, Richard Wright, Robert Anderson, and others, Merton was engaged in a search for his father. With these other writers, he wanted more from his father, more of his father. Merton wanted more even after his father's death—which did not provide closure, which did not end the relationship for the son, which left an emptiness he could never fill. He becomes a companion along the way for all of us struggling to make sense of our relationships with our fathers.

Merton grasped, with mingled joy and pain, that he and his father were "in each other all along." And he further grasped that the search for his father was, as it invariably must be, a search for himself. What comes through in Merton is that the struggle isn't easy. Where there is pain, it may be too much to bear, far too much to express. We may be unable to separate what we want our fathers to *be* from what our fathers are or were. He once remarked: "Most men cannot live fruitfully without a large proportion of fiction in their thinking."[2] As he engaged in the search for his father, Merton's experiences remind us over and over again that a certain amount of "fiction" may influence and color the search. The answers we find may be no answers—either because we cannot see the answers, or because we reject the answers, or because the answers fail to fit into the picture we are limning of ourselves and our fathers. We may go looking for one thing and find another. We always want "more" somehow and so we may, as Merton did, go looking for something and find it because that is what has impelled our search.

Thomas Merton entered Gethsemani at age twenty-six, fifty-two days short of his twenty-seventh birthday. The date was December 10, 1941. Twenty-seven years to the day later—fifty-two days short of his fifty-fourth birthday—he died near Bangkok, Thailand, on December 10, 1968. His life divided—quite neatly in fact—in half, one half before the monastery and one half in the monastery. It has been pointed out, frequently and often tiresomely so, that to understand Merton and his place in the experience of our century, we must understand monasticism and the monastic structure which gave discipline and substance to his life and writings. Certainly! No one can deny that. The monastic structure is important in understanding Merton, but it is also important to know how and why that structure worked for him. He brought a great deal of baggage into the monastery with him, and what he "unpacks" in his writings—about human values, human relationships, human aspirations, even about monasticism itself—comes from deep-seated feelings inside him, feelings instilled in the half of his life before he was a monk. Nexus after nexus connect the two halves of Merton's life.

Clues to Thomas Merton lie in his father's story. Owen Merton's story is as palpable to the twentieth century as is his son's, for it, too, is a story of "what went on in the heart of man in this cruel century."[3] We have a staggering amount of autobiographical material which the son produced about himself. Owen didn't write about himself *per se,* but a surprising amount of material about him has survived in letters, in biographical novels, in accounts by people he knew. As Thomas Merton searched for his father, he may not have known that so much material existed—had survived—about Owen. The son had not, partially because he simply wasn't there, been privy to a lot of information. The search, then, was impelled in part because he didn't know a great deal about his father and he wanted to know, to have more. In a 1957 letter to A. A. MacGregor, for instance, he couldn't remember when his father was born.

Nevertheless, Owen Merton had bequeathed a great deal to his son—a certain way of looking at the world, a certain self-contradiction, a predilection for a particular lifestyle, a commitment and dedication to "vocation." He also bequeathed pain and angst. While pain and angst may inevitably be part of the father's bequest and may just as inevitably be a catalyst in the son's search, Thomas Merton is more interested in the "positive" parts of the father's bequest. Where he expresses pain or despair or other emotion, as in the quotation which began this essay, it is more the pain of *not* being with his father. It is rarely the pain of what his father may have done or failed to do. It is never the pain of blaming his father for the bad things in his life. The search for Owen Merton is not that kind of search.

Owen Heathcote Grierson Merton (1887–1931) was born in Christchurch, New Zealand. His life, like his son's, divides in half: he was in New Zealand basically until he was twenty-two (1909), and he spent the latter twenty-two years (1909 to 1931) in Europe, America, and Africa. He thought of himself as a *painter,* in much the same way his son would later think of himself as a *writer.* Thomas Merton survived his father, but the relationship didn't end with death. Owen died of a brain tumor in a London hospital when his son was almost sixteen. It had been a long, drawn-out illness, and his death came after some years of increasingly erratic behavior (caused in part, no doubt, by the brain tumor). At the end, he was unable to speak, though he had moments, his son tried to believe, of lucidity. On January 20, 1931, the day of his father's funeral, young Tom Merton wrote to Owen's art teacher, Percyval Tudor-Hart: "I naturally will feel his absence greatly, for he was always so awfully good and kind to me, and we enjoyed life so much together in the South of France. I cannot quite accustom myself to the knowledge that he and I shall never visit our old haunts together anymore."[4]

This short note contains many clues. Tom enjoyed their life *together*. He wanted to be with his father. He wanted to pal around with him. Owen left, and it is his absence that gives pain. What comes through—in this note and later—is that Tom Merton saw his father as a kind of buddy, someone to knock about with. Owen was not paternal in the usual sense of the word, nor was he much of an authority figure to or for his son. Owen once wrote: "He is exactly like his mother in most ways, which means I am a bloody fool to him, except when my foolishness is thought interesting by authority, then I must be wonderful."[5] Owen does not appear in his son's accounts as a domineering, tyrannical father—not as one whose authority was exercised or heeded (as authority). That was not Owen's paternal style. He felt (as had Tom's mother) that their son must be independent, learning to live and to think for himself. Owen had written earlier: "Tom *is* good about understanding he has to look after himself. He always cries when he gets the importance of something I lecture him about."[6] There are other reports that Tom Merton cried when told what to do. (Are there shades here of his later chafing at times against abbatial authority?) He was described as "intractable" and Owen's mistress, Evelyn Scott (of whom more later), remarked: "Tom is and will be until he is big enough to be set adrift a constant obstacle to piece [*sic*] of mind."[7]

Owen stated about Tom: "It came on him all of a heat when he got away from me, that I was pretty good to him."[8] Echoes of this appear in Tom's statement to Tudor-Hart that his father was "always so awfully good and kind" to him. He never wavered in this judgment. He later said: "My father wanted to [take] care of me, but he did not precisely know how."[9] He didn't know how! What does this mean? Was it that Owen didn't know how, or was it that he didn't take care of his son as his son saw other fathers doing, or was it that he didn't take care of his son as his son wanted? Is what we are to see unfold in the son a kind of repentance for recalcitrance while his father lived, an apology for not appreciating Owen while he was alive? Can this explain why Owen's good intentions come to loom larger than his failures?

Something was left unsaid, unspoken between father and son. Selima Hill, daughter of Owen's friend, James Wood, has noted: "He didn't tell his son he was dying."[10] Is it possible that Owen, remembering Tom's reaction when his mother told him she was dying, feared to tell his son? The possibility of Owen's death only came clear to Tom when he visited him in the hospital in the summer of 1930. It had been several months since he had seen his father. He later said: "When I saw him, I knew at once there was no hope of his living much longer."[11] But, by that time, Owen could no longer talk. Whatever may have been left unsaid—because saying was impossible—in Owen's last months started his son toward a resolution of his relationship with his father in which Owen becomes larger than life. In 1933, when he was eighteen, Tom wrote again to Tudor-Hart, "I wish either my brother [John Paul Merton] or myself had inherited even a small part of our father's genius" (*RJ,* 57).

Geniuses are often allowed behavior which is not brooked in other people, and Thomas Merton, it seems, made such allowance for his father. Years later in *The Seven Storey Mountain,* he attributed even more extraordinary qualities to his father: "[His] was a great soul, large, full of natural charity. He was a man of exceptional intellectual honesty and sincerity and purity of understanding" (*SSM,* 83). In writing of his father's death, he said: "Here was a man with a wonderful mind and a great talent and a great heart: and, what was more, he was the man who had brought me into the world, and had nourished me and cared for me and had shaped my soul and to whom I was bound by every possible kind of bond of affection and attachment and admiration and reverence: killed by a growth on his brain" (*SSM,* 84).

Thomas Merton was not ready for the relationship to end and parting was painful. An aside in *The Seven Storey Mountain,* prompted by Tom's visit to his father in the hospital, gives us a quick glimpse of the pain. The aside is about suffering, but the suffering is as much Tom's interior pain as it is Owen's physical pain. "The one who does most to avoid suffering is, in the end, the one who suffers most: and his suffering comes to him from things so little and so trivial that one can say that it is no longer objective at all. It is his own existence, his own being, that is at once the subject and the source of his pain, and his very existence and consciousness is his greatest torture" (*SSM,* 82–83).

Was Merton his own prophet here? Did he try to avoid "suffering"—the pain of separation from his father? At fifty-one, he still felt the pain of what he called his "lost childhood."[12] A year after that, he could write to his friend Ed Rice: "You think I no got angst? Man, think again. I got angst up to the eyes" (*RJ,* 291). Did he continue to suffer in the search for his father and himself? Did he suffer because he tried to avoid suffering? Was the overblown view of Owen in his public pronouncements at variance with what he felt within himself? Did he fictionalize Owen, for himself and for others? Is this why Merton never faced certain facts about Owen in his writings? Did he deliberately set out to edit from his accounts of his father anything that was negative, anything that caused him to suffer?

The answer would seem to be yes and no. Thomas Merton does not tell us everything about his father (or his mother), but what he does tell us is not, to him at any rate, fiction. His view of his father's legacy to him is not a distortion. To realize why it is not distorted, we must go back to who and what Owen Merton was. Thomas Merton was proud of his parents, proud of who he thought they were, proud of the fact that they were artists, proud of the fact that they had not run with the herd—many of the qualities that would later be attributed by others to him. He said: "Being the son of an artist, I was born the sworn enemy of everything that could obviously be called 'bourgeois'" (*SSM,* 133). His good friend—some say his best friend—Robert Lax has recently commented: "I certainly got the impression that he liked and admired his father, and liked his paintings. That he liked his mother's painting too . . . I think that Merton liked being the son of two artists and being an artist himself. (I feel now he felt he was part of a tribe, and knew where he belonged in it.) Some of our gang, not I but others, felt more like changelings in their families. Couldn't imagine how they could have been born to parents so unlike themselves. Not Merton."

Owen and Ruth Jenkins Merton (1887-1921) were bohemians of the first water, part of that complex of artists and writers who wafted through London, Paris, and Greenwich Village before, during, and after the First World War, and who would be dubbed by Gertrude Stein "a lost generation." Owen and Ruth thought of themselves as artists, and they were both, studiedly and intentionally, "marginal persons." This was to leave deep and pervasive influences in their son. He wrote:

> *After all, from my very childhood, I had understood that the artistic experience, at its highest, was actually a natural analogue of mystical experience. It produced a kind of intuitive perception of reality. . . . I had learned from my own father that it was almost blasphemy to regard the function of art as merely to reproduce some kind of a sensible pleasure or, at best, to stir up the emotions to a transitory thrill. I had always understood that art was contemplation, and that it involved the action of the highest faculties of man. (SSM, 202–203)*

Ruth Jenkins, an American, was self-consciously "daring." She had gone to Paris in 1909, alone and unchaperoned, to study art (hardly the thing for a young woman to do in 1909). There she met and fell in love with Owen Merton. Both tried to assure their anxious families that there was no cause for alarm, but what the families feared did happen: Owen and Ruth lived and slept together before their marriage. They preferred the company of artists and writers whom they considered *avant-garde,* who espoused ideas and techniques congenial with their own. They, too, were searching—and they did not look to traditional values as final answers, in lifestyle or in art. Merton gave a rare insight into this aspect of his parents when he wrote in 1965:

> *[Rabindranath] Tagore is the kind of writer whom my Father and Mother admired and whom I therefore grew up to respect. . . . Why was Tagore popular with my parents' generation? Because so many of them were open to the East without knowing precisely what they were open to. They wanted some Eastern figure with whom they could, to some extent, identify themselves, and Tagore made a definite enough impression to fill this role admirably for the West. Hence his popularity, and hence the readiness of the Europe of the turn of the century and World War I to listen to him with reverence as a spokesman of Asia.*[13]

What his parents respected, he respected. They were open to new ideas and to areas ordinary people—the bourgeoisie—were not. Though he respected his mother, the picture he paints of her is much harsher than the one of Owen. Yet he does not relate that her New York neighbors found her "weird." She dressed "artistically" and, it has been said, people avoided engaging her in conversation as she walked through the neighborhood because she expressed ideas that seemed far-out and unconventional. She was a person who could provoke embarrassment in others. And she had decidedly "modern" ideas about child-rearing. What came through to her young son, in her desire to make him his own person, was that she was demanding. She *expected* a great deal from him, more, in fact, than he later felt he was able to deliver. In his late poem *Cables to the Ace,* he asks a mother (his mother?): "What do you teach me . . . What do you want of me . . . What do you seek of me" (*CP,* 400–401).

Ruth Jenkins Merton died of stomach cancer at Bellevue Hospital in 1921. Her older son was six-and-a-half years old. To the end, she "expected" things of Tom. She wrote him a letter telling him she was dying and expected him to understand. He didn't. Despite social practice which kept children isolated from dying and death, despite hospital rules which proscribed visits by children his age, he blamed his mother for writing him a letter, and he never forgave her for not telling him in person that she was dying. It left deep scars in young Tom, and the pain was to emerge in different ways for the rest of his life. The usual interpretation has been that Ruth's death ended family life for Owen, Tom, and John Paul—that her death started Tom on the lonely path of "lost childhood" and plunged him into a knockabout existence. It surely did in a way, but things had not been settled and smooth before her death.

At eighteen months, little Tom had been uprooted from his birthplace in the south of France (he was later to say "I am mortally homesick for the South of France, where I was born"[14]) and the small family fled to the United States. Tom was born in Prades on January 31, 1915—"in a year of a great war," as he put it (*SSM,* 3). Owen and Ruth had gone to the south of France, ostensibly to paint, but also because they could live there on next to nothing. But World War I was raging and, as the war encroached and as their "pacifist" feelings made them reject the idea of Owen's entering the army, they attempted to leave France. They managed to secure passage from Bordeaux in July 1916.

In the United States, they tried to avoid taking money from Ruth's affluent American parents. But Sam and Martha Jenkins ("Pop" and "Bonnemaman" to Tom), anxious over the welfare of their grandsons, often underwrote the finances of the little household. This only increased tension and conflict in a family already afflicted with tension and conflict. Tom later wrote: "Our family had been one of those curious modern households in which everybody was continually arguing and fighting, and in which there had been for years an obscure and complicated network of contentions and suppressed jealousies" (*SSM,* 160). Sam Jenkins didn't much like Owen Merton, nor did Ruth's unmarried brother Harold who still lived with his parents. Owen didn't seem interested in "work" as Sam defined it, though he did try various things to make a living. It was simply never the kind of living Sam found appropriate. Things weren't without conflict on Owen's side of the family either. His mother (in New Zealand) had had extreme doubts about the regularity of his relationship with Ruth—despite remonstrances to her from both of them. It was later reported that Ruth was "*not* good friends" with Owen's sister Gwynned, who had followed her brother to England.[15] When Owen's mother, Gertrude Grierson Merton (1855–1956), visited on Long Island in 1919, she was not delighted by what she found. Michael Mott points out in *The Seven Mountains of Thomas Merton* that something seems amiss in the family photographs taken during the visit, that Tom in particular is scowling and seems, at age four, unhappy with the proceedings (Mott, 18–19).

Owen and Ruth continued to pursue their "art" and continued to associate with "artistic" types. They knew or met several Greenwich Village and New York bohemians, such as Marianne Moore, Djuna Barnes, Lola Ridge, Kay Boyle, and others. Owen managed to exhibit some paintings, including a small show at Alfred Stieglitz's "291 Gallery." But he didn't make any money, and this consternated Sam Jenkins. (Tom was later to portray his grandfather as a blustery, though amiable and somewhat silly, Babbitt-type of American.) Through it all, Owen reiterated to his in-laws and others: "Painting is the only thing I want to do. . . . it takes all I have—and satisfies me—and I have no time to think of anything else."[16] The chronology is hard to follow, but it is clear that Owen was gone from his family, pursuing his art, a great deal of the time. There are strong hints that the marriage was headed for divorce when Ruth was diagnosed with terminal cancer. Even then, Owen was away much of the time. He was in England through much of her illness. As late as July 1921 (three months before her death), he was teaching art classes outside London. He *was* in New York when she died, and his son recorded that he wept. But then comes one of the most curious passages in *The Seven Storey Mountain:* "Mother's death had made one thing evident: Father now did not have to do anything but paint. He was not tied down to any one place. He could go wherever he needed to go, to find subjects and get ideas, and I was old enough to go with him" (*SSM*, 16).

Curious, yes. Unfeeling, even more so. Is this the payback for expectations which had become too much for Ruth Merton's son? She had become an encumbrance to Owen and his vocation. Her death liberated both father and son. Here we find the major key to Thomas Merton's continuing search for his father: he wanted to be with him! Ruth's death enabled it. The passage also exonerates Owen from responsibility for stability in his sons' lives. He is exculpated from the post-Industrial Revolution role of the father as "provider." Tom, like Owen, was more than willing to let Sam Jenkins pay the bills while deriding him as crass and materialistic. In a strange twist, Tom could even excuse his father's absences due to his "business" (painting). It was not, he says, always possible for him to be with Owen, but this, he also says, did not bother him. No, even in his later search—though desperate and despairing and anxious to be with his father—the son sees his father's commitment to painting as a valid, legitimate, spirit-based *vocation*!

So, in Thomas Merton's version, the knock-about existence of the next few years makes sense. He was to say more than once that he accepted with equanimity anything his father did, or did to him. As we shall see, he was not always so equable as he later pretended. He could accept being dragged here and there by his father. That gave him freedom and got him away from his grandparents, though he could even accept being deposited for periods with them. He could accept, with remarkable composure, Owen's abandoning him in Massachusetts in 1923. But he could not accept—and would not accept—his father's affair with novelist Evelyn Scott.[17]

Tom had been delivered from one woman—his mother—whom he saw as austere, dominating, demanding. Even at age seven, he was not about to come under the control of another such woman. It would probably have been the same with any woman Owen met since he didn't want to share his father, but Evelyn was, from all reports, even more demanding than Ruth had been. In the pages of *The Seven Storey Mountain,* Owen becomes after Ruth's death a kind of contemplative *manqué* to his son, a man devoted to his art. Yet this is at variance with the facts before about 1926. Tom knew—what child wouldn't?—that his father wanted for years to marry Evelyn and make her his stepmother. We glean nothing from the son about this: about his father's having an affair, about his desire to remarry, about his sexual being.

Granted, like many sons, Tom may have had little knowledge of his father's sexuality. What he might have known, I suspect he would have rejected. He may not have known that Owen had probably had homosexual experiences and that he may well have been bisexual.[18] At age seven, he may not have realized in Bermuda—where Owen dragged him in 1922—that his father was actually sleeping with Evelyn *and* her common-law husband, Cyril Kay Scott. (Owen tried to "protect" Tom from the milieu by lodging him, for a time, alone in a boarding house across the island.) But Evelyn's son Creighton—the same age as Tom—grasped then or later what was going on and recorded with great repugnance facts about the *ménage à trois* in Bermuda.[19]

Merton was later to say: "That beautiful island [Bermuda] fed me with more poisons than I have a mind to stop and count" (*SSM* [BC], 36). There was some good reason why he made this remark, and it was almost certainly pointed in some way toward Evelyn and the *ménage.* We gain clues from a lengthy aside, a sermon really, which was cut from the published version of *The Seven Storey Mountain.* The passage is convoluted, full of suggestion and pious mutterings, but one can sense resentment and hurt in it as well.

> *What a terrible thing is the plasticity and gentleness of the mind of a child! How quickly it takes on shapes and forms of distortion! With what simplicity and love it welcomes disorder and accepts disfigurement! How hard it is for the most careful and conscientious parents to foresee all the unsuspected occasions when sickness and corruption can seep into a child's soul! Sometimes they themselves are the cause of what they would give their lives to prevent, by some word or gesture or an action which perhaps because of some completely subjective context in the child's own mind, something that utterly avoids detection and diagnosis, turns into a seed of one of the deadly sins.*
>
> *It takes all the special understanding and sympathy of the love that only exists between parents and children, to even begin to protect a child against moral disfigurement: and, by the way, when I speak of moral disfigurement, I have in mind more than the one kind of sin. The godless think that all religious people are preoccupied, as they themselves are, with unchastity, as if there were no other disorders. And against all of them, is needed the watchfulness of a Father's and a Mother's special love. More than that, even the natural solicitude and sympathy of parents for their children is not strong enough or sure enough without grace from God.*

> *When I think of my own childhood, and of the love and conscientiousness of my Father, and his well-meaning desires to bring me up an intelligent and happy person: and when I think how completely impossible it was for him to succeed, under the circumstances in which he had placed himself and me, I cease to wonder at the wars and the crimes that have filled this century with blood. Because of all the millions of children that have been born and have grown up in it, how few have reached maturity under the constant protection of religion and grace, and how many have grown like weeds on any dung they could find to put their roots in! . . .*
>
> *When I was eight years old, running loose among the rocks and the prickly pears of Somerset Island, Bermuda, I was in just about the same position as the child of divorced parents. (SSM [BC], 35–38)*

Thomas Merton refers first to the Scotts as "some people he [Owen] had met" (*SSM,* 19). Later he calls them Owen's "friends, who were literary people and artists" (*SSM,* 19). And thus, he dispensed with Evelyn. She was a difficult person, but she found young Tom equally difficult. She wrote to her friend Lola Ridge: "Tom is a morbid and possessive kid and Owen is made morbid about Tom through various things that occurred in connection with Ruth."[20] After she and Owen finally separated in 1926, she wrote: "Little Tom *hated* me. What was there to do?"[21] And Owen himself admitted after the affair had ended: "I know I could not have reconciled the children & the question of either living with or marrying Evelyn. Tom's jealousy and irreconcilableness are perfectly enormous."[22] Young Tom Merton did not want his father to remarry. He didn't want a stepmother, a rival for his father's affection and attention. He especially didn't want any such woman telling him what to do and getting in the way of the life he wanted to live with Owen. Evelyn may not have been particularly nice to Tom, but he was reported as "devilish"[23] toward her. He may have known, as well, that he had allies in his grandparents and uncle who strongly disliked Evelyn (though he may not have known that they referred to her as a "whore"[24]).

While his role in "eliminating" Evelyn at the time makes sense, his subsequent public elimination of her from his life *and* his father's raises several questions. What nine- or ten-year-old boy forgets the woman who might have been his stepmother? Why would such a woman, no matter how much she was hated, *not* be mentioned in an autobiography hailed as "candid, revealing, and utterly honest"? But the elimination of Evelyn goes even beyond that: Merton never—anywhere—mentions her by name. Robert Lax has said: "If I heard anything of father's lady-friend (and I must have)—it surely wasn't much." For some time I thought that the hatred and pain ran so deep in Thomas Merton that he could not, even years later, face the specter of Evelyn Scott. That may be true to an extent, but I now suspect it was more than hatred and pain that caused him to edit Evelyn Scott out of his life and out of his autobiography. She didn't fit into his "search for his father" as the story was unfolding in his version.

Now I play with a scenario like this: Isn't it likely that young Tom Merton, who was from all reports a precocious and unusually sophisticated boy, knew that Evelyn Scott was a novelist? The fact that he refers to her and to Cyril as "literary people" suggests he did know. Knowing this, might he not in 1933, at age eighteen, have recognized her name and picked up a copy of her novel *Eva Gay* which was published that year? If he did, it wouldn't have taken Tom Merton long to realize that much of *Eva Gay* is a thinly disguised biography of Owen Merton. He would have realized that Evan Garrett is his father and Louise his mother—and that Eva Gay is really Evelyn herself. The novel would, no doubt, have shocked young Tom. He would certainly have rejected the description of his father as "a fumbling, brutal, and fragmentary man."[25] In fact, he probably would have rejected *all* that Evelyn had to say about Owen. One can imagine—in this scenario—his hatred for Evelyn rekindling. His father, his wonderful father, had died and he had now been betrayed by this harridan of a woman. If he also happened to read Evelyn's *Bread and a Sword*, published in 1937, it would have compounded things. It is also based, though more loosely, on Owen Merton's life as an artist. It is, as D. A. Callard puts it, "a story of economic necessity versus artistic integrity" (Callard, 151). Owen Merton is Alexander Williams, whose marriage collapses because he cannot support his family. His wife dies and by the end of the book, he is "hopelessly compromised and defeated" (Callard, 151). Tom had, by that time, fallen under the spell of Mark Van Doren at Columbia—a man who remained a mentor for the rest of his life. Did he know that Van Doren's wife, Dorothy, reviewed *Bread and a Sword?* Did he read her words: "Mrs. Scott does not convince us that her artist is worth saving" (see Callard, 153)?

If he read these novels, one can imagine that he would not have wanted anyone else to know that Evelyn's unflattering depictions were of his father. Her portrayals didn't square with his developing view of his father. And so, Evelyn had to go! When he came to write his autobiography (and even his later writings), I find it reasonable to assume that he feared to mention her lest it lead people to her novels. He needn't have feared, but he couldn't have guessed that Evelyn would be a quickly forgotten novelist (forgotten actually by the time he wrote *The Seven Storey Mountain*) and that her books would not be much read. In fact, the connection with Evelyn Scott was not discovered until a dozen or so years after Thomas Merton's own death. But, once Evelyn was eliminated, once she was reduced to an anonymous and innocuous footnote in *The Seven Storey Mountai*n, it no doubt became easier to ignore her in subsequent writings. I doubt, though, that he ever managed to eliminate her from his private thoughts, any more than his father managed to do.

The Bermuda *ménage* ended in the spring of 1923. Owen, Evelyn, Cyril, and Creighton left in late summer for Europe. Thomas Merton later wrote: "I was deposited, of all places, in the house of a very rich lady at Buzzard's Bay, in Massachusetts" (*SSM* [BC], 40). That didn't last long. Sam Jenkins came and fetched him back to Long Island where he was to live with his grandparents until August 1925. He may have felt at age fifty-one that these years with his grandparents were a time of despair, but he was wary when Owen returned from Europe in June 1925. He recorded: "As he landed in New York, he was a very different person—more different than I realized—from the man who had taken me to Bermuda two years before" (*SSM,* 28). Merton doesn't tell exactly how he was different, but Owen himself said he was in "a violently hysterical condition."[26] He had, a year before, suffered a strange illness. It was thought he was dying. The irrationality which he displayed was undoubtedly a precursor of his subsequent illness. He may already have been suffering from the brain tumor which eventually killed him. But we don't see, in the son's account, Owen as he was at the time: still weak from illness, undernourished, strained in body and soul, exhausted from the affair with Evelyn and from years of living in poverty. No, Tom only tells us he had grown a beard—which he didn't like! He also says he returned "in a kind of triumph" (*SSM,* 28) because he had sold some paintings. In actual fact, Owen had come to make a last ditch effort to reconcile his in-laws to a possible marriage with Evelyn, to extract funds from them so he could live and paint, and to take his sons back to Europe with him. The Jenkins family was as wary as Tom and, as things developed, they were not receptive to Owen's plans.

Michael Mott reports that there was "a bitter and angry dispute between Owen and Sam Jenkins, with Harold Jenkins now taking a strong part against Owen" (Mott, 26). The basic problem was Evelyn. Sam refused to finance any arrangement which included her. She wrote to Lola Ridge: "If Tom is to live with him, he and I, living together, would need to marry at once. If we married at once there would be no help whatever from Jenkins or people here [London]."[27] It was clear that Sam Jenkins wanted the relationship regularized if Tom was to live again with Owen, but he wouldn't provide money if Owen married Evelyn. Tom himself wasn't happy: he didn't want to go to Europe, and he certainly wanted no arrangement which included Evelyn. As Sam Jenkins stood firm, Owen said: "I just busted!"[28] The situation reached denouement at the Jenkins summer home in Ashuelot, New Hampshire, when Owen attempted to commit suicide. This apparently swayed Sam Jenkins who relented, forked over money, and let Owen take Tom back to Europe. Though Owen had mentioned "children" in his letters, John Paul was not allowed to go.

Thomas Merton was later to say of going to France with Owen: "It really saved me" (*LL*, 12). The obvious conclusion is that, as he looked back, he found life with Owen more "nourishing" than life with his grandparents would have been. But was he with Owen? At first he was at school, but living with his father who wrote: "He depends on me very much."[29] Owen was already looking forward to a time when Tom could be left elsewhere. That time came soon. Tom was packed off to a *lycée* at Montauban; hustled off to live with peasants in the summer; jerked from the *lycée* in 1928, and taken to England where he was dumped on Owen's aunt and uncle and then, as in France, packed off to boarding school.

After 1925, Owen withdrew into self-imposed solitude. He wanted, again, to devote himself to his painting. He wrote to Evelyn: "I think I had better stay quietly by myself for a long time."[30] It is at this point that we can see parallels between Owen's life and Tom's life as he related it in his writings. Father and son had both engaged in "illicit" (did they believe "sordid"?) sexual escapades. Both came to see such involvement as detrimental to themselves, their spirits, and their vocations. Both came to see sexual abstinence as necessary to their lives. Both withdrew to the fringes of society—Owen to the French countryside, Tom to the knobs of Kentucky. Owen called the house which he started to build at St. Antonin his "hermitage." Tom was to call at least two places at Gethsemani his "hermitage." But Owen's solitude was not long-lasting, and it may have been no more eremitical than his son's. Illness struck again, and he died in 1931. At sixteen, Tom was not ready for the relationship to end and the struggle to "find" his father remained with him for the rest of his life.

The story, as the search progresses, is a positive one. The important period, to the son, is the one in which his father lived in solitude and pursued his art. Little bitterness—about anything—surfaces through the years. No, Owen was responsible for Tom Merton's becoming the person he became. It was Owen's ideas and spirit which "shaped" his son's soul. For this, the son is grateful. And, in his gratitude, his affection, attachment, admiration, and reverence—he tried constantly to convey what a good artist his father was. But beyond the fact that an artist father inspired an artist son, Owen was instrumental in starting Tom on the path of finding himself and his God. In *The Seven Storey Mountain,* Owen becomes, as D. A. Callard puts it, "the lodestar of his life" (Callard, 71). Anthony T. Padovano put it this way: "Merton's entire adult life is a search for artistic and spiritual excellence, one sustaining the other, both converging into a striking unity, each initiated by his father."[31] Merton himself said: "Of us all, Father was the only one who really had any kind of a faith. And I do not doubt that he had very much of it, and that behind the walls of his isolation, his intelligence and his will, unimpaired, and not hampered in any essential way by the partial obstruction of some of his senses, were turned to God, and communed with God, Who was with him and in him" (*SSM,* 83).

To Merton, his father was a religious man, and he died, in his son's view, in a state of grace. Yet, this was said of a man who had agreed with his wife to give his son no religious training—this of a man whose own mother was shocked to find in 1919 that her four-year-old grandson did not know "the Lord's Prayer" (see *SSM,* 9)—this of a man who wrote in 1926 that if there were a just God, "I could believe in him."[32] But Owen was to do even more. He was to figure, after death, in his son's first real religious experience, which took place in Rome in 1933. Merton related:

> *I was in my room. It was night. The light was on. Suddenly it seemed to me that Father, who had now been dead more than a year, was there with me. The sense of his presence was as vivid and as*

> *real and as startling as if he had touched my arm or spoken to me. The whole thing passed in a flash, but in that flash, instantly, I was overwhelmed with a sudden and profound insight into the misery and corruption of my own soul, and I was pierced deeply with a light that made me realize something of the condition I was in. . . . And now I think for the first time in my whole life I really began to pray. . . . There were a lot of tears connected with this, and they did me good, and all the while, although I had lost that first vivid, agonizing sense of the presence of my father in the room, I had him in my mind, and I was talking to him as well as to God, as though he were a sort of intermediary. . . . I do not offer any definite explanation of it. How do I know it was not merely my own imagination, or something that could be traced to a purely natural, psychological cause—I mean the part about my father? It is impossible to say. I do not offer any explanation. . . . But whether it was imagination or nerves or whatever else it may have been, I can say truly that I did feel, most vividly, as if my father were present there, and the consequences that I have described followed from this, as though he had communicated to me without words an interior light from God, about the condition of my own soul. (SSM, 111–12)*

After this experience, the search for Owen Merton continued—even if expression of it was intermittent. In April 1939, Merton returned to Bermuda. Was the trip supposed to be a cathartic one? Robert Lax said some years ago that it was a "David Copperfield" kind of trip, one on which Merton was mining "the darkest things" in his past (Mott, 21). Yet, Merton's letter to Lax from Bermuda is enthusiastic, referring to where he had last lived with Owen: "Bermuda is the place in the world most like the South of France. It is, hear me, splendid!" (*RJ*, 145). And the poem he wrote while there—"Aubade: Bermuda"—is a sunny, joyous little poem (*CP*, 691–92). Lax has more recently said: "He had a good feeling about Bermuda (which he passed on to me)—because he'd been there with his father." Where were the poisons in 1939? Part of Merton's search always seems to have been to visit "old haunts" where he had been with his father. It fits into his later search in the 1960s, when he tried to collect materials and paintings.

The search merged and submerged after his entrance into Gethsemani into a search for a kind of spiritual father, a search which meshes, of course, with that for his physical father. In the late 1950s and early 1960s, he returned to thoughts of the "lost father." He was, by that time, literally without immediate family. His American grandparents died in the 1930s, and his brother, John Paul, died in 1943 in an airplane crash. His other grandmother died in New Zealand in 1956—at the age of 101. He began the attempt to re-establish contact with family members in the United States, England, and New Zealand. He had been alienated from some of them for many years, particularly his uncle, Harold Jenkins.

In this period, some materials were sent to Merton at Gethsemani. He was especially delighted with letters written by his father—and these letters renewed his interest and reconfirmed him in his opinion of Owen. His aunt, Gwynned Merton Trier, sent two letters in 1966. He wrote to her: "For a long time I have been thinking of looking into all that [Owen's paintings]. I never got down to doing anything about it. . . . Have you any notion where his paintings are? . . . [D]o you think there is any possibility of finding Father's pictures, if they survived the war, and doing something about them? Perhaps an exhibition could be arranged in this country and then those not sold could be placed somewhere where they could be seen" (*RJ*, 80).

It becomes clear here that there was a lot Thomas Merton didn't know: that his father had left forty paintings to Cyril Kay Scott, a number of paintings to James Wood, and had left over 150 in Tudor-Hart's possession (these had been brought to Canada). Merton took one of the letters sent to him by "Aunt Gwyn" and edited it for publication. He called it "Sincerity in Art and Life," and it was published in *Good Work,* the quarterly of the Catholic Art Association, in the spring of 1967.[33] He remarked in his introductory note: "It is typical of my Father's outlook on art and on life also, and expresses what seemed to him essential to 'good work'." The letter confirmed Merton's impression of his father as a good and sincere and dedicated artist, and it must definitely have confirmed—with its references to Christ—his view of his father as a spiritual, if not a religious, man. It must have reinforced the picture he had drawn of Owen nearly twenty years before in *The Seven Storey Mountain.* He wrote again to Aunt Gwyn: "If more of Father's letters turn up, please send me copies or the letters themselves if you can: I think they are well worth preserving and perhaps publishing in one way or other. Really it would be a pity to let all the good things he did be forgotten" (*RJ*, 81). His New Zealand aunts also sent materials: early letters, clippings about Owen's exhibitions and about his death, information about the Merton family. He became interested in learning more about his father's family, and was particularly intrigued by the supposed Welsh connection. (Wales figured prominently in his late poem, *The Geography of Lograire* [*CP*, 459–61]). Oddly, he displayed no interest in learning more about his mother's family, about his American forebears.

As Anthony Padovano has said:

> *His conversion begins when he senses his father's presence after death. As his life draws to a close, he searches again for that presence. His father has something to do with his artistic temperament, with the development of a religious instinct in him, with the conversion experience that begins his vocation, with the search for home and father culminating in Gethsemani, with the later poetry, and with an emptiness in him nothing could satisfy. (Padovano, 113)*

We can learn from Merton's search, though it is, in many ways, not a typical one. It was a search for presence, but it was not posited, despite pain that may have existed, in dwelling on the bad things his father may have done to himself or to his son. It is not a journey of recrimination. Merton does not, as so many twentieth-century writers do, fulminate against his father, nor does he wallow in the kind of anguish which stultifies and festers. Rather his search is to demonstrate (to himself and to others) the "good things" Owen did, the good things about him. Merton is responsible for himself, just as his father had been responsible for himself. In a reaction rare in our time, Merton is comfortable in emphasizing those good things, the qualities which contributed, for better or worse, to shaping his son. What matters to Merton is that his father had a vocation, a dedication to art, which allowed him, in his son's view, to integrate his person and his spirit. He wanted more, but it was the "more" of wanting to know more, to learn more from and about Owen. He wanted the world to see Owen as he saw him. The relationship never ended. Emptiness, a certain void, lingered on, yes, but Merton thought his father had shaped him—and that was, for him, the important part.

Photograph by Thomas Merton

Used with the permission of the Thomas Merton Legacy Trust.

With the Eye of the Heart: Thomas Merton on Faith

Christine M. Bochen

Faith is "the opening of an inward eye,
the eye of the heart,
to be filled with the presence of Divine light."[1]

In an essay written in 1966 for *Harper's* magazine, Thomas Merton characterized himself as a "solitary explorer" whose "own peculiar task" in his church and world was "to search the existential depths of faith in its silences, its ambiguities, and in those certainties which lie deeper than the bottom of anxiety."[2] Elena Malits has observed that Merton's calling himself a solitary explorer was "no casual metaphor."[3] It was at once a statement of identity and mission. The phenomenal success of his autobiography, *The Seven Storey Mountain*, had cast Merton into a unique, if paradoxical, role. Committed to a life of silence, the contemplative monk became a famous writer whose narrative of conversion claimed the attention of a post-war generation. The story of how he had found faith made for compelling reading, and the story of how he kept faith during the changing seasons of his life would continue to move readers during the next two decades of his life and long after his death. With candor and conviction, Merton told the story of faith awakened and nurtured, accepted and kept, treasured and shared. In everything he wrote, Merton documented his interior journey, testifying to the ways in which faith transformed, sustained, and challenged him, and showing how faith illumined his way. As he mapped faith's geography, Merton moved easily between an inner and an outer landscape, between the inner realm of the heart and the outer realm of monastery, church, society, and world, first experiencing and then showing how the interior reality of faith must express itself in committed action. While the theme of faith is always implicit in his writings, Merton explicitly addressed the subject of faith in a number of his works. Over the years, his vision of faith remained clear and consistent: it was a contemplative vision.

A Gift Received and Shared

Some of Merton's earliest reflections on faith are embedded in his autobiography, *The Seven Storey Mountain*, which was itself hailed as a "hymn of faith." In it, Merton tells the story of his awakening to and first steps of faith as he describes the process of his conversion, from faith's initial stirrings during adolescence and his growing attraction to Catholicism, to his reception into the Roman Catholic Church and his becoming a monk of the Abbey of Gethsemani. He explains what drew him to the Catholic faith: how he was moved by ordinary Catholics at prayer, the witness of non-Catholic writers such as Aldous Huxley and William Blake who opened him to the mystical life, and the writings of Catholic intellectuals such as Étienne Gilson and Jacques Maritain who challenged Merton to a fresh understanding of God. These influences were so many "external graces . . . arranged, along my path, by the kind Providence of God" and, working together, they laid "the groundwork of conversion."[4]

But it is in telling the story of how he helped prepare his brother, John Paul, for baptism that Merton articulated what he saw as central to the meaning of faith. When John Paul visited the monastery in 1942, Merton recalled asking his brother "if he didn't want to get baptized." "I sort of hoped I could be," John Paul responded (*SSM*, 394). During the next few days, Merton helped prepare his brother for baptism. We will never know exactly what the two brothers said to each other. Merton simply tells us that he talked about "everything" he could think of that had "something to do with the faith" (*SSM*, 395). There was much to be said about what Catholics believe and practice but, more importantly, Merton also shared what he knew from experience: that God was a Mystery that could be fully known only in silence. Words were inadequate to express the mystery of his own encounter with God. Nevertheless, the young monk admitted to "talking [his] head off" (*SSM*, 395). "I spoke about faith. By the gift of faith, you touch God, you enter into contact with His very substance and reality, in darkness" (*SSM*, 397). Merton's statement captures two insights that are key to his understanding of the *gift* of faith. Faith is an experience of intimate *contact* with the Divine. Faith plunges one into the divine Mystery in all its *darkness*. What Merton captured in these words was the essence of a contemplative vision of faith.

As a writer, Merton would continue to search for ways to express this contemplative vision of faith. There would be many other times in his life when he would speak and write about faith—with fellow monks and novices, with friends and readers, with believers and unbelievers—but few exchanges would have the poignancy of what, as it turned out, was his last visit with his brother. The newly baptized John Paul left Gethsemani to fight in the war that would claim his life. In April 1943, Merton would learn that his brother had been reported missing in action and then that he had died at sea. In the years that followed, everything that Merton would say about faith would, in some sense, build on the vision of faith he remembered sharing with his brother in the summer of 1942.

A Contemplative Vision of Faith

Already evident in his understanding of faith was Merton's realization that faith is intimately linked to contemplation, and writing about contemplation provided Merton with occasions to reflect on faith at some length. He devoted a chapter to "Faith" in *Seeds of Contemplation*, published in 1949,[5] and then expanded his discussion of faith from one chapter to two in *New Seeds of Contemplation*, published in 1961.[6] In *New Seeds*, he retained, with very minor changes, what he had written in *Seeds* and added a substantial amount of new material.[7]

"The beginning of contemplation is faith" (*SC*, 77; *NSC*, 126), Merton wrote in the opening line on his chapter on "Faith" in *Seeds of Contemplation*. He elucidated the statement in three movements. First, he stated what faith is not.[8] It is "not an emotion, not a feeling. . . . not a blind sub-conscious urge towards something vaguely supernatural. . . . not simply an elemental need. . . . not a conviction that one is somehow saved. . . . not something entirely interior and subjective." Faith is "not an opinion. . . . not a conviction based on rational analysis" (*SC*, 77–78). Second, he states that faith is "first of all an intellectual assent" which accepts the truth of propositions "revealed" by God and that faith involves submission to the authority of the God who reveals. Third, Merton explains that faith is "the way to a vital contact with a God Who is alive, and not to an abstract First Principle worked out by syllogisms" (*SC*, 78). Faith, Merton insists, is more than assent to revealed truth; it is an assent to God. The intellect knows God by "loving" and in faith one knows (and is known) by the "living God, the God Who is God and not a philosopher's abstraction" (*SC*, 79). Concepts of God, however useful they may be, are only a pale analogy. They are *only* concepts *about* God. Fourth, the way of faith is dark; language gives way to silence. The kataphatic way which knows God by the use of concepts and language opens into the apophatic way in which God is encountered in silence and darkness. "The closer we get to God," Merton writes, "the less is our faith diluted with the half-light of created images and concepts" (*SC*, 81–82). It is in the *darkness* of contemplation that we *see* God. Faith, in Merton's understanding, opens the door to contemplation and contemplation deepens faith.

It is this integral relationship between faith and contemplation which Merton explores at greater length in *New Seeds of Contemplation*.[9] Merton's deepened understanding of faith, an understanding rooted in his own experience of contemplation, informs his expanded discussion of faith in *New Seeds*. While he retains the material he wrote for *Seeds* (with only an occasional change here and there) in *New Seeds*, he develops the idea of faith as communion with God, introduces a discussion of faith as a "dimension of depth" that informs all of life, and discusses faith's potential for both *revealing and integrating the self*.

Faith as Communion

Although Merton insists, as he had in *Seeds*, that faith is "primarily an intellectual assent," he quickly adds that "if it were only that and nothing more . . . it would not be complete."[10] Faith has to be "something more. . . . a grasp, a contact, a communion of wills." In faith, one not only assents to propositions: "One assents to God Himself. One *receives* God. One says 'yes' not merely to a statement *about* God, but to the Invisible, Infinite God Himself" (*NSC*, 128). Faith is "communion." It terminates not in a statement, not in a formula of words, but "*in God*." Without discounting the significance of language about God, Merton again makes it clear that verbal formulas cannot be "the final object of faith. Faith goes beyond words and formulas and brings us the light of God Himself" (*NSC,* 129). Formulas are "means," not ends. As such, formulas "must be clean windows"—through which God's light can shine clearly. And though "we must make every effort to believe the right formulas . . . we must not be so obsessed with verbal correctness that we never go beyond the words to the ineffable reality which they attempt to convey" (*NSC,* 129). Although he does not use the term, Merton cautions against fundamentalism, against an obsession with "verbal correctness," which, in its preoccupation with the literal, fails to go beyond the words themselves to realize what the words express. "Faith, then, is not just the grim determination to cling to a certain form of words, no matter what may happen. . . . [A]bove all, faith is the opening of an inward eye, the eye of the heart, to be filled with the presence of Divine light" (*NSC,* 129–30).

Faith involves submission, but submission is not the whole of faith, "as if a mere unloving, unenlightened, dogged submission of the will to authority were enough to make a 'man of faith.'" Real faith is more than "mere unloving, unenlightened, dogged submission of the will to authority" (*NSC,* 133).

And faith is not incompatible with doubt. Doubt is not a hesitation to "accept the truth of revealed doctrine" but rather "the weakness and instability of our spirit in the presence of the awful mystery of God." And this helplessness is not only normal but entirely compatible with "true faith" (*NSC,* 134). As Merton had already noted in *Seeds of Contemplation* (81), the "more perfect faith is, the darker it becomes." Relying less and less on "the half-light of created images and concepts," faith becomes more obscure but, paradoxically, more certain (*NSC,* 134). "Deep belief" opens "the eye of the heart." Without the "light of faith" and its interior illumination, there can be no "real faith." It is "in the deepest darkness that we most fully possess God" (*NSC,* 135).

A Dimension of Life

Faith is not "just one moment of the spiritual life, not just a step to something else. It is that acceptance of God which is the very climate of all spiritual living." Merton continues,

> *As faith deepens, and as communion deepens with it, it becomes more and more intensive and at the same time reaches out to affect everything else we think and do. I do not mean merely that now all our thoughts are couched in certain fideist or pietistic formulas,*

> *but rather that faith gives a dimension of simplicity and depth to all our apprehensions and to all our experiences. (NSC, 135)*

To say that faith is a dimension of life means that faith has the potential to transform all of life. "Faith does not simply *account for* the unknown, tag it with a theological tag and file it away in a safe place where we do not have to worry about it. . . . On the contrary, faith incorporates the unknown into our everyday life in a living, dynamic and actual manner" (*NSC*, 136).

Faith informs the whole of life, not just its *spiritual* aspect. In fact, although he wrote a great deal about the "spiritual life," Merton realized that the term itself could be misleading by suggesting that the spiritual aspect is "a part, a section, set off as if it were a whole." "Our 'life in the Spirit,'" he explained to Etta Gullick in a 1963 letter,

> *is all-embracing, or should be. First is the response of faith receiving the word of God, not only as a truth to be believed but as a gift of life to be lived in total submission and pure confidence. Then this implies fidelity and obedience, but a total fidelity and a total obedience. From the moment that I obey God in everything, where is my 'spiritual life'? It is gone out the window, there is no spiritual life, only God and His word and my total response. (HGL, 357)*

In *Day of a Stranger*, Merton quipped, "The spiritual life is something that people worry about when they are so busy with something else they think they ought to be spiritual. Spiritual life is guilt."[11] His tone may have been jocular, but his observation was serious and substantive.

Realizing the True Self

Faith, as a dimension of depth, penetrates mystery—in us and in God; faith opens up "the true depths of reality, even of our own reality" (*NSC*, 137). So we no longer live on the surface; we are no longer limited to our external selves. Faith opens the door to the divine within, to God within. At this level, faith brings us "into contact" with our own inmost spiritual depths and "with God, Who is 'present' within those same depths" (*NSC*, 138–39).

The "function of faith," Merton explains, "is not only to bring us into contact with the 'authority of God' revealing; not only to teach us truths 'about God,' but even to reveal to us the unknown in our selves, in so far as our unknown and undiscovered self actually lives in God, moving and acting only under the direct light of His merciful grace" (*NSC*, 136–37). Faith is life itself—"the only way of opening up the true depths of reality, even of our own reality." Until a person yields to God, "he must inevitably remain a stranger to himself, an exile from himself, because he is excluded from the most meaningful depths of his own being: those which remain obscure and unknown because they are too simple and too deep to be attained by reason" (*NSC*, 137). In *New Seeds* and elsewhere, Merton names this deepest inner reality the "true self": the self that knows itself to be one with God.

A few years earlier, Merton had reflected on this very aspect of faith in "Notes for a Philosophy of Solitude," observing that "the actualization of a faith in which a man takes responsibility for his own inner life" is essential to inner solitude. Facing his "full mystery, in the presence of the invisible God," the solitary takes up "the lonely, barely comprehensible, incommunicable task of working his way through the darkness of his own mystery until he discovers that his mystery and the mystery of God merge into one reality, which is the only reality. That God lives in him and he in God."[12]

Faith unites and integrates and thus enables us to overcome ignorance with wisdom and fragmentation with wholeness. Faith "opens to us this higher realm of unity, of strength, of light, of sophianic love where there is no longer the limited and fragmentary light provided by rational principles, but where the Truth is One and Undivided and takes all to itself in the wholeness of *Sapientia*, or *Sophia*" (*NSC*, 141). This view of faith as wisdom leads Merton to define the human as at once *animus*, *anima*, and *spiritus*—and so whole. Although Merton viewed both *animus* and *anima* in a gender-stereotypical way—with *animus* representing mind and intelligence and *anima* representing passion or emotion—he saw that the union of *animus*, *anima*, and spirit makes possible "a life of wisdom, a life of sophianic love" (*NSC*, 141).

What does Merton the contemplative teach us about faith? Simply put, it is this: Faith is experiencing the mystery of God. By insisting on the relational and experiential nature of faith, Merton counters a reductionist understanding of faith—which reifies faith, viewing it primarily in conceptual terms and reducing it to a set of propositions about God. Such a distorted view of faith is an impoverished and poor substitute for true faith. True or real faith is not merely a matter of adherence to the correct formulas but a commitment of the heart. It is not saying "yes" to words about God; it is saying "yes" to God.

Faith requires not merely intellectual assent but personal commitment. Such commitment affirmed and reaffirmed over the course of a lifetime expresses itself in living faith.

Merton's own vision of faith is a dimension of his contemplative spirituality. It is impossible for Merton to speak of faith without speaking of contemplation. Contemplation, as Merton understands it, is awakening to the presence of God within. Faith opens the door; contemplation invites us inside, and contemplation names the experience that follows. Just as Merton defines faith in terms of contemplation, so, too, he defines contemplation in terms of faith. Contemplation, he writes, on the first page of *New Seeds*, is "a more profound depth of faith, a knowledge too deep to be grasped in images, in words or even in clear concepts" (*NSC*, 1).

Living Faith

One who sees with "the eye of the heart" looks inward to glimpse God *and* outward to see the world in a new light. For Merton, faith opens the way to contemplation *and* compassion. Merton's own faith story illustrates the movement from contemplation to compassion. His interior journey impelled him outward to a renewed vision of the world around him. The monk who renounced the world and withdrew to a monastery in rural Kentucky soon realized that he was involved in the world and implicated in its problems. The faith that drew him inward in prayer and into solitude also compelled him outward to speak out against injustice. Writing to Latin American poet Ludovico Silva, Merton explained what faith demanded of him.

> *One's whole being must be an act for which there can be found no word. This is the primary meaning of faith. On this basis, other dimensions of belief can be made credible. Otherwise not. My whole being must be a yes and an amen and an exclamation that is not heard. Only after that is there any point in exclamations. . . . One's acts must be part of the same silent exclamation.*[13]

Merton's silent exclamations erupted in an articulate and resounding Amen—voiced and echoed in a flurry of writings on war and peace, Auschwitz and Hiroshima, discrimination and racism. Although he remained a monk living in the monastery, he also became a prophet calling a world to justice.

Living faith became for Merton a matter of keeping faith. And keeping faith required that he respond to the signs of the times—the times of his birth and of his life: "That I should have been born in 1915, that I should be the contemporary of Auschwitz, Hiroshima, Viet Nam and the Watts riots, are things about which I was not first consulted. Yet they are also events in which, whether I like it or not, I am deeply and personally involved" (*CWA*, 145). Speaking out on social issues became a way of living faith. Beginning in the late fifties, he recognized that he had a responsibility to be "a peacemaker in the world, an apostle, to bring people to truth, to make [his] whole life a true and effective witness to God's Truth."[14] Merton felt himself called to witness to his faith in a new way. His writings on war and on violence, on racism and genocide, serve as a public witness to living faith. Merton's passion for peace and justice underscores faith's ethical implications.

True faith, Merton had written in the mid-fifties, is not "a kind of diversion, a spiritual amusement, in which one gathers up accepted, conventional formulas and arranges them in the approved mental patterns, without bothering to investigate their meaning, or asking if they have any practical consequences in one's life" (*DQ*, 180). Faith that functions as a kind of diversion—*divertissement*—"anesthetize[s] the individual" and "plunge[s] him in the warm, apathetic stupor of a collectivity which, like himself, wishes to remain amused" (*DQ*, 178). Almost a decade later, in 1968, Merton opened the preface to a collection of essays that ranged over an array of contemporary topics, which included the practice of non-violence, the atrocity of Vietnam, religion and racism, and the death of God, with a parable that was at once a critique and a challenge:

> *The Hassidic Rabbi, Baal-Shem-Tov, once told the following story. Two men were travelling through a forest. One was drunk, the other was sober. As they went, they were attacked by robbers, beaten, robbed of all they had, even their clothing. When they emerged, people asked them if they got through the wood without trouble. The drunken man said: "Everything was fine; nothing went wrong; we had no trouble at all!"*
>
> *They said: "How does it happen that you are naked and covered with blood?"*
>
> *He did not have an answer.*

> *The sober man said: "Do not believe him: he is drunk. It was a disaster. Robbers beat us without mercy and took everything we had. Be warned by what happened to us, and look out for yourselves." (FV, ix)*

The drunken man was both blind to the reality of his experience and unable to speak. The sober man, aware of what happened, was able to speak out and warn others. "For some 'faithful'—and for unbelievers too," Merton explained, "'faith' seems to be a kind of drunkenness, an anesthetic, that keeps you from realizing and believing that anything can ever go wrong." This kind of faith "whether in a religious message or merely in a political ideology" is a kind of drunkenness. It is the kind of faith that blinds us to the reality of violence in our world and in our selves and functions as a "narcotic" rather than "an awakening" (*FV*, ix–x).

Merton's own experience had taught him that faith could dispel illusion. He knew, firsthand, faith's liberating potential. His own liberation had begun with his conversion to Christian faith. "I was . . . the prisoner of my own violence and my own selfishness," he had written on the opening page of his autobiography (*SSM*, 3). In the pages that followed, he had testified to a gradual liberation from the captivity of sin and violence through his conversion to Christ, his becoming a Catholic and then a monk. "My conversion to the Christian faith, or to be precise my conversion to Christ, is something I have always regarded as a radical liberation from the delusions and obsessions of modern man and his society," he observed two decades later.[15]

Choosing Between Two Faiths

Thomas Merton recognized that the "delusions and obsessions" of modern society—however false and misguided—actually constitute a kind of faith. Consequently, humans must choose between two faiths:

> *One, a human, limited, external faith in human society with all its inert patrimony of assumptions and prejudices, a faith based on fear of solitude and on the need to "belong" to the group and to accept its standards with passive acquiescence. Or, in the second place, a faith in what we do not "see," a faith in the transcendent and invisible God, a faith that goes beyond all proofs, a faith that*

demands an interior revolution of one's whole self and a reorientation of one's existence in a contrary sense to the orientation taken by mundane prejudice. Such faith as this is a complete acceptance not only of the existence of God . . . but [the acceptance of God] as the center and meaning of all existence, and more particularly of our own life.[16]

What at first glance appears to be simply a choice between "human" faith and "religious" faith is more complex. Implicit in Merton's description of "religious" faith is a distinction between extrinsic and intrinsic ways of being religious. The former contents itself with the externals of belief and behavior; the latter involves a re-centering and reorientation of one's whole existence in God. It is not just "human" faith that can become self-serving—absorbed in the search for security and "psychological comfort." Christian faith can be self-serving when it is reduced to accepting truths about Christ and professing belief in Christ without answering the call "to become like Christ," that is, to become a new creation. True Christian faith is "the beginning of a new life"—a life lived in community, for we do not go to Christ "as isolated individuals" (*LH,* 111–12), and a life lived in charity, for "[w]ithout love and compassion for others, our own apparent 'love' for Christ is a fiction" (*LH,* 113).

"Keeping the Faith"

There is no question that Thomas Merton considered his faith a treasure for which he was deeply grateful. "There is nothing more important than the gift of Catholic Faith—and keeping that faith pure and clear," he wrote in his journal on the vigil of the twenty-seventh anniversary of his baptism.[17] But what did keeping the faith entail? In a commemorative booklet, written in 1962 to celebrate the 150th anniversary of the founding of the Congregation of the Sisters of Loretto, Merton observed that "the ideal of 'keeping the faith' can sometimes dwindle into something very negative, resentful, and obtuse: a mere 'no' to everything that we do not agree with."[18] Although Merton's comments emerged in the context of a piece honoring a group of women religious, his message has broader relevance and still broader implications. "Keeping the faith" means saying "yes": "yes" to God within ourselves and others and "yes" to "all that is valid in human culture and civilization" (*LG,* 7). "Keeping the faith" entails a contemplative dimension which expresses itself in responsible and compassionate action.

Eschewing an attitude of dualism and world denial, Merton insists that Catholics can "no longer afford to barricade ourselves in our Catholic environment and regard it as a smug little fortress of security in a world of pagans" (*LG*, 7). He had come to see the world as the arena of God's action *and* of human responsibility. Merton's view of the world was not naïve. He recognized that it was a world where evil happens: it is the world of Auschwitz and Hiroshima, of Watts and Vietnam. But it is also a world sanctified by Christ who restored "all nature . . . to the Father by his Resurrection" and "we, too, have our work to do in extending the power of the Resurrection to the whole world of our time by our prayer, our thought, our work, and our whole life" (*LG*, 7). To do so, we must overcome the tendency to divide our lives into compartments, "God and prayer in one compartment, work and apostolate in another" (*LG*, 7). Those living in the shadow of the Cross of Christ, which is "the sign of contradiction, but also and above all the sign of reconciliation," must face the profound reality of "Gethsemani" and realize that "Christian life is not an enclosed garden in which we can sit at ease, protected by the love of God. It is, alas, a wilderness into which we can be led by the Spirit in order to be tempted by the Devil. Or, a garden where, while Christ sweats blood in an agony beyond our comprehension, we 'struggle to keep awake under the moonlit olive trees'" (*LG*, 7–8).

Some years later, Merton would express his understanding of what "keeping the faith" entailed in two essays, reprinted posthumously in *Contemplation in a World of Action*: "Is the World a Problem?" and "Contemplation in a World of Action." To keep the faith, one must do more than barricade oneself against the intrusion of the "world." If faith is to be kept, it must be kept *in* the modern world. Keeping the faith means "turning to the world" (*CWA*, 149). *Contemptus mundi* has no place in the modern world. "If the deepest ground of my being is love, then in that very love itself and nowhere else will I find myself, and the world, and my brother and Christ" (*CWA*, 155–56). "Keeping the faith" requires balancing faithfulness to the tradition with openness to "the signs of the times," recognizing that the Christian tradition is a *living* tradition and that Christ is found in the midst of life.

While Merton spoke boldly of what keeping faith entailed, he readily admitted that finally it is God who keeps faith. We struggle and fall short. "Speaking in monastic terms, of fidelity to the truth, to the light that is in us from God," Merton wrote to Czeslaw Milosz in 1961,

> *everyone has been more or less unfaithful, and those who have seemed to be faithful have been so partially, in a way that sanctified greater evasions (the Grand Inquisitor). Perhaps the great reality of our time is this, that no one is capable of this fidelity, and all have failed in it, and that there is no hope to be looked for in any one of us. But God is faithful. . . . This, I think, is the central reality. (CT, 73)*

The same is true of the church, as Merton observed in a letter two years later to another friend, the French philosopher Jacques Maritain: "it is this Church, with all her wounds, her masks, and the rest, that remains in some fantastic sense 'faithful' and we are faithful in her and with her, but after the manner of survivors in some awful cataclysm. The truth is, of course, that it is not so much the Church that is faithful to Christ, as Christ Who is faithful to her and faithful unto death" (*CT*, 42).

A Crisis of Faith

In the late sixties, Merton recognized and responded to a contemporary crisis of faith. Fewer than thirty years had passed since he himself had found faith. Fewer than twenty years had passed since his autobiography had met with the enthusiastic reception of a postwar generation, hungry for faith and ready to applaud the Trappist monk's articulate witness. But it was a new age. The decade of the sixties was the era of "the secular city." A new theology declared God dead and talk about God meaningless. It was a time of change and crisis, reaction and protest. Merton was well aware of the winds of change blowing in church and society alike and recognized that, for some, faith itself was a problem. Reflecting on what he was reading, Merton confessed:

> *I do not underestimate the sincerity and difficulty of those who have problems of faith, for whom God is so easily "dead" all at once. But for my own part, the gift has been too great to be trifled with. The faith is not something that can be set aside while one is putting on a display of cleverness. One feels that this purity of faith suffers much more than it did then—there is a lot of good will; idealism, but much confusion and a sort of "why shouldn't I*

> *believe this if I want to?" attitude. You pick your faith like your clothes!! (DWL, 317)*

Nevertheless, those struggling with faith found Merton an understanding and empathic ally. This man of faith living in the simplicity and solitude in a monastery in rural Kentucky understood better than most how difficult it was for some to believe. Perhaps it is not so paradoxical after all when one considers that Merton saw himself as something of an outsider, as a marginal person: "There are by and large two Mertons: one ascetic, conservative, traditional, monastic. The other radical, independent, and somewhat akin to beats and hippies and to poets in general."[19] The man who appeared to be so much a part of the establishment easily identified with those who felt marginalized. While Merton denounced false faith and criticized bad faith, he empathized with people—inside and outside the church—who struggled with faith, people for whom belief seemed if not impossible, then at least difficult.

Already in *The Ascent to Truth*, published in 1951, Merton had explored the subject of belief and unbelief. He described three groups of unbelievers: first, atheists who once having believed in God have "formally rejected" God; second, those who accept the existence of God intellectually but find themselves "unable to believe"; and third, nominal Catholics who may continue to receive the sacraments, remain loyal to Catholic society, and have "almost entirely lost their faith" but "still cling to the outward forms of religion without a living faith in God" (*AT*, 38–40). Merton found the second group the most mystifying. They "know" God but cannot "believe" in God. They may even envy believers and want faith for themselves. Merton advises this group to "start the journey." "It is only when faith, by the action of the will in charity, takes full possession of our being that the so-called 'light of faith' becomes what one might classify as an 'experience'" (*AT*, 48). Understanding follows upon belief. Submitting oneself in love, one may begin to understand.

In a move that anticipated themes he would develop more fully in the sixties, Merton observed that if we "sometimes fail to meet this problem of unbelief in those who would 'like to believe but cannot,' it is generally because we are merely apologetes when we ought to be Apostles. We have been trained to feed men not with Christ, the Bread of Life, but rather with apologetic arguments" (*AT*, 41). An apologete focuses on resolving intellectual difficulties by rendering them intelligible, and so is concerned with "credibility rather than faith." An apostle "engenders 'new beings' in Christ, by the word of God." It is the "word of faith," planted in our hearts, that "starts an interior activity which results in a 'new birth' or the fundamental spiritual transformation from which emerges a new self, a 'new creature,' united with Christ by faith" (*AT,* 43-44). Citing Saint Thomas Aquinas as his source, Merton explains that the truth, which we believe, "must take possession of our entire being." The problem of unbelief is not centered in the mind but in the will. Accepting faith demands "a transformation" of one's whole life. One has to be "uprooted and transplanted" (*AT,* 45). It is the prospect of the radical consequences of accepting faith that can keep a person from doing so.

When Merton returned to the subject of belief and unbelief in the sixties, he did so, not in the classical terms of scholastic theology, but in a framework shaped by the content of a contemporary debate—resounding with the voices of Dietrich Bonhoeffer, Bishop J. A. T. Robinson, Thomas Altizer, William Hamilton, and Gabriel Vahanian—who championed a "religionless Christianity," radical theology, and the Death of God. These "theologians" challenged the assumptions taken for granted by past generations. They proclaimed God-talk meaningless and declared God irrelevant. Merton was both attentive and responsive to the debate engendered by the new theology. In a series of essays written in the middle to late sixties, Merton took these theological developments seriously. As he read the work of the new theologians, Merton critiqued their conclusions, but he recognized and readily admitted to points of agreement. For example, in a response to Bishop Robinson's *Honest to God,* Merton acknowledged that he and Robinson had much in common. Not only had they both studied at Clare College at Cambridge, but they shared the realization that "God is not a God 'out there,' not seated on a throne in the empyrean heaven, not overseeing an earth-centered universe" (*FV,* 225). However, Merton was quick to point out that the realization was hardly a new one. "I am . . . used to thinking that no conceptual knowledge of God is perfectly adequate, and therefore when I see the Bishop busy with 'framing new concepts' I would be inclined to say he still had not grasped the extent of the problem" (*FV,* 226). Merton confessed that he "discovered the meaning of Christian faith when [he] found out that the usual mythological and anthropomorphic picture of God was not the true God of Christians" (*FV,* 228–29). Merton's discovery played a key role in his conversion to Catholicism.

Reviewing Martin Marty's *Varieties of Unbelief*, published in 1964, provided Merton with another opportunity to consider the phenomenon of unbelief. That book review, which first appeared in *Commonweal* in January 1965, was one of several articles that Merton later published in *Faith and Violence*. More serious than the "vague presentiment of rampant godlessness in America" is "the phenomenon of a general pervasive indifference and complacency which are spread out among believers and non believers alike," Merton wrote in his review (*FV*, 199). Invoking a God of security who makes no demands, Americans embrace a "Christianity" that "is built on vaguely pragmatic securities, on flimsy and sentimental images, and on the tepid reassurances provided by conformity and togetherness in this world" (*FV*, 201). In the midst of apparent orthodoxy, Marty "detects the 'nearness of unbelief'" and in the end "bad faith" (*FV*, 201). Christians, Merton concludes, "can no longer afford to equate faith with the acceptance of myths about our nation, our society, or our technology; to equate hope with a naive confidence in our image of ourselves as the good guys against whom all the villains in the world are leagued in conspiracy; to equate love with a mindlessly compliant togetherness, a dimly lived and semi-radiant compulsiveness in work and play, invested by commercial artists with an aura of spurious joy" (*FV*, 203–204).

One of the most important of the essays included in *Faith and Violence* is entitled "Apologies to an Unbeliever." Originally published in *Harper's* magazine in November 1966, and later revised and expanded, the essay reveals Merton's interest in extending the discussion of faith beyond his already faithful circle of readers to promote a dialogue between believers and unbelievers and to challenge those who considered themselves believers to consider their faith. Merton seemed to be looking for a fresh approach to the subject of faith and belief, a way of speaking that would enable him to make contact with those for whom traditional theological terminology no longer had meaning. For Merton, the discussion of belief and unbelief was not just a theoretical matter. He was interested in communication. Merton had witnessed friends and readers struggling with faith and he listened. Most importantly, he recognized that the "religious problem of the twentieth century is not understandable if we regard it only as a problem of Unbelievers and atheists" (*FV*, 213).

"I think the whole business of faith and the message of faith is in the process of finding a whole new language—or of shutting up altogether," Thomas Merton wrote in a letter to Katherine Champney in November 1966.[20] Champney had written to Merton after reading "Apologies to an Unbeliever" in *Harper's*. Merton wrote back on November 10. The next day, with Champney's letter and his response still on his mind, he reviewed the exchange in his journal. This was unusual for Merton but perhaps not surprising given his misgivings about the article. After finishing the first draft in March, Merton noted that he had done so "[i]n spite of" himself, "with many hesitations." When he asked himself why he wrote it, Merton said he didn't know and then admitted to a very personal motive: "Compassion for Victor Hammer, who is after all a very believing 'unbeliever' and for so many others who have to be alone and confused, penalized for the sincerity which prohibits facile options! Perhaps it was well that I wrote this."[21] A few days later, he sent the article off "tentatively," confessing that he did "not like the tone of it" and would have to make changes "if they want it" (*LL*, 30).[22] Perhaps it was this personal investment in the topic that made him tentative. The discussion of belief and unbelief was close to his heart. He knew that real human beings struggled with faith and belief.

Champney wrote that she appreciated the article but confessed that "she never 'hears God.'" Reflecting on her letter, Merton observed: "The whole question of 'hearing God' has become extremely ambiguous. So ambiguous that the very way it is talked of makes some people incapable of 'hearing' anything. Their defensive reflex is basically healthy and perhaps more radically religious in some cases than the 'faith' of those who 'hear'" (*LL*, 158). It is clear that the line between believers and unbelievers was blurring for Merton. No longer was he inclined to categorize and group unbelievers as he had in *The Ascent to Truth*.

"Apologies to an Unbeliever"

Merton's essay demonstrates how he continued to develop and express his contemplative vision of faith. As the rigid boundary between believers and unbelievers eroded, Merton searched for a way of speaking about faith that would be meaningful—outside and inside Christian circles. He wrote "Apologies to an Unbeliever" to "apologize for the . . . affront [which] has been, and still is, daily and hourly perpetrated on you [Unbelievers] by a variety of Believers, some fanatical, some reasonable; some clerical, some lay; some religious and some irreligious; some futuristic and some antique" (*FV*, 208). Although Merton directs the essay to "Unbelievers," he is also speaking to "Believers." As he sees it, an apology is in order; it is demanded by his faith. "If I, as a Christian, believe that my first duty is to love and respect my fellowman in his personal frailty and perplexity, in his unique hazard and his need for trust, then I think that the refusal to let him alone, the inability to entrust him to God and to his own conscience, and the insistence on rejecting him as a person until he agrees with me, is simply a sign that my own faith is inadequate" (*FV,* 208). Could Merton have had his friend, Victor Hammer, in mind when he wrote this? Certainly so. "Where authentic religious concern degenerates into salesmanship," he continues, "it becomes an affront to the honest perplexities of the vast majority." These "honest perplexities" must be taken seriously and especially so in the changing cultural context inhabited by "'Diaspora' Christians in a frankly secular and non-believing society" (*FV,* 208–209).

Three elements essential to Merton's contemplative view of faith emerge in "Apologies to an Unbeliever." Each concerns listening. "Faith comes by hearing," as St. Paul says, but Merton asks, "by hearing *what?* The cries of snake handlers? The soothing platitudes of the religious operator?" One must listen to the "the inscrutable ground" of his or her own being. What must be heard can only be heard in the silence of one's spirit. This is the hearing that leads to faith. The limits of speaking about and to God must be recognized. Acknowledging the apparent "absence of God" and "silence of God," Merton notes that these are metaphorical expressions that refer "to another metaphorical concept, that of 'communication' between man and God. To say that 'God is absent' and 'God is silent' is to say that the familiar concept of 'communication' between man and God has broken down" (*FV,* 210). For Unbelievers, communication with God is itself "incredible." But Believers have not only insisted that God speaks but also that God speaks through them: "When *we* spoke, *God* spoke." Furthermore, Believers "keep insisting that we and God deal with each other morning, noon and night over closed-circuit TV" (*FV,* 210). Such "pious metaphors" may have some truth in them but, when forced on people, the metaphors "border on blasphemous idiocy." The "absence of God" and "silence of God" are "facts of profound *religious* significance" (*FV,* 210–11). Listening to God's silence fits into Merton's contemplative view of faith. Finally, one must listen to the world. The contemplative understanding of faith requires that one be attentive to the many voices speaking in the world today, hearing them, critically, but hearing them nevertheless.

Merton concluded this essay by characterizing his "own peculiar task" in the church and world as that of "the solitary explorer," searching "the existential depths of faith."

> *In these depths there are no easy answers, no pat solutions to anything. . . . On this level, the division between Believer and Unbeliever ceases to be so crystal clear. . . . Everybody is an Unbeliever more or less! Only when this fact is fully experienced, accepted and lived with, does one become fit to hear the simple message of the Gospel—or of any other religious teaching. (FV, 213)*

The religious problem of the twentieth century is a problem shared by Unbelievers and Believers alike. In fact, Merton's critique of the faith of Believers is pointed:

> *The faith that has grown cold is not only the faith that the Unbeliever has lost but the faith that the Believer has kept. This faith has too often become rigid, or complex, sentimental, foolish, or impertinent. It has lost itself in imaginings and unrealities, dispersed itself in pontifical and organizational routines, or evaporated in activism and loose talk. (FV, 213–14)*

Contemplation and Faith

Early on in his monastic life, Merton had learned that the language of faith was linked to contemplation. As he wrote his way through the forties, fifties, and sixties, it was with the conviction that the contemplative life pointed the way to faith. In "Contemplation in a World of Action," he put it this way: to reach "a true awareness" of God and ourselves,

> *we have to renounce our selfish and limited self and enter into a whole new kind of existence, discovering an inner center of motivation and love which makes us see ourselves and everything else in an entirely new light. Call it faith, call it (at a more advanced stage) contemplative illumination, call it the sense of God or even mystical union: all these are different aspects and levels of the same kind of realization: the awakening to a new awareness of ourselves in Christ, created in Him, redeemed by Him, to be transformed and glorified in and with Him. In Blake's words, the*

> *"doors of perception" are opened and all life takes on a completely new meaning: the real sense of our own existence, which is normally veiled and distorted by the routine distractions of an alienated life, is now revealed in a central intuition. . . . This "loving knowledge" which sees everything transfigured "in God," coming from God and working for God's creative and redemptive love and tending to fulfillment in the glory of God, is a contemplative knowledge, a fruit of living and realizing faith, a gift of the Spirit. (CWA, 161)*

Merton left us with a contemplative vision of faith: nurtured by prayer and meditation and committed to action. It is a vision that honors experience over formula, practice over words. It is a vision rooted in an awareness of the mystery of God. It was a vision Merton lived. His words mirror wisdom gleaned in living faith.

Photograph by Thomas Merton

Used with the permission of the Thomas Merton Legacy Trust.

Interiorizing Monasticism

Lawrence S. Cunningham

Let me take a small space to pay tribute to the late Bob Daggy, to whom this essay is dedicated. Bob was a friend whose memory I cherish. We spent many happy moments at Merton meetings, at various watering holes on the old Bardstown Road in Louisville, and in the Merton Studies Center. He did his job so well that he served as a conduit for all those folks, serious and not, who trudged to the Center to commune with the works of Thomas Merton. In writing about how Merton interiorized monastic life and made it available to others, I am, in a sense, attempting to explain why so many people came and still come to the Merton Center—a center forever marked by the love and energy that Bob lavished on it. Bob rests today in the secular graveyard at Gethsemani. On that day of resurrection, he will meet the old hermit, Herman Hanekamp and Father Dan Walsh; the three of them can walk to the flank of the monastic church to find Merton in the company of the Gethsemani community. Until then: Requiescant in pace. *Amen.*

This essay poses a simple question: How do people who are not formally monks learn from, and find sustenance in, that great tradition which is called monasticism? The question is posed since at least part of the explanation for the continuing pertinence of Thomas

Merton is to be found in the fact that he was a monk and, further, exemplified that monasticism to a heroic degree and in a new fashion. No attempt will be made to explore Merton's monastic witness as such, but attention will be paid to the way in which he attempted, especially in his mature years, to give an account of monastic wisdom. This essay, then, is a reflection on the phenomenon of monasticism and its role as being a purveyor of certain values and insights to the larger world of religious seekers.

The New Testament's Acts of the Apostles testifies that one of the earliest descriptions of the believers in Jesus was that they were followers of The Way (Acts 9:2; 18:26; 19:9, 23; 22:4; 24:14, 22). Since Jesus called himself the Way (Jn 14:6), it is as apt a description as one could hope for. Nonetheless, one can say that in the long history of the Christian tradition, there have been many ways to follow The Way.[1] Among those ways, of course, is the way of monasticism.

Since the Second Vatican Council recovered for us the rich concept of *charism,* it has been common in theological circles to see monasticism as one of the many rich charisms which exist in the Christian tradition. The Dogmatic Constitution on the Church (*Lumen Gentium*) tells us that along with the sacraments and the ministries of the church, the Holy Spirit gives gifts "among the faithful of every rank" in order to equip them to be "fit and ready to undertake the various tasks or offices advantageous for the renewal and upbuilding of the church."[2] The important point to note in that citation is that these gifts are not for the sole benefit of the recipient alone but for the renewal and the upbuilding (i.e., edification in the strict sense of the term) of the church.

Monasticism, thus understood, is a way of following The Way whose roots go back even before the third century when monasticism becomes a visible historical reality. It is interesting that when the Second Vatican Council discusses—as it does only briefly—the role of contemplatives in the church, they refer to the men and women who follow this way as contributing to the overall mission of the church by their very role as contemplatives and their witness to the inestimable value of prayer and their place as such witnesses for the evangelization of the world.[3] In other words, the conciliar documents discuss monasticism as a charism available for the good of the larger community and not only as a grace for the person who might adopt such a way of living. In fact, Estevao Bettancourt, writing shortly after the closing of the Council, lists, along with monasticism, such charisms as asceticism, virginity, martyrdom, poverty, and movements favoring mysticism, social virtues, and the theological sciences as "ways in which charisms are manifested."[4]

Monasticism, of course, is not a phenomenon peculiar to Christianity. Monasticism and movements that bear, as Wittgenstein would say, a "family resemblance" to monasticism are found in all of the world's great religions. Scholars have attempted, with varying degrees of acceptance, to articulate the essential character of the monastic impulse as a phenomenon in religion.[5] Such an undertaking is far too complex to be discussed here, but a simpler question might be raised with profit. If monasticism is a charism that builds up the community, what is it in that life that those who are not monks might learn from the monastic experience that nurtures their own way of following The Way? The question is raised precisely because it is one characteristic of a charism that it is given to a person or a movement not exclusively for that person or group but for the benefit of the whole.

Such a question wishes to go beyond the "soft" understanding of edification, that is, the idea that monks "edify" us by the example of their holiness of life or the severity of their path in order that we might be spurred on to greater fidelity to The Way. Nor does it help much if we consider the monastic charism solely as a form of surrogacy by which we leave to the monk the task of making reparation for the sinfulness of the world or rely on them to say the prayers to which we have failed to attend. As readers of Thomas Merton well know, he had little patience with those who would see the monastery in general (or Gethsemani in particular) as some kind of spiritual "powerhouse" generating grace by the ceaseless prayers of monks. Nor did he see the monk as a scapegoat accepting penitential discipline upon his or her back to "make up for" the failure of others to be penitential people.

The question which we ask is not unlike the traditional inquiries made of the early desert monastics: "What must I do?" or "Give me a good word." When people went to these solitaries and asked for such wisdom, it was not because they wished to become monks (though some did or were monks to begin with) but because they saw in the lives of those desert figures a certain valuable wisdom which would be of use to them even though they were not monks. So, our questions are pretty much like this: What are the good words that the monastic tradition can provide us?

The great Russian Orthodox theologian, Paul Evdokimov, approached this question by arguing that every Christian is able to "interiorize" the monastic values (or, more properly, the monastic vows) for their own life even though they were not called to the monastic life.[6] Evdokimov's argument is fully consistent with the spirituality of the Christian East. Saint John Chrysostom, after all, refused to distinguish monastic from lay spirituality since the scriptures want "all Christians to lead the monastic life even if they are married."[7]

While I have borrowed Evdokimov's language for the title of this paper, my intention is not to follow his line of argument but rather to look into the writings of Thomas Merton for clues that might help us to see how monastic life in general, as he described it, and his experience of monasticism in particular, "crossed over" into the consciousness of his millions of readers as an aid for their own spiritual journey. While many people tried the monastic life in the late 1940s and 1950s under the inspiration of Merton, it is what he perceived in the monastic life and was able to articulate that most captured the hearts of those who read (and continue to read) him for spiritual nourishment.

It is true that today many people look to monasticism as a resource for nourishing their personal lives. The popularity of such authors as Basil Pennington, Thomas Keating, Kathleen Norris, Esther DeWaal, the late John Main, Bede Griffiths, and the many other monastically inspired authors (think of the widespread appreciation for the practices of *lectio* and/or "centering prayer") draw on the traditional *praxis* of the monastic tradition. The enormous popularity of monastic guest houses testifies to the attraction monasticism still holds for people. Merton himself certainly fueled much but not all of that interest in our time. What made Merton *sui generis*, however, was his capacity to remain rooted in traditional monastic disciplines while, at the same time, constantly pushing for clarifications in his own mind for what was at the very heart of the monastic experience. His well-known disdain for the ceaseless chatter about superficial "reforms" of the monastic life in the wake of the impulses following Vatican II requires no documentation. That impatience is a leitmotif of most of the letters he wrote after 1965, as is attested by even a cursory examination of his correspondence collected by Brother Patrick Hart under the title *The School of Charity*,[8] or his remarks collected in *The Springs of Contemplation*,[9] which is a transcript of conferences he gave to contemplative sisters, or the essays collected under the title of *Contemplation in a World of Action*.[10]

Merton constantly circled back to one fundamental issue: What is at the heart of our lives as monks?[11] In other words, he exemplified the beautiful interrogative *mot* attributed to his European confrère, Dom André Louf:

What is a monk?
A monk is a person who every day asks:
What is a monk?[12]

To answer that question in terms of the evolution of Merton's life and thought fully would require a book in its own right. It is a commonplace to note that how he perceived the monastic life in 1941 was not the way he saw things around 1960 and still less as he departed for the East in 1968. Furthermore, there is a whole range of images, metaphors, pseudonyms, and biblical, patristic, and monastic topoi which he employed to discuss his own sense of the monastic life. The very titles of his books give some small sense of his range: the purgatorial penitent;[13] the reluctant prophet in the belly of the sea monster;[14] the bystander who stands guiltily at the margins;[15] (*l'étranger; peregrinus*) the stranger; the hermit; and so on. In one extravagant conceit, he even imagines the contemplative in the hermitage or cloister as John the Baptist in the womb of Saint Elizabeth who leaps for joy at the coming of the Word carried by the pregnant Mary: "Planted in the night of contemplation, / Sealed in the dark and waiting to be born."[16]

Merton's writings often contained, either explicitly or implicitly, lists of words or litanies of monastic practices which he found essential to an understanding of monasticism in general and for his own spiritual life in particular. As a young monk, he loved to repeat and meditate on words like "purity" or "solitude" or "silence." Indeed, books like *Thoughts in Solitude* can be seen as the end product of such meditations.[17] As a mature monk, he would grapple with the interior meaning of those (largely) Buddhist concepts of mindfulness, attention, and compassion as touchstones for his own understanding of spirituality. He wrote compellingly throughout his life of those standard practices of monasticism like common prayer, *lectio*, the value of work, the necessity of cultivating the counter-cultural spirit, the right ordering of asceticism, and the meaning of monastic *conversatio* and so on. None of these emphases need any documentation since they run like threads from *The Sign of Jonas* to the posthumous collection of essays in *Contemplation in a World of Action*.

The closest Merton came to thinking through in any sustained and systematic fashion what he conceived the essence of the monastic life to be reveals itself in some observations he made while on his Asian journey. In the fourth appendix of *The Asian Journal,* we find notes sketched out for a talk he gave in Calcutta to an interreligious group centered at the Temple of Understanding. In those notes, Merton set out three characteristics of what he considered to be root monastic values which characterized that life across religious traditions as well as being pertinent for anyone who wished to incorporate monastic values in their lives. The three characteristics are: (1) a certain distance or detachment from the ordinary secular concerns of life; a solitude of varying intensity and duration; (2) a preoccupation (Merton's word) with the radical inner depth of one's religious and philosophical beliefs, the grounds of those beliefs, and their spiritual implications; (3) a particular concern with inner transformation and the deepening of consciousness of a transcendent dimension of life beyond the empirical self and of "ethical and pious observance."[18] Each of those characteristics requires some comment.

The "distance or detachment" of which Merton speaks in his first characteristic of the monastic charism is, of course, close to the ancient monastic idea of *fuga mundi*—that "flight from the world" under which one could group all of those monastic impulses that emphasize simplicity of life, sharing of goods, abstention from luxury and sensuousness, the valuation of asceticism in style of life, and a certain prophetic stance vis-à-vis the larger culture. Distance and detachment sums up, in a phrase, the fact that the monastic impulse is profoundly counter-cultural. The phrase is not unlike the analogous phrase also ancient in monastic literature: *contemptus mundi*. Contempt for the world sounds harsh in our contemporary parlance, but in monasticism, it has the more precise sense of relativizing the values (success, display, ambition, etc.) which are the goals of worldly achievement. The great gift, of course, is to learn how to live with *contemptus mundi* not out of hatred for the goods of the world but because of the prophetic character of such a stance. Such a conversion is to build what Francis Kline has called the most difficult of all attitudes for the spiritual person who is not a monk—namely "an interior cloister in this frenzied world of ours" (Kline, 45).

To adopt such a style of life, which means to construct an interior cloister, is in itself a sign of how one stands with regard to the world. That stand requires one, at the very least, to undervalue achievement, status, and advancement. Relativizing the values of the world allows the monk to balance work (required for sustenance and maintenance) in such a way that there is enough leisure to live in a contemplative fashion. Monastic culture has always put a high premium on what the ancients called *otium*—that leisure which permits the life of the spirit to flourish.[19]

What the monastic emphasis on living "counter-culturally" has taught every religious seeker is the necessity of the right ordering of one's life so that the temptations of acquisition and success do not disfigure what is authentically human and fundamental. That "ordering of life" is what is called in traditional terminology "the regular life" (*vita regularis*), which is, literally, life under a rule. It is one of the more interesting phenomena of our time that those who are reformed Christians, especially those who are evangelicals, have attempted to recover the concept of the "regular life" by articulating a post-conversion way of living that does fair justice both to the exercise of piety and ascetic practice and the need to flesh out one's conversion into a style of life that seeks to turn biblical wisdom into performative practices. In a similar fashion, spiritual seekers who are not professedly Christian seek after expressed forms of the regular life centered around meditative and ascetic practices. These impulses are in harmony with Merton's insistence that one basic teaching of monasticism is "living out the full consequences and implications of what they believe" (*AJ*, 309).[20] Such a stance helps us to see, one might note in passing, the true meaning of asceticism, since asceticism is, almost by definition, the ordering of lesser goods for higher or better or more perfect or more fulfilling ends.

The second characteristic of the monastic charism Merton mentions is a preoccupation with the radical inner depths of one's religious and philosophical beliefs, as well as the experimental "ground" of those beliefs. It is clear from Merton's orientation that by "experiment" he means both turning thought into practice and having some reflective sense of what that practice entails. In that sense, "experiential" is a synonym for "experimental."

If the "distance and detachment" of the first characteristic provides us with the *where*, the preoccupation with radical inner depth singles out the *subject* of the monastic charism. What Thomas Merton, and all great masters and mistresses of the spiritual life understood, was that religious faith is not mere assent to faith propositions but being grasped by the depths of God's reality. Every religious tradition has set out ways of bringing such an awareness to a deep level of consciousness; the inscription "God Alone" is not merely a pious slogan but a program for life for a monastic house.

This sense of the "radical inner depths" involves both a going in and a going out. What monastic culture and experience teaches us is a way to do that if we are spiritual seekers. There is a first step in this process, and it can be summed up by the first word in the *Rule of Benedict*: "Listen."

With the willingness to listen, we can see the link between the first and second characteristics outlined by Merton in his Calcutta talk. Listening requires a certain ascesis of place, style of life, and human practice in order to acquire the capacity to listen. To listen is to be a person who understands interior solitude, who watches (think of monastic Vigils), who sits before the Word of God, who is sufficiently detached from the exigencies of success and promotion to make listening possible. In other words, to reach the "radical inner depths" one must be alert and prompt to receive. Perhaps monasticism, more than any other source in the Christian tradition, has given us the clues about how to understand the presence in our lives of God who is, as Augustine says famously, "nearer to us than we are to ourselves."

When we have found the *place* and the *subject* of our religious search, we can then, with God's grace, reach the third goal of the monastic search: that deepening of consciousness which leads to an "eventual breakthrough and discovery of a transcendent dimension of life beyond that of the ordinary empirical self and of ethical and pious observance" (*AJ*, 309–10). It is at this level that a person, while remaining faithful to his or her own tradition, achieves a breakthrough to the deep ground of human existence which is variously named in different religious traditions. Merton, as a Christian, calls it "life in Christ," although others may name it the Void or self-realization of the Atman, among other terms. Merton emphasizes that such realization is not only for the single perfection of the individual who experiences it but is a gift by which a person stands as representative of his or her community but in communion with others who have had such experiences. Such experiences, he goes on to say, do not typically come from individual revelations or illuminations but as the result of following from the discipline and teaching of a "traditional religious *way*" (Merton's emphasis) which is a certain "mode of life and of consciousness" (*AJ*, 310).

When one glosses those three simple characteristics set forth by Merton in some notes which formed the basis of a talk given over three decades ago, one sees that he was on to something terribly important. It is crucial to remember that he was preparing notes for a conference to be given to persons who came from a wide religious spectrum. His task was to "translate" monastic interiority into something understandable for an audience who would not understand the ethos of Christian monasticism in a fashion more than cursory.

Precisely because Merton was thinking of an interreligious audience, his remarks become salient when one asks the question about his immense influence over large numbers of people. He was a monk who had immersed himself thoroughly in the monastic way of being. He turned that experience into language, both in poetry and prose, for the edification of the world. His strategy, then, was an old and honorable one. He handed on to others what he himself had experienced and learned: after all, monks "specialize" in living a certain way in order to plumb the depths of what it means to be a person of faith, so that in their radical transformation into contemplatives, they can then share their path with others.

That sharing, however, was a two-way street. Merton mediated his grasp of the search for "inner transformation," but he also went to others to learn how others have achieved that goal and by what path. In other words, he was both a teacher and a learner. That latter task—of learning—comes in faithful obedience to monastic listening.

A final observation. The title of this essay advertised a reflection on the interiorization of monasticism. This interiorization is meant in a double sense. First, Merton did not simply join a monastic community; he was, in the deepest meaning of the word, a monk.[21] When one speaks of the interiorization of monasticism in that sense, one speaks of the ways in which he absorbed the life and ethos of his chosen path in life. It is clear that his understanding of what a monk was evolved over the decades, but the resources he drew on to allow that evolution to happen were consistently monastic.

While it is true, as *The Imitation of Christ* says, that the "habit does not make the monk," there are many people in the history of monasticism who have deeply interiorized their monastic lives (think of the tradition of spiritual directors, elders, etc.), but not everyone has had the gift of articulating their lives in such a way that others might draw nourishment from them. Merton had that gift. He had the capacity to transmit what he had learned in a fashion that has made him a spiritual master for countless people of countless persuasions. What Merton once wrote for a Latin American audience about the value of contemplation came from deep within his own life and was offered to others:

> *Without contemplation we remain small, limited, divided, partial: we adhere to the insufficient, permanently united to our narrow group and its interests, losing sight of justice and charity, seized by the passions of the moment, and, finally, we betray Christ. Without contemplation, without the intimate, silent, secret pursuit of truth through love, our action loses itself in the world and becomes dangerous.*[22]

A recent sociological study by Robert Wuthnow of the evolution of spirituality in American life[23] argues that American religious sensibilities have evolved from locating the search for greater spiritual understanding in commitment to a church community to a search in various sources and with a wide willingness towards eclecticism. Wuthnow calls the former the "spirituality of dwelling" and the latter the "spirituality of searching." These are ideal types and should not be seen as antinomies in which one chooses one over the other. The temptation of "dwelling" is complacency and smugness, while the temptation of the "seeker" is to fall into trendiness or illusion. Traditional Christian spirituality seeks a balance between the two types. One sees in Merton how this balance works out in creative and fruitful ways. He committed his life to the ancient "dwelling" of monasticism, but from within that tradition, he set out, intellectually and spiritually, to explore.

It may be that one of the greatest gifts Merton has given to us is the lesson derived from his capacity to be in place and to explore from that place. In other words, Merton understood that to say that monasticism was a tradition did not mean that it had to be traditional or, what is worse, a museum of past observances. His lifelong vocation was to root himself in a tradition and exploit its wisdom, while at the same time living as a contemporary human being. He managed that task, at least in part, by showing that traditional monastic usages like silence, contemplation, prayer, work, and so on were not evasions for the nervous, but deep gifts which, when cultivated, spoke to the world and, in certain ways, passed judgment on it.

Those who wish to interiorize monastic values would be well warned that their desires should not be framed as becoming ersatz monks by imitating the superficial characteristics of the monastic life. What Merton teaches us is that the deepest truths of monastic spirituality are simple and direct: the cultivation of listening, watching, and openness to God; the right use of goods; the desire for a deeper consciousness of self and others; drawing from the spiritual wisdom of the Christian tradition; and openness to the future (monks, after all, are the most eschatological of people!). This is what Merton had in mind when, in 1967, he had the opportunity, after a suggestion from Pope Paul VI, to write a letter "to the world" in the name of the contemplatives of the church. He said, toward the end of that letter, that one does not need to navigate the jungle of language and problems that surround God. The message of the contemplatives is simply this: "That whether you understand or not, God loves you, is present to you, lives in you, calls you, saves you, and offers you an understanding and light which are like nothing you ever found in books or heard in sermons."[24] To absorb that lesson which Merton offers to others is, in the most profound sense of the term, to interiorize what monasticism is all about.

Photograph by Thomas Merton

"Crisis and Mystery": The Changing Quality of Thomas Merton's Later Journals

Victor A. Kramer

Merton's journals were composed with definite patterns in mind, yet the configurations of ideas shift considerably during his final decade of keeping them. Early, and especially through 1952, he sought and emphasized patterns suggesting spiritual progress as he himself moved from novitiate to ordination. The clear structures employed in the earliest published journals suggest Merton felt positive stages in his forward movement in the spiritual life were documented. Both *The Secular Journal*[1] and *The Sign of Jonas*[2] imply significant spiritual progress was experienced. Later, the patterns observed and recorded were often less ordered and positive as he came to realize he should also record experiences which seemed occasionally to move him down psychologically and spiritually rather than up, as he searched for knowledge of God.

Throughout Merton's complete journals, recently published in seven volumes, the clear patterns both of progress and of his occasional disappointment are apparent. The publisher and the editors responsible for the structuring of the seven books, however, have chosen titles which stress the quite distinct positive patterns as this personal narrative unfolds: *Run, Entering, Search, Turning, Dancing, Learning, The Other Side*.[3] Implicitly all these upbeat titles, partly chosen by the publisher for commercial appeal, stress Merton's spiritual life as one of clear and positively developing stages. Certainly there is considerable truth in such an assumption; yet in fact, what this journal composer seems to have realized was that as his vocation unfolded, he was also learning that he could not always observe such clearly structured positive rhythms. Merton then came to affirm the mystery of life, while not being much concerned with finding discernible patterns suggesting spiritual progress.

By looking carefully at the middle parts of Volume 4, 1960–1963, *Turning toward the World*, it can be demonstrated that by the midpoint of this immense journal project, Merton was apparently even consciously shifting his methodology. He was becoming less concerned with documenting spiritual progress and was much more aware of the wavering patterns in his life—surprises, disappointments, and gifts within his experiences—which he then sought to record honestly as a part of a document which revealed that "[i]nexorably life moves on towards crisis and mystery" (*TTW,* 152). What I argue here is that the complete journals subtly shift in the 1960s toward a far greater emphasis upon acceptance of mystery along with concurrently less emphasis on personal assurance. Merton, therefore, puts energy into recording particular reflections, while such entries often were sometimes frustrating, even unclear. This shift in strategy which reveals his acceptance of mystery is at the core of what I will analyze. Such a reading helps to explain that Merton's journal became more and more a record of his honesty, acceptance, and patience rather than a documentation of strides accomplished in pursuit of a spirituality of perfection.

Such a shift is already in process during the period 1953 to 1959 (after *The Sign of Jonas* was published) and as Merton lived through the crisis of vocation which helped him to reorient himself in his relationship to the world and concomitantly as he became less concerned with private worries, plans, and desires. Then, and especially in 1961 to 1962, a period which seems to provide a paradigm of the writer's shift in strategy away from emphasizing positive patterns, he begins to put considerable stress on letting patterns which cannot easily be explained emerge in their mystery as journal entries.

Merton's decade of journal writing from 1953 through 1962 reflects an increasing awareness of his changing sense of vocation and of a developing awareness and responsibility about the world concerning issues of war, political power, race, peace, and even in regard to the relationship of Cistercian monasticism to the church. Ironically, during this same period, Merton documents in the journal a growing realization that he must now include detailed information about his own lack of peace, his worries, and his own willfulness. By 1961 and 1962 we can observe significant changes in intensity as Merton becomes more intrigued with determining how he must (in life and journal) shift away from concerns with self. This decision also called for a change in tactics to include as journal entries things which are often less clear-cut, or edifying. It is as if the rules of censorship (self-imposed or otherwise) are lifted, and this writer begins to provide a journal which reflects more of his own contradictions and fallibility. It is precisely because of this conscious shift of methodology that we have materials which make his mature journals of most value for today's readers who live in a world of little certainty, while nevertheless a world full of graces to be celebrated.

I. Stages in the Making of the Complete Journal

Merton's sustained journal, something which it is clear became a quite systematic project for him, operates for readers as a *catalyst* for thinking about him, his life, his work, and even as reflection of his probable planning for projected future readers. These patterns, chosen, reiterated, and even sometimes manipulated by him, as he systematically became more aware of the complexity of what he had to do as a journal keeper, have been additionally channeled in the editing process of the seven volumes—not in a way which is wrong, yet, as readers, we should be aware that the organization of this publishing project does affect how we read it and how we think about Merton.

Many factors are at work: the decision to publish the journal in *seven* volumes, not, for example, year by year in blocks; the decision to create individual *titles* for each of these seven volumes, with a different kind of organizing *structure* for each of the seven separate books (because of the nature of the raw materials); and the *freedom* which was allowed different editors to identify materials and annotate as they chose (within parameters set by the publisher). Readers must be aware that all these factors provide significant assets and liabilities, while one definite factor is that readers tend to think of all seven books as constituting progressive movements forward.

We cannot know if Merton would be dissatisfied with this project as it has recently been published; yet he would understand it might have been done in a quite different format. Imagine that we had a multi-volume project utilizing Merton's religious name, entitled simply: "The Journal of Fr. Louis Merton." Imagine it were published with considerably more extensive footnotes and cross-references which would allow readers to be aware of his many other writing projects—autobiography, essays, letters, poetry, devotional books, the working notebooks, and his notes for teaching—in greater detail than possible with the present edition. With such an edition, much of the journal would radiate outward quite differently. All of a sudden, it would not seem so much a private enterprise, and it could be perceived less as a means of storing ideas about self, and more as a storehouse of ideas for projects, and for community, and thus for others. Now, in fact, Merton came to see his journal as a repository that did work, and would continue to function, on many different levels. Increasingly it moved away from an almost obsessive concern with self and his spiritual progress, although, of course, it had to center on his experiences.

With more scholarly apparatus, it would be much easier to apprehend the myriad connections that need to be made. I predict this will eventually happen, and especially with electronic publishing, one can imagine a textual apparatus that will keep growing as layers of identification, annotation, corrections of Merton's holography, and more are added to the transcriptions. This is to say that when the seven volumes of the complete journals are read, in a very real sense, our reading will have only begun because Merton's monastic career and his "turning toward the world" was an exceedingly complex movement that included a deepened appreciation of his monastic calling *and* an acceptance of the mystery of all life.

Merton's contribution in the journal is, then, an exceedingly complicated one, made more complicated by the publisher and by the *good* intentions of the six editors of this seven-volume edition, myself included. Think how strange and exciting it is to come up with seven good titles, which direct the reader to seven distinct periods in Merton's exciting life. While I think all the titles are excellent, what I am suggesting is that the publisher and the editors have put a distinct slant on this narrative. A different and perhaps more subtle method of manipulation could be provided, and that is what I want to begin to suggest now.

A slightly different organization, with different titles, for example, would have provided a different set of options for much subsequent interpretation. There are, for example, significant gaps in the journals as a whole. Little seems to exist for 1943 to 1946, three years; and similarly from mid-1953 to 1956, we have another three-year omission. Arranged differently, the existing blocks of material could be used to suggest a slightly different story, perhaps a less outwardly exciting one than what is suggested by the editors and publisher with the imposition of titles assigned by HarperCollins for the first seven volumes: *Run*, *Enter*, *Search* (as monastic) and *Turning*, *Dancing*, *Learning* (as a somewhat unhappy monastic becoming familiar again with the world), and then finding the "*Other Side*." Consider if these journal entries were published in blocks of years as they were written—beginning with a new book volume when there is a significant gap. Imagine that all the volume titles were less metaphorical. We might then have eight books with volumes titled to stress Merton's continual re-examination within his monastic vocation. Father Louis's journals could have been entitled: 1) *Preparation for Ordination* (through 1949); 2) *Acceptance of Vocation* (through 1942); 3) *Teaching Students* (through 1953); 4) *Guiding Novices* (through 1960); 5) *Wondering about the World* (through 1963); 6) *Part-Time Solitary* (through 1966); 7) *Distracted Hermit* (through 1967); and 8) *Ecumenical Traveler* (through 1968). My suggestion is that the "raw" materials presented within such a structure would be received much more as the record of Merton's continuing questions about the meaning of his vocation as a monk while the circumstances experienced by him, and others like him, changed enormously. If this had been done, the writer's continual *re-examination* of the monastic life would assume a considerably more prominent position in any attentive reading of the cumulative journal project. Such a continual reexamination in the midst of change, surprise, and frustration is a key to seeing Merton's complete journal enterprise.

These "raw" journals are not just a record of what Merton does or encounters. They are, it seems to me, a continual reexamination of what it means to be called to a dual vocation: *silence* and *speaking* during a particular historical era. Read in this way the journals might become recognized as much closer to *The Education of Henry Adams* than to Henry David Thoreau's daily records in his meticulous, but sometimes boring, journal. Even more so, Merton's entries could still function like Thoreau's in the many particulars observed, while his journal as a whole could be perceived as much closer to an *emblem* of the modern monastic life when predictable patterns in that life were so rapidly changed.

Several points are significant: as a writer, Merton thought with his pen. Thus, all these "raw" journals are his record of his selective thinking about life, his spiritual journey, and other matters, and from this original material he sometimes crafted books, including *The Sign of Jonas* and *Conjectures of a Guilty Bystander*. But, I stress, all these journals are also the record of a Merton *fully aware* that he is—already as he selects particular items, and styles, and as he returns to certain subjects—also *crafting* materials about the contemplative vocation, which are almost certain *to be published* as is. It is hardly ever just happenstance that something occurs and he records it. No, things happen and then he *chooses* some of those items as things to write about by including them in his journal.

One constant subject throughout this intense journal project is Merton's obvious concern about writing, and particularly writing this journal; thus we have (sometimes indirectly) a record of someone thinking consistently from beginning to end about life and spiritual journey, while he is also consistently thinking about the nature of his writing *and* the dynamics of writing this particular journal, while he also learns, like Henry Adams, that many of the patterns he earlier sought were often never really ever there. A significant theme in the three books of journal that precede the one I've edited, *Turning toward the World*, is the nature of journal writing itself, and the fact that Merton appears to be in control. Later he is not so sure, and by 1960 to 1963 Merton is fully aware that his journals (no doubt) will be published almost exactly as he composes them and this awareness becomes even more important as a basic structuring factor. He did not choose titles for every movement in this documentation, but he is nevertheless giving readers a picture of his gradual education. Of course, had he lived, he might well have mined all this raw draft material as he did for *Conjectures of a Guilty Bystander*.

Merton's realization of what he is learning about changes in the monastic life becomes especially clear in the later volumes, specifically the fourth, *Turning toward the World*, which covers the period from May 1960 through July 1963, and the fifth, *Dancing in the Water of Life*, from August 1963 to December 4, 1965. This is perhaps even more true in Volume 6, *Learning to Love*, where Merton chooses to record the troubles and pain of his romantic excursion with "M" while he still remains very much committed to the monastic life, and therefore charts his need for re-examination about the contemplative life.

II. A Decade of Change: 1953–1963

In the decade 1953–1963, Merton had a growing awareness of the nature of his vocation and craft; his "raw" journal, therefore, changed during this decade. First, we must examine the period that involves the journal composed just after the selections published as *The Sign of Jonas* (1953): *A Search for Solitude* and *Turning toward the World*, volumes that are the basic materials for what feeds into the composition of *Conjectures of a Guilty Bystander*. There are various ways of characterizing this period: I think that the years from 1953 forward can best be called a period of doubt along with a corresponding acceptance of mystery, rather than, as is suggested by the volume titles assigned, a period of searching for solitude and then an abrupt moving on toward the world. A point to be emphasized is that it was never simple for Merton to know what to do, and as he himself came to learn, there are far more complicated ways to think about vocation than those simplistically suggested by the titles which the publisher of this posthumously published project selected.

It is hard to put this complexity into simple terms, but what must be stressed is that really good things about Merton unfold during this period, and what becomes especially evident is his coming to know that immediacy is important; living in the moment is what is important; being attuned to others is crucially important. There are all kinds of wonderful anecdotes about Merton, and many from the 1950s suggest his growing ability to live well in the immediate. I once heard Jim Finley remark in a talk that, as a novice, he would go into a conference with Merton, his Novice Master, and how, as a young monk, he was extremely nervous. Merton was well known, and Jim Finley was young. The weekly conferences were difficult. Finley recalled that he had a job in the monastery feeding the pigs, and Merton announced: "Well, I want you to think about your job a little bit, and when you come back next week, we'll talk about your spiritual life." Then, when Finley returned a week later, the first thing Merton said was, "Tell me something about those pigs." So Finley said, "Well, there was this big pig and then there was a little pig, and the big one pushed the little pig." They started laughing. This laughter changed Finley's relationship with Merton. Every week thereafter, they joked and laughed, and Finley felt at ease with the famous Thomas Merton. Clearly Merton was learning to live in the immediate.

There must be lots of other good stories like that about Merton. The point is there is something fundamental there about immediacy that is important. I talked with Dom Augustine Moore, who was the Abbot at the Monastery of the Holy Spirit, the first daughterhouse of Gethsemani. His recollection of Merton stressed that when he and Merton were novices together from 1941 through 1943, it was always Merton who lingered longest in the chapel after Mass.[4] There was apparently a quality in Merton that allowed him to live well in the moment, and what the journals reveal is that this became increasingly important. What is also observed looking at the complete journals, 1953 to 1963, is that Merton was also quite capable of often "living in his head," and it was hard for him to realize that the business of immediacy was so very important. This conflict is why we might call this a decade of doubt along with the gradual acceptance of mystery.

What we observe in this decade is that Merton changed immensely. He matured enormously spiritually. He learned to take himself less seriously. He was never much concerned about his physical appearance, but he was putting on weight and he could make jokes about that. Perhaps he was a bit vain, but he was also becoming aware of the fact that he had to stop thinking about himself and how he fitted within accepted monastic conventions. Throughout this decade and into the mid-1960s, he is, in fact, learning how to accommodate himself to a constantly changing set of circumstances in the church, in the monastery, and in the world, as well as in himself, while at the same time keeping certain kinds of monastic ideals alive.

This decade is a time when Father Louis was heavily involved as a teacher, and then from 1955, for a full decade, as Novice Master. It is a period of great activity working with and for others, but it is also a time of intense questioning about his role and his progress as a monastic. One of the most important questions to which he kept returning throughout these years—after he had sung that triumphant song which concludes *The Sign of Jonas*, the wonderful prose-poem "Fire Watch"—is about the nature of his vocation. He keeps asking himself what would be the right place for him to fulfill his vocation. In Volume 3 of the journals, which Larry Cunningham had originally planned to call "A Solitude Beyond Geography," using Merton's own words, so much of what is basic there for the seven years up to 1960 has to do with fulfillment of vocation. For Father Louis, these are often questions about where he would best live his monastic life.

His dreams about the Camaldolese, or the Carthusians, or going to some monastery in Latin America or Mexico provide real struggles. And, if we pursue all the references to questions about vocation during this period, we find that there is no doubt that a fundamental struggle was in process. We can assume that this is an extension, to some degree, of his earlier rather romantic ideas about Gethsemani as "*Paradisus Claustralis*," his view of the monastery as a kind of paradise or gateway to heaven. Such earlier ideas were attractive, but such concepts were never unvarnished fact. The fact is, as Merton slowly came to realize, that any monastery both is and is not paradise. So, when Cunningham wanted to use Merton's phrase to name this section, "Solitude beyond Geography," as an editor, he was emphasizing that during this time period, Merton was continually struggling with the question of how to perfect a life of solitude, and simultaneously struggling with how to accept the realization that "place" is not as important as it had seemed. So much of what is going on during the middle to late 1950s is finally a matter of Merton coming to understand that obedience is the key to his needs. It was, therefore, never a matter of his search for a different place, but rather more a matter of acceptance and stability. The same type of lessons about acceptance had to be learned in later years concerning matters beyond place. How does one connect with a world beyond the monastery, yet remain a Christian monastic?

Merton had to learn during this decade that he could never make all the decisions about his life. He knew that he had ideas and desires and plans and hopes, but finally all of this became much less important than learning that he had to accept the mysterious plans of God often manifested through the decisions of others. Vocation in relation to interpreting the call he heard is at the core of these years documented in *A Search for Solitude*. At first, Merton thought his job was to find the right place. What he had not learned, although he had already stated it at the end of *The Sign of Jonas*, was that he was already in that place. This decade is a time when Merton as monk and writer is seeking a balance. He realizes that he needs to be a successful contemplative, and he is spending a lot of time writing journal entries that are concerned about place, alternate plans, and so on. Ironically, what is finally realized is a gradual clarity about place not being so important if one can stop dreaming about being somewhere else.

In the period 1960 to 1963, covered in *Turning toward the World*, we have a somewhat different and even more complex situation unfolding. Merton continues to wonder about place. Should he have a hermitage? What does that mean? He is looking for more contact with the world. What does this mean? He does not know, and then all of a sudden in 1960, he has been given a different set of circumstances and a good place where he can retreat, a place that will eventually become his hermitage. But in this fourth volume of the journals, he is also asking questions about how he is going to have *both* solitude and contact with a world for which he has developed a new respect.

My working title for Volume 4 was "Towards Crisis and Mystery." That phrase, written in 1961, is significant: "Inexorably life moves on towards crisis and mystery" (*TTW,* 152). Merton is trying to figure out what it is that is going to allow him to retain solitude, and not be restless, yet at the same time allow him to make sense of a vocation that is going to have to combine solitude and going out toward the world. I think he is beginning to think of himself as an emblem of a new type of monastic, in fact a new type of Christian, who must at times retreat and at other times assume a missionary role.

III. Changing Sense of Vocation and Craft

In terms of building the argument underlying this essay, Merton's learning to accept the mystery of his monastic life is basic. The next step is to give attention to the journals as a record of this acceptance, yet also as his carefully crafted record of an artistic process. Always a balance is being sought, but also I think it is quite clear that Merton remained foremost a writer. He was, in fact, despite claims to the contrary, a professional writer and an ambitious professional. So what we have throughout the journal project is someone recording all of this about vocation, yet doing it in a very artful and craftful manner as his life surprisingly changes. The part-time solitary; the hermitage; living alone full-time; the eventful relationship with "M"; the return to the discipline of the solitary life—all demanded disciplined writing. What we have is this artist personality struggling with vocation, trying to figure out what to do, and then finally coming to a new view about acceptance of circumstance. But we also have a monk who is writing all this down, and he controls the record.

The journals are *not* a daily record of what occurs. They are highly selective. If we look at any one month, there are approximately ten or eleven entries—moments when he has time to write and when he is also choosing those thoughts and events which are really important for him and which he thinks will be of value for readers later. So what is present in these not-so-"raw" journals is a rather systematic arrangement of things so that what we read is not so much a record of spiritual journey, but rather a very highly selected record of events wherein we are provided a picture of a spiritual life unfolding. During this decade, there is a fundamental concern reflected in the journal material about spiritual development, Merton's spiritual awareness, and while often carefully focused, it is not necessarily about "progress." My obvious point is that it was not clear sailing. As Emerson says in "Self-Reliance," the true voyage of a sailing ship is to reposition and correct and begin again.[5] In the complete journal, there are, therefore, episodes which are going to say something to readers not just about Merton's progress, but about his distractions and how he chose materials for future readers which reveal his developing awareness that he could never be in complete control. Also we have to remember that Merton was becoming fully aware that every word of journal he wrote would eventually be published word for word. And while that is basically what we have done with editing them, we have imposed a structure which seems to stress clarity and progress.

The most fundamental lesson to be learned in reading all these journals (and especially in what we observe in reading *Conjectures of a Guilty Bystander* as it grew out of the latter part of this period) is that Merton increasingly wants his readers to be aware of how all persons must accept where they are, even if life seems to become more mysterious in the process. Simultaneously, another thing that Merton was learning throughout this period was how he could both make his journals honest and still craft them so they would be of value to later readers. In the complete journals, especially in the early parts, and in the early years of *A Search for Solitude*, we often have entries that are quite clearly private, while they are focused so that anyone anywhere later can use these entries such as they might read Pascal's thoughts. Merton, in fact, refers to Blaise Pascal at one point. Such journal entries are going to work like a prayer book. These are entries planned so that you can go back and re-read. The earlier parts of Merton's journal are most successful precisely because of this quality.

In the entries written after 1960, what we have is a situation where a more mature Merton is becoming attuned more and more to how he must continue to write to get at the essence of a moment—moments which are selected and crafted remembrances, but maybe more difficult moments. The result is a new variety of journal entry, which is quite carefully crafted to be meditative; yet this is not like a diary, and it does not chronicle "progress," nor is it at times even edifying. Certain entries make sense only in terms of what he is learning about moving away from concerns about self.

When examining *A Search for Solitude*, certain places can be noted in the September 1952 to February 1953 sections that contain moments relatively early when he is celebrating solitude and enjoying being by himself. One might examine these entries at one's leisure (February 9, 1953; February 24, 1953). These are interesting moments which, as suggested, work almost like prayers. In the journal, there are no entries at all for the entire period from March 10, 1953, to July 17, 1956—only a gap. In this context, the entry of February 16, 1953, is quite interesting because it is as if somehow Merton has found some really good material, which he chooses to record and to which he knows others might return. He then chooses to stop. The gap is intriguing. One might even argue Merton must have found other outlets for writing. He was not interested in keeping a journal at this time. Thus, a search of the correspondence might reveal that he was putting energy into detailed journal-like letters or other activities.

Within this volume, the "raw" journal resumes after a three-year lapse, at which point—July 17, 1956—there is some significant material. Merton is, in fact, analyzing what he is doing in this journal and how it is slightly different than what he has done previously. Now he again feels a necessity to write, and explains that now he feels he must somehow write not just about himself. In fact, he suggests, he has to consider the whole universe. He admits he always wants to "write about everything." And then he qualifies: "That does not mean to write a book that *covers* everything—which would be impossible. But a book in which everything can go. A book with a little of everything that creates itself out of everything" (*SS*, 45). What is being suggested is that he needs to think not just about his life, but how any life reverberates with all other things observed. Immediately in the same passage, many separate items follow, items which unfold together and items which allow one to see what he seems to be planning and what he is executing. As suggested, in his opening paragraphs, this necessity to write and to write about everything is stressed; but note then he is not writing about the universe. He remarks instead about particular things observed: slender young black oaks; the sun suddenly touching the woods; how proverbs work for him; and indeed in that sequence, we are given a formal prayer. It is all very carefully done, and it suggests a newfound aesthetic. His entries are his day-by-day record, yet they are very carefully crafted by the monk/writer to reflect a wide range of thought. What I mean by crafted is that this writer is now bringing skill to the body of the material so that he can shape it, and then readers can later use it for meditation or reflection. Merton, later, will extend this type of specific technique by also focusing upon events and remembrances that may be quite disturbing.

Merton's focus in writing was clearly developing over a long period, over decades. His craft develops on several levels: as a user of words; as an observer of himself; and as someone increasingly aware of the relationship of his work to future readers in the years and decades to come. Merton was clearly terribly ambitious as a writer. And so what we observe in the developing complete journals is someone who is eager to write and to write well, but someone who is eventually also aware of the fact that his very ambition is in some ways getting in the way of being honest. Then what we actually see, and this is significant, throughout Volumes 3 and 4 (during this period from 1953 to 1963), is a gradual diminishment of the documentation of Merton's ambition and the corresponding growth of his awareness of others and his awareness of insights offered to him, and sometimes accepted or rejected.

All this is done the way a writer does it. First, we observe a lot of struggle; next, we observe a writer increasingly aware of his unique responsibilities, and then we have a writer who is raising lots of questions, especially questions about vocation, and still later, in 1960 to 1963, wider questions about his changing relationship to the world.

The next emphasis has to do with how questions regarding vocation are handled during the decade in question, 1953 to 1963. Merton is learning that it is never just a matter of place, and it is much more a matter of attitude. Here I will not pursue in any great detail these passages, but if one examines the period from 1953 to 1960, much of that journal records a life very much concerned with how he, Merton, would best pursue God, holiness, the sacred. What is perhaps most interesting about the patterns revealed in *The Sign of Jonas* and *Conjectures*, and within the four complete volumes which cover the years leading up to 1963, is the shift from focus in, and on, self to a more significant awareness of God's presence and how that presence can be manifested in others, in nature, and in flashes of the transcendent.

All this occurs while Merton continues to be fundamentally aware that, paradoxically, his primary responsibility remains to himself. That paradox gives hope to many of the late 1950s to mid-1960s journal entries. In the third volume, we observe a slow, often painful, movement away from dreams of perfection—if this or that change might occur. One of the most intriguing patterns in this period through 1960 is Merton's near obsession with the idea that he must somehow move to another monastery. What happens when he finally gets a letter in 1959 saying, "NO, you're not going to move, Rome says you're going to stay put," is quite interesting. What happens in just two quick pages is that the crucial letter comes and he recognizes this is an important event; and then, almost immediately, he says fine, I accept it, no questions, and that is the end of that particular series of questions (*SS*, 358–59). In only a few hours, he is able to muster the strength to articulate that the solitude he needs is "beyond geography." So he has come to know concretely that his most important work is interior work. Or, perhaps, he is relieved he no longer has to think about these questions. Of course, that does not mean that he will not continue to dream dreams about Mexico, Alaska, New Mexico, or California. Also it does not mean that he ceases to have problems. He learns by the end of the decade that a change of place is more a matter of convenience; that the spiritual life is a matter of how one lives.

In *Turning toward the World*, for the period 1961–62, similar patterns are revealed. This is a period that I call pivotal in the journal, and maybe also for the life. I regard two basic patterns occurring throughout this decade: monastic vocation and openness to the world. At the core, we always have questions about vocation; what it means to fulfill a monastic vocation. There are wonderful things in *The Search for Solitude*, in effect providing a definition of vocation and how one finally has to learn to do what is the will of God, to simply accept life without reservation. Yet by the time we get to the end of Volume 3 (1960), we have a far different Merton than the writer of earlier moments in these journals, someone who is going to raise many other questions: how, for example, he can combine his calling, his concern for developing an interior life, with responsibility for the world, and how he is to begin turning more toward that world.

Maybe the chief difference between Volumes 3 and 4 could be defined by saying that the earlier Merton (1953–1959) is still concerned almost too much with his own feelings. There is an entry

(August 15, 1952) where he notes his joy in being "cleansed by [his own] bitterness" (*SS*, 9). He realizes he is sort of reveling in his own emotions. I think those kinds of passages are less available in later journal entries. (*Learning to Love* is a special case.)

When one examines Volume 4, what can be demonstrated is that we have someone who is concerned much less with himself, but rather with how he is going to take what he has learned about himself and turn it toward a focus on the world. So from 1960 to mid-1963, we have a Merton who wants contact with the world while he also senses he needs much more quiet. We have someone who wants to speak out about issues in the world, while he does not know exactly how he is going to do this. We have someone who is learning to speak in all kinds of ways that will allow him to be heard beyond the monastery, but we have someone who wants to remain quiet. There are many contradictions here, and what is significant is his shift as he records these contradictions.

Merton cannot, we learn, just be quiet. This is especially true in the fast-changing world of the 1960s, when he finds himself asking, "What must I do? Am I, Merton, innocent or guilty?" He wrote a valuable essay called "Letter to an Innocent Bystander"[6] where he argues no one is really fully innocent. That (to some degree) mutated into the concept for the book that became *Conjectures of a Guilty Bystander*. Part of what is revealed in the earlier essay, written as a letter, and in the revised journal entries for the book, is an assurance that we are neither innocent nor guilty; we are all living in an ambivalent situation. That ambivalence is a large part of what is being recorded in Volume 4, *Turning toward the World*. Year by year, we see Merton asking certain kinds of questions and then trying to figure out what he should do.

When I edited and structured that volume which covers parts of four years, I entitled the first part "The Promise of a Hermitage"; permission had just been given to begin to build a new gathering place and it seemed possible that a new kind of life might unfold for him. I called the second part (1961) "The Continuing Need to Question" and then part three (1962) "Seeking the Right Balance." The fourth part, 1963, is labeled "Gifts of Quiet and Nature." It was not possible for me to be aware of what was included in Volumes 5 or 6 when I was doing the transcription and editing for *Turning toward the World*, and I did not, for example, know how Larry Cunningham was structuring his volume for the years preceding. But it is exceedingly interesting to look at the total project—Larry Cunningham's volume covering seven years, this volume, *Turning toward the World*, spanning four years, and then *Dancing in the Water of Life* and *Learning to Love*, the volumes that follow, because they all work together, and Merton knew this. As the controller of this record, Merton saw how they worked together as an increasingly honest record of his struggles and simultaneously his acceptance of ambiguity and doubt.

IV. Honesty and Documentation in 1961–1962

With this necessary foregrounding, it is now possible to concentrate on a critical period of change, just two months in 1961 and 1962, wherein Merton, as journal writer, reveals his own ups and downs and finally his acceptance of the ambiguity of his role as monk and writer. Clearly, what was created in *The Sign of Jonas* and later in *Conjectures*, both pulled from the raw material of the complete journals, are crafted pictures that are designed to encourage the reader. But in *Jonas,* the encouragement stresses predictable monastic patterns; in *Conjectures,* it is more a matter of complexity and mystery. I think all the "raw" journal entries work this way too, and even more so as this pivotal change in his life is accepted, while it is sometimes hard to see all this because so much seems to be going on and so many types of journal entries are included.

A section from the complete journals for December 1961 and January 1962 can be read as a model of how the journal as a whole seems to be developing. These entries often reflect hope, and they frequently work as encouragement for the reader, but this is often hard to perceive when absorbing separate entries. If we look at individual "raw" entries, we find a Merton who is sometimes depressed, often discouraged, someone who is wondering what his monastic life is all about. But we also have a controlled record of a Merton who is frequently also indicating: "OK, I've got what I need right here, I can accept where I am right now" even though it is not always clear what all this means regarding the future.

This is an alternating pattern about which Merton is never completely clear, while he is always seeking or being surprised. Readers can study this December and January and watch how it is structured. Then it might be possible to do a similar thing for the whole of Volume 4; the same thing can be done for the decade (1953–1963); and, I suggest, it can be done for a whole life. That's Merton's most important strategic point.

The later complete journals are wonderful in that they include a multitude of entries that reflect Merton's quest, his myriad ideas, and lots of dissatisfaction with himself, with his role, with his relationship to the world. But there is also a new stress upon acceptance and mystery. What is revealed within just these two months of entries demonstrates Merton's growing willingness to accept ambiguity. This is fundamental to the bulk of the later journals and to the spiritual life as Merton was coming to understand it. For him, the contemplative life is really becoming more and more a matter of integration—with contemplation come darkness, and trouble, and emptiness.

Here is an observer who writes about 1960s life with all of its horrible nuclear threats and all the problems of civil unrest perceived as a kind of foreboding about the drift of all western civilization, but here also is a monk coming to realize that one has to keep struggling and not worry too much about winning. Thus, what I examine now are some twelve entries from December 22, 1961 through January of 1962. These entries—crisis and mystery—are wonderfully honest. They are also sometimes like a roller coaster ride; Merton's implied point is that this is the way life works. Every day cannot be the same day, and one has to deal with the experiences which one is given. This is, therefore, Merton, the writer, composing a literary work that is his roller coaster, while it is also a reflection of him as spiritual seeker providing hope for future readers. So, in these entries, it sometimes seems as if Merton is overwhelmed with the complexity of a world that is, for him, so hard to interpret. Such a feeling of loss or abandonment is also basic for this entire period of ten years. But, and most importantly, Merton learns one need not worry so much about interpreting the world. That is the key to what is going on in this decade of journal, and this key gets Merton through December 1961 and January 1962.

Here is an ambitious spiritual interpreter little by little saying, "So what—but I have to keep the journal to stress that point." By the end of 1961, clearly his journal entries indicate that Merton is not in a particularly good mood, while he also acknowledges that he possesses many gifts, many advantages, and that things do have a way of working out given Divine Providence. That is what I want to demonstrate: It is truly amazing if one glances at these dozen entries that reflect aspects of the overall structure of the book, keeping in mind the titles that I assigned for each of the four years: "The Promise of a Hermitage," "The Continuing Need to Question" in

1961, and then "Seeking the Right Balance" in 1962, which leads to "Gifts of Quiet and Nature" in 1963. My point is that all four of these themes and patterns are crucial within this very short period of only about a month from December to January. Merton's cumulative journal choices reveal him returning to these overlapping and recurrent themes of promise and struggle and then surprise.

There are lots of things to think about in terms of Merton's roller coaster ride. In one significant entry, he draws a distinction between preachers preaching about peace and the kingdom of peace. He then notes in a somewhat discouraged manner, "My vocation seems to be only to preach peace, and perhaps only as a voice in the desert preparing the way for those who will 'announce' it" (*TTW,* 186). But then, a couple of days later, he goes back, he reads the entry preceding, and he notes as if he is picking up the same passage—or rather it just continues as if he never stopped thinking about it: "It is even doubtful whether my vocation is to preach peace. More and more the conviction haunts me, that I shall sooner or later be silenced" (*TTW,* 186). And, in fact, he was. But he notes he is also corresponding with John Ford, SJ, and he is thinking about how he is going to write about issues of war. He is clearly trying to figure out what all this means because there are so many conflicting things taking place during this period.

On December 20, Merton writes, *"Clama in fortitudine qui annuntias pacem in Jerusalem"* ("Cry out loud, you who announce peace to Jerusalem") (*TTW,* 186). He is quoting from the Nocturne prayer of that day and obviously thinking about the meaning of peace and peacefulness. If one looks at the entries for most of the rest of December, there are numerous questions raised about the wider issues of peace and how he himself is going to be peaceful and write about peace and war. There are lots of different things going on simultaneously. In the passage immediately following, Merton testily reports receiving a letter from the Papal Secretary of State, and, sure enough, this is a sign of things to come: that letter urges a diminution of contacts with Protestant ministers and scholars. Merton writes: "My inference is that I have been delated" (*TTW,* 187). That is, someone has reported him to the Vatican. Within the same entry, he suggests maybe the best thing to do is to say all that he thinks at once, and then let the blows fall.

But, importantly, we must note what happens with the entry on December 24, on Christmas Eve (*TTW,* 188). He is reading the Divine Office and sees the word *maiestas* (majesty), and then he reports thinking about the anguish of the word "peace" in the community prayers and in the offices, while the realization comes to him that it is totally serious and perfectly simple: "Above all our confusions, our violence, our sin, God established His kingdom no matter what 'the world' may do about it. He sends the Prince of Peace. The message of Christians is not that the kingdom might come" (*TTW*, 188) but that somehow it is here right now. What is especially significant is that this same reassuring line of thought can be observed through several other entries here in late 1961 and early 1962.

The entry for Christmas day pulls together many of Merton's conflicting ideas; it is *not* a matter, he indicates in this entry, of living and also condemning others who don't agree with you. He notes: To live and say to all who would destroy, you are scoundrels is simply not the answer. For we cannot keep peace by calling one another "scoundrels." Maybe he learned this from reading Gandhi, whose writings he was then editing. Peace within oneself must come first.

In the entries that follow for December 27 and 31, a wonderful calmness is included. He is writing about Julian of Norwich and how he learned much from her. (Significantly, in part three of *Conjectures*, within the central part of that book, he reworks this same entry.[7]) Now I think what is important about what Merton is recording here is his being disturbed and not feeling peaceful; yet also his realizing that there is somehow right there in this particular monastery, in this liturgy, great peacefulness to be celebrated.

Merton also is almost simultaneously dealing with the fact that he is not happy, as, for example, in the entry about the distress and confusion of this past year (*TTW*, 190): "Life is madder and madder"; yet he insists the woods and fields are always a relief. And so on. Then go to the next entry, the beginning of 1962, and watch what occurs. The point is we continue to raise all kinds of questions, but we have also acknowledged the realization that Christ has given us what we need, and we should acknowledge the fact that He can be experienced. Persons like Julian of Norwich have answers.

But Merton remains agitated, and this provides the drama of the journal. We examine the other early parts of the 1962 journal, and we watch him again dealing with the fact that he might not be able to write; or he might not be able to do as much as he would like to do, while he also realizes that there is a certain beauty and calmness and correctness in his present circumstances. These entries—January 2, 3, and 9—work well together. They all show Merton accepting the fact that he may not get to be the spokesman he wants to be, while, at almost the same time, he acknowledges there are many other things he might be able to do. The allusion to some reading he has been doing about Fr. Metzger, who was a World War II conscientious objector, is a kind of answer to his own needs (*TTW*, 193).

At the same time, he stresses the beauty to be observed throughout the monastery itself and in its rituals. He notes a particular psalm, "that I may be pleasing to God in the light of the living." He notes he is deeply moved, as if he had never seen that psalm before (*TTW*, 193). What he is admitting, therefore, is that he is still learning to pray and pay attention to particularities of the moment. One gets the impression that this psalm was being given to him almost as if it were brand new.

If we study the following entry, January 12, on the next page, this also is valuable precisely because it introduces still another mood of conflict. Merton reports that he had gone off to visit Asbury Methodist Seminary, and returned by way of Shakertown, a nineteenth-century settlement close to where he lives, between Lexington and the monastery (*TTW*, 194). Both events were stimulating. He has had a chance to go out and speak with other people; yet he is not sure if he should even be going to this seminary, and in the paragraph that follows, he reports how he had stopped at Shakertown to take photographs. He observed something in the simplicity of that architecture that reflects the earlier Shaker community life and that he realizes he can draw upon. What Merton is doing is reminding himself of the fact that he himself needs to insist on simplicity, the simplicity that he had already noted in those Christmas offices, or in moments when he was calm ten days earlier, around December 24 or 27.

But he also has to deal with the real fact that he must *now* continue to deal with so many personal problems of his existential life. The January 21 entry reflects his personal "struggle against pessimism and desperation. How can we believe that the tragedy that is being prepared can be avoided?" he asks. "Everything contributes to the inexorable preparation" which the weapons systems dictate, and so on (*TTW*, 195). In the entry immediately following, while he is on retreat and thinking about his own intense interior confusion of the past few days, the struggle continues. Then he records an important insight: on January 25, 1962, he includes an entry where he says his problems are "false problems" (*TTW*, 197). So much of what he is writing about, he notes, is necessary precisely because he has created his own problems. And so much of what he needs is already present. This, again, is real honesty.

All this "raw" material is a carefully planned and detailed record of Merton dealing with this internal struggle. It is also a beautiful example of how with words he is able to put together a kind of dialogue with himself which people are later able to read and ponder. Now there clearly are many other ways of talking about what is going on in this key period linking 1961 to 1962; but if we examine these twelve or so entries, what we find is a precise record of someone wondering how is he going to speak about such complicated issues relating to violence, justice, and war, and how he himself is going to become more peaceful.

Merton frequently wonders: What is the difference between preaching peace, which he fears may be all he has been doing, and being peaceful? What is the difference between getting excited about whether you're going to get published, or if you are going to write about this or that public issue, and praying for a wise heart, or remembering that Julian of Norwich says too many activities distract? Always, however, he remains focused on his evolving understanding of his monastic vocation.

These 1961–1962 entries are a basic "raw" record of Merton, as journal composer, dealing with his struggles and learning slowly that somehow trust is what is most necessary. Living in the immediate is what is necessary; and then all kinds of small joys are observed when one takes a moment to observe them. That is what is most important. Such is Merton's way of revealing God's Providence for him. By implication, his revealing his struggles becomes a source of encouragement for his future readers. He senses readers will feel similar tension.

Merton's developing journal is a story carefully structured by him. Maybe the patterns of surprise and instability and contradiction are ones we, as editors, might have paid more attention to. In the early 1960s, Merton is increasingly reminding himself and his readers that a spiritual journey forward is not easy, or ever straightforward. One therefore keeps reexamining. As readers, we keep beginning again and again in our reading of this journal and therefore in our understanding of the journey of life. This is the real significance of what Merton so honestly recorded.

Photograph by Thomas Merton

Loving Winter When the Plant Says Nothing:
Thomas Merton's Spirituality in His Private Journals

Jonathan Montaldo

Joy is natural in the spring, and celebration is easy with all that thrives in summer's stiff, green heat. October through December produce in us their transient harvests of delicious melancholy. But how do we learn and who can teach us the hard art of always needing to begin again, of "lov[ing] winter when the plant says nothing"?[1]

Scholars of repute call Thomas Merton a "spiritual master," and publishers lace the back covers of his books with avowals that he is one of the most important spiritual writers of our century. Merton's own assessment of his achievement was more modest. He even insured a more complex reception of his spiritual legacy by writing journals that scandalize the reader who seeks in them a spiritual success story to emulate.

His extant journals, now wholly exposed, do not chronicle an ascent to ever higher stages of human and spiritual development. They reveal instead a disconcerting journey of his descent into an ever-deepening spiritual poverty. Merton's journals manifest scant evidence of spiritual mastery. They disclose its salvific opposite: Merton's being mastered by the Spirit as his willfulness is purified in the furnace of failure, and his self-absorption is transfigured into compassion for everyone else.

Merton's mature journals are a sustained narrative of redemption from his having to wear the self-fabricated public mask of holy monk. In them his readers have a final accounting of the "lucky wind / That blew away his halo with his cares" and of the "lucky sea that drowned his reputation."[2] His journals elaborate his parable of hard-road enlightenment through a loss of status. Readers of his journals witness their "spiritual master's" deepening foolishness and the manner by which his polished ego arrived at tarnishment: an inveterate exhibitionist's happy fall from a public grace.

This is not to say that the "great affair" of Merton's being purified of his false public self was fully accomplished. His life enjoyed no happy, neat ending. Like all of us humans, who come wet from the womb and end in dust, the cosmos requiring neither our coming nor our going, Merton died just as he was born: in the middle of the world's ten thousand things.

As his hand reached out for that hot-wired fan, we imagine he was reminding himself that his recent esthetic experience before the Buddhist statues at Polonnaruwa[3] was not, unlike for many of his critical readers, the definitive "word" for him. More an icon for persons who never fully settle into fixed ideological positions but who are always departing them to follow the Spirit which blows wherever the Spirit wills, Merton, we surmise, died just as he had lived: happy and in full-throttle-up flight.

The year 2003 marks the sixty-fifth anniversary of Thomas Merton's baptism into the Roman Catholic Church and his first eucharist at the age of twenty-three, when he was a student at Columbia in New York City. Merton always understood that the singular narrative of his redemption paralleled a common salvific pattern for every Christian: "the great affair," he called it, "of saving my sinful soul, in which grace and 'psychology' are sometimes in rather intense conflict."[4] Merton's story, like any serious Christian's, is a chronicle of yearning for the inbreaking of God's living face into his personal history and into the history of his imperfect times. This eschatological yearning, echoing the prophet Isaiah's cry, "O that you would tear open the heavens and come down" (Is 63:19), is the ground of Merton's vocation to be both monk and writer.

Merton's spiritual journey was a persistent yearning that he might be fully converted to God's presence to and pressure upon his life, a pressure and a presence that Merton apprehended under the particular metaphors of God as "Merciful Father" and as "Holy Wisdom." Like many an adult convert, Merton declared himself to have been dramatically redeemed through baptism, only to discover himself forced on a pilgrim's march down a dark path toward his God in rhythms of complaint punctuated by praise, of struggle syncopated by rest, and of obstinacy modulated by obedience. Baptism simply sealed forever this rhythmic pattern of a sustained groping forward through which Merton heard his God's "voice" beckoning to him, though often muffled, through all his experiences.

At his death in 1968, Merton bequeathed to his readers a legacy of extant journals written over twenty-nine years (1939–1968). Two self-edited and selected portions of his journals, *The Sign of Jonas* (1953) and *Conjectures of a Guilty Bystander* (1966) were among his personal favorites and remain two of his most popular books. Merton had restricted publication of his surviving journals for a period of twenty-five years after his death. By June 1998, the project to publish his extant journals in seven volumes had been completed.

This essay represents a work in progress, a too-brief reflection on elements of Merton's spirituality culled from his journals. This harvesting should thus be read as suggestive and ruminating rather than as analytical and systematic. In all his writing, Merton is acutely conscious of his intended reader: he incites personal engagement, he overcomes and bridges distancing, he invites personal response to his autobiographical art of confession and witness.[5] In his preface to the Japanese edition (1963) of *The Seven Storey Mountain,* he made this extraordinary declaration:

> *Therefore, most honorable reader, it is not as an author that I would speak to you, not as a story-teller, not as a philosopher, not as a friend only: I seek to speak to you, in some way, as your own self. Who can tell what this may mean? I myself do not know. But if you listen, things will be said that are perhaps not written in this book. And this will be due not to me, but to One who lives [within us] and speaks [to us] both.*[6]

This meditation on Merton's spirituality will disclose something of my singular though hardly unique appropriation of Merton's journals. As have so many other readers, I too have accepted his invitation to converse with him, one human being to another. In my case, this conversation continues with critical sympathy, with poetry, and even with prayer.

Merton's "Voice" in his Journals: Opening the Heart's Inner Ear

To open a reader's heart by revealing his own heart so that heart could speak directly to heart was the primary motivation behind all of Merton's expressive, autobiographical writing. Early in his writer's career, failing to have his fiction accepted for publication, Merton realized that his major literary asset was in writing about what he personally experienced and about what he loved in that experience. Writing in his journal in December of 1939, while living on Perry Street in Greenwich Village, Merton acknowledged:

> *I have tremendous preoccupations of my own, personal preoccupations with whatever it is going on inside my own heart, and I simply can't write about anything else. Anything I create is only a symbol for some completely interior preoccupation of my own. . . . I only know I am writing well [when I am writing] about the things I love: ideas, places, certain people: all very definite, individual, identifiable objects of love, all of them.*[7]

Merton invites his reader to engage his autobiographical *persona*. Merton's literary gift is inducing his reader to love the ideas and the places and the particular people he loved. His reader gradually incorporates Merton's mental climate as a phenomenon affecting the reader's own spiritual temperature. Merton's artful presentation of himself and his experience first seduces and then powerfully constrains his readers to examine themselves in the mirror of his autobiographical art.

I have been reading Merton consistently since I was thirteen years old, for more than forty years. I have read him even through my bad times, when I would sporadically conclude that everything he had ever written on the spiritual life was junk. I remember one night in the early seventies, having recently returned from Vietnam, cursing him and throwing one of his books against a wall. At that moment, the gap between Merton's rhetoric and my experience was too large. But the episode was just another of my many quarrels with his literary mask over the years.

Reflecting on my long experience of reading Merton, I seem in retrospect almost destined to have heard his "voice" so early in my life.

His voice has always educated me. Merton's writing still opens my heart's inner ear. He still animates me to lead with him, in the company of his text, an "examined life." Through Merton's writing and my responses to it, we have always waited together, writer and reader, at the far end of our experiences, for a Mercy neither of us could ever bequeath to ourselves.

When a writer elicits sustained and deeply affecting responses in a reader, responses which are reproduced with varying intensities in hundreds of thousands of other readers, he has no doubt mined a mother lode of universally shared human and religious experiences. Merton's reaction to John Henry Newman could well describe his readers' own reactions to him: "There are people one meets in books or in life whom one does not merely observe, meet, or know. A deep resonance of one's entire being is immediately set up with the entire being of the other (*Cor ad cor loquitur*—heart speaks to heart in the wholeness of the language of music; true friendship is a kind of singing)."[8]

To expose the chasm between his ideals and his realities, to delineate the gap between his published rhetoric and his struggling practice, was a second major motivation that impelled Merton to write journals. In his pre-monastic journals (*Run to the Mountain*), he was more practicing the art of writing and auditioning his writer's voice. He maps out his vocational goals, and he exposes the process of his deciding to enter a Trappist monastery, but many entries are, in his own words, mere "exercises."

In the early monastic journals (*Entering the Silence*), a self-conscious romanticizing marks an obvious and, unfortunately for him, successful attempt to secure a publicly recognized holiness. The piety of these early monastic journals is real but could not survive. He would look back on the monastic-honeymoon period of his journaling with dismay. Three months before the publication of his autobiography in 1948, he wrote in his journal:

> *I just read some of the notes I wrote in the journal a year ago ([the] end of 1946) and I am wondering what I thought I was talking about. The first thing that impresses me is that practically all I wrote about myself and my trials was stupid because I was trying to express what I thought I ought to think, and not for any especially good reason, rather than what I actually did think. . . . What was painfully artificial in that diary was that I was trying so much*

> *to write it like every other pious diary that was ever written: "I resolve this"—"I pray that." Well, I am very slow to learn what is useless in my life!*[9]

Precisely because *The Seven Storey Mountain* had freeze-framed for his readership a glowing portrait of his pious self in deep shades of rose, the color of choice for enthusiasts, his journals (beginning with *A Search for Solitude* and continuing through four more volumes) began to function for him as a practice of honesty with regard to the false literary mask he had created and of mindfulness with regard to the crooked road his life had taken by the pursuit of both monastic vows and the exigencies of a literary and public career. His journals became "part of a documentation that is demanded of me—still demanded, I think—by the Holy Ghost."[10] His journals, while a source for future books, became consciously confessional writing. They revealed his spiritual journey's paradoxes and inconsistencies. Merton allowed his later journals to expose the sins that marred his publicly professed religious life.

When writers, such as Merton, confess themselves to be spiritual seekers and reach their goal, perhaps unconscious, of finding themselves sought after as "sages," then pride becomes for them as debilitating a sin as lust. Self-righteous criticism of others sins against the communion of saints. Excessive self-concern and self-analysis implies a form of unbelief in the forgiveness of sins. Ambition in a "spiritual master" insures spiritual failure. The Chinese Taoist Chuang Tzu warned those who believe their good works place them above other human beings: "Achievement is the beginning of failure. Fame is the beginning of disgrace."[11] In a journal entry dated January 19, 1961, Merton admitted:

> *Someone accused me of being a "high priest" of creativity. Or at least of allowing people to regard me as one. This is perhaps true. The sin of wanting to be a pontiff, of wanting to be heard, of wanting converts, disciples. Being in a cloister, I thought I did not want this. Of course I did and everyone knows it. St. William, says the Breviary this night, when death approached, took off his pontifical vestments (what he was doing with them on in bed I can't imagine) and by his own efforts got to the floor and died. So I am like him, in bed with a mitre on. What am I going to do about it? . . . I have got to face the fact that there is in me a desire for survival*

as pontiff, prophet and writer, and this has to be renounced before I can be myself at last.[12]

Merton was always first to admit that any treasures of spiritual insight embedded in his autobiographical writing were a graced harvest from poor soil. A major theme of Merton's journaling is his acknowledging that real fissures in his character rendered him a weak vessel in which, by God's grace, strong things were nevertheless contained and were being poured out for others. This is, of course, a major theme in the Pauline corpus of the New Testament. While Merton is no Saint Paul, what theologian Karl Barth said of Saint Paul can be applied to Merton. Barth wrote:

> *When pilgrims on the road of God meet one another, they have something to say. A man may be of value to another man, not because he wishes to be important, not because he possesses some inner wealth of soul, not because of something he is, but because of what he is not. His importance may consist in his poverty, in his hopes and fears, in his waiting and hurrying, in the direction of his whole being towards what lies beyond his horizon and beyond his power. The importance of an apostle is negative rather than positive. In him a void becomes visible.*[13]

The deep significance for us of Merton's witness may consist in his errors and in his acknowledged failures. He incarnates in his journals his quintessentially human fate to stand with his feet straddling a divide between what he longed to be and what he actually was. Merton's limitations illuminate. His more than occasional ability to transcend them, by moments of insight which recall him to his vocation to move forward in spite of himself toward God, both motivates and encourages.

Readers misunderstand the false steps, the backsliding, the being caught in the same old compulsive thinking that Merton regularly discloses in his journals if they fail to understand his persistent dedication to the evangelical task of being "pure of heart." Merton's personal integrity in his later journals is missionary: "I am thrown into contradiction," he wrote from his hermitage in 1966. "I am thrown into contradiction: to realize it is mercy, to accept it is love, to help others do the same is compassion" (*LL*, 355).

As Merton elaborates the paradox of his desiring purity of heart, while witnessing in himself the ability to evade the humility and self-disregard necessary for its procurement, he places before the eyes of his readers their own struggle with conflicting desires, which attends their own spiritual journeying.

Merton focuses his reader on the inadequacy of confining religious experience to the esthetic or only to the intellectual and academic. Writing to Étienne Gilson, he had begged: "Please pray for me to Our Lord that instead of merely writing something I may *be* something, and indeed that I may so fully be what I ought to be that there may be no further necessity for me to write, since the mere fact of being what I ought to be would be more eloquent than many books" (*SC*, 31).

Merton's nervousness at finding himself, after years of self-discipline, still more complicated and impure mirrors our own nervousness as we, without his discipline, give ourselves over to any technique marketed to us as a painless solution for calming our distracted selves. We grasp at any pill that will quick-fix the attention deficit disorder we are suffering *en masse*, we who are always nervously changing the channel and the subject.[14] Merton witnesses our dilemma for us and suggests its hard cure by exposing his own nervousness and then embracing his weaknesses as an essential means of identifying with his life's only spiritual master, Jesus Christ. His journals testify to the necessary self-emptying of his idealized personality into the total catastrophe of his being enfleshed in an imperfect time.

Merton exposes the deep layers of his weaknesses that he might assume and incorporate them. His practice of writing journals is thus akin to the ancient asceticism of the Desert Fathers and Mothers: "He who manifests his thoughts is soon healed; he who hides them makes himself sick."[15]

As Merton incorporates into his own consciousness his heart's dark cellar rooms, he invites his readers to incorporate their own hearts' dark rooms into their own biographies. Gregory of Nazianzen in the fourth century had already elucidated this psychological and religious principle: "That which has not been incorporated has not been healed."[16]

Voicing himself to himself continuously over the years simply kept Merton honest. He needed the hard evidence at hand, which his journals provided, when he paused—often and persistently—to examine his conscience. Writing journals kept Merton authentic. The written evidence prevented the blind admiration of his readers from blinding him to his misguided, and often misguiding, quotidian self.

When I was a teenager, I was taken up into the cloud of Merton's romance with the monastic life. Now that I am in my fifties, the tone of his voice in his maturity captures my attention most. Merton's voice from his hermitage, on the cusp of his own fifties, and beyond, has a more broken and uncertain modulation, which strikes me, from where I am hearing it now, as utterly convincing. After finally getting everything he always thought and said he wanted—being solitary in a hermitage—Merton is sad with disbelief, in his journals of 1966–68 (*Learning to Love* and *The Other Side of the Mountain*), at finding himself acting much like the same crazy young man he was on Perry Street in the Village. Away from his monastic community, Merton discovered himself much too easily and once more acting "wild."

Merton's voice from the hermitage rivets his reader as he talks himself through encounters with dangerous seasons of insecurity, which tore away at the disguises he wore to hide hard truths about his more visceral self. In his long-hoped-for hermitage, Merton experienced a "dread" for which his prayer, although he did not know it fully until then, had always been preparing him.[17] After decades of publicly theorizing on the spiritual life and of practicing monastic disciplines, Merton in his hermitage found himself humbled, his back to the wall, as he discerned himself making a mess of his "answered prayers" for a solitary life by becoming "a priest who has a woman" (*LL*, 79).

Merton appeals at this end-game stage of his mortality because his hermitage experience allowed him no more mirrors to reflect upon himself garbed in the saffron robes of a "spiritual master." It is precisely at this juncture in his experience of unmitigated defeat for his self-idealizing personality as hermit that Merton's spirituality of humbly waiting for a Mercy, which he now knew by hard experience he could never bequeath to himself, is positively revealed.

A Spirituality of Vigilance and Listening

The spiritual practice flowing through Merton's journals like an underground stream is an attentive, faithful, and sober listening. His path toward human wisdom was an ancient one: Merton was Benedictine to the bone. The first counsel of *The Rule of St. Benedict* is "Listen carefully, my son, to the master's instructions. . . ." Your very salvation, Benedict implies, depends on your opening the "ear of your heart." This culture of listening (*cultus auris*)[18] permeates Merton's autobiographical writing and witnesses to his traditionally monastic spirit.

In the face of his recurring desires for a more perfect place to become his idealized self, Merton acquiesced, although often with loud complaint, to voices of authority, especially those of his abbots. Merton's grace was to doubt himself. No matter how much his sacred ideals might be challenged, he listened for and then obeyed the definitive abbatial instruction and submitted himself to the Rule's yoke to which he had pledged himself at his profession of First Vows. He inclined his heart's ear in obedience to the mercy of God, which had baptized him as Thomas, and to the mercy of the Cistercian Order, which had called him to itself and given him the new name Louis. He wrote in May 1947: "Gethsemani—the place and the community, *locus et fratres*—is the spring where I am to drink the waters of life, and if I look somewhere else, it is to a broken cistern as far as I am concerned because, no matter how excellent it may be in itself, [another place] *is not God's will for me*" (*ES*, 71–72).

Merton's spirituality of vigiling was most embedded in his listening for "a word" from those who wrote the sacred scriptures. For twenty-seven years, he listened to the biblical writers' words on the Word of words, and he sang their words with them seven times a day every day. While he had a ferocious appetite for the latest word in the latest book, the sacred writers were his hourly companions, and they always whispered in his ears. He wrote in his journal for 1949:

> *Isaias, Job, Moses, David, Matthew, Mark, Luke and John are all part of my life. They are always about me. . . . They are my Fathers. They are the "burnt men" in the last line of* The Seven Storey Mountain. *I am more and more possessed by their vision of God's Kingdom, and wonder at the futility of seeking anything else on earth but the truth revealed in them and in tradition—the Church's treasure to which she holds the keys. (ES, 362)*

This passionate listening to the church's music, her chorus of witnesses to the Living God in both Scripture and Tradition, a music with which Buddhist, Islamic, and Hindu voices for Merton could only harmonize, particularizes Merton's spirituality of "mindfulness" as essentially western and ecclesial.

By temperament always tempted to go his own way alone, an Adam without an Eve to encumber him, Merton's journals also witness to the gradual feminization of his heart's inner ear as he listened for voices that could call him out of his chronic self-analysis to a more inclusive, other-oriented appreciation of God's presence to him on every level of his experience. The voices of women permeated Merton's life. He listened to his birth mother Ruth's voice, telling him he must be "original" and "independent."[19] He listened to the Mother of Mercy's voice consoling him every evening as he sang to her in choir "mourning and weeping in this vale of tears."[20] He listened to Gethsemani's voice, his community's maternal nurturing, which kept him rooted in one Kentucky place.

Merton's dreams were populated with women: He dreamed of a "Chinese princess" who knew and loved him,[21] of a black mother who danced with him (*DWL*, 202), of a young Jewish girl, a recurring dream figure whom Merton called "Proverb," [22] who symbolized for him Holy Wisdom, and the Mother of God who called him to recognition of their merciful activity in his life. The feminine would significantly enflesh itself for Merton in a young nurse who turned her face toward him and overturned his lifelong strategems to keep clear of love. Merton's listening to this chorus of feminine voices, whether in flesh or in dream, were types of Merton's faithful and obedient listening to the voice of the church, calling him to herself as the only possibility for his finally being made whole. The church, in the guise of women's faces, companioned Merton's fragmented life, taught him to love and, more significantly, to accept love, and orchestrated the gradual but unfinished knitting of his life into a more integrated, hidden wholeness.[23]

Singing "Viva Voce" in a Fraternity of Bums

"Sometimes I want to turn away and be a tramp and hang around on the roads without anything, like Humble George or Benedict Joseph Labre" (*ES*, 209).

After having read and written so much, after having taught and directed the spiritual journeys of so many others, and after having experienced the incommunicable spiritual insights that must have accompanied his abundant reading, writing, and teaching, and yet, through all of it, to have voiced himself as continually insecure, to have questioned everything as if he always needed to start over, as if he never knew his life's next move, even relishing his insecurity and finding a happy solace in his ignorance, is a mysterious, though ponderable, reality that informs all of Merton's autobiographical writing.

In his review of Volume 4 of Merton's journals, *Turning toward the World*, Ernest Daniel Carrere, a monk of Gethsemani, observes: "It is almost scandalous that an adult of forty-six years was such a problem to himself, but this is to neglect the foundational hermeneutic of kenosis. The very contortions of Merton's drama indicate a healthy spirit robustly facing the challenges of incarnation."[24]

Merton's kenotic dilemma, how to live wisely when one is enfleshed imperfectly in an imperfect world in an imperfect time, is an important lens through which to conduct a fruitful, though necessarily complex, examination of his life and his writing.[25] Carrere correctly senses that an apparent Merton character flaw, an inability to become comfortable with himself or to nest contentedly in the approved ideologies of his time, is also, in fact, a genuine religious experience of homelessness for being in the presence of the Divine Person in whom all creation is personable and comfortable.

To be human and alive is to search. The grace building upon Merton's instincts accentuated his compulsive restlessness and transformed his natural, inner transiency into an authentically religious search for the Divine Person in whom all ideologies and experiences originate but who is yet more than any human ideology or experience. His spiritual poverty, finding himself continually exiled from his past ideologies and experiences so as to hear the Voice and voices that spoke to his heart in the present moment, was the positive experience hidden below Merton's appearing never to have "gotten his act together." Journeying through an experience of such relinquishment demands hard and necessarily imperfect practice because to undergo such an impoverishment—for the best of motives—is unnatural to the human need for security and anti-cultural to the human need for group approval.

Merton had a natural, perhaps even a pathological willingness to explore self-exile as an inner experience, rather than a geographical experience, of monastic *peregrinatio*: an interior journeying without knowing where he would firmly land. If elements of pathology in his personality account for Merton's often voiced desire to be "without status," to be a "no one" and not "to know where he was going,"[26] grace built upon the pathological and transfigured Merton into a sign for his generation.

Merton's intellectual and emotional poverty of spirit signifies that the deepest humanism in the following of Christ is learning to have no place upon which to lay one's "head" (mind-heart-spirit) except in obedient vigilance, attentive listening, and active response to the present moment of one's experience as communicating God's loving Voice. This fits precisely at least one Mertonian definition of "contemplation":

> *Contemplation is essentially a listening in silence, an expectancy. . . . In other words, the true contemplative is not the one who prepares his mind for a particular message that he wants or expects to hear, but is one who remains empty [spiritually poor] because he knows that he can never expect to anticipate the word that will transform his darkness into light. He does not even anticipate a special kind of transformation. He does not demand light instead of darkness. He waits on the Word of God in silence, and when he is "answered," it is not so much by a word that bursts into his silence. It is by his silence itself, suddenly, inexplicably revealing itself to him as a word of great power, full of the voice of God. (CMP, 122–23)*

Leo Stelten's *Dictionary of Ecclesiastical Latin* (1995) defines a *peregrinatus* as "a stranger, wanderer, pilgrim, traveler, foreigner," upon which denotations can be further nuanced Mertonian connotations of being "an exile, a prodigal, an orphan, a marginal person, a bystander to the main road, one who gets lost in order to find a right way, a spiritual bum." Merton's self-images in his journals are exactly these of the archetypal *peregrinatus*.

The real journey of Merton's life was interior.[27] He lashed himself to the mast of Gethsemani for twenty-seven years so as to weather his interior storms and move forward through them into further encounters with his God's mercy toward him, which anchored him through all his experiences. His stability at Gethsemani, "the belly of the whale" as he had called it in *The Sign of Jonas*,[28] was his way of converting himself to endure the deepest of human mysteries, the Christlike catastrophe of being incarnated in an imperfect place in an imperfect time and yet seeking to love and be loved perfectly by his neighbor and his God.

In 1960, he wrote Jacques Maritain that he was experiencing the paradox and mystery of his vocation:

> *This is my place and yet I have never felt so strongly that I have "no place" as I have felt here [at Gethsemani] since becoming fully reconciled to this as "my place." My place is in reality no place, and I hesitate to act as if I were anything but a stranger anywhere, but especially here. I am an alien and a transient, and this is the last happiness that is possible to me: but a very real one. More real than all the others I thought I knew before it.*[29]

As it authentically should, Merton's "last happiness" exudes minor chords of bitterness. Spiritual poverty is naturally unpalatable as one truly waits for a Mercy one cannot give to oneself. A "spiritual poverty" that is professed solely as a consolation is possibly something else: another method for self-aggrandizement, an "as if" pose for the gushing crowd viewing one's "mastery," or perhaps just another means of placing oneself above (or below) social obligations. Merton confronted himself with his pseudo "as ifs" too often for him to have been dishonest in his interior poverty. His compunction at his failures was too visceral not to have been authentic.

An authentic inner poverty will display itself positively as a more simple and carefree love of life, qualities Merton exhibited with an abundance of exuberance and gusto. Although he might have been uncomfortable in the company of a Jack Kerouac, familiarity could just as easily have bred consent. Merton was connaturally "beat": his natural inclination was always to be "on the road." Lonely for his sweet M. and writing in his "Midsummer Diary" for her, he reports how glad he was that there were obstacles to their being together:

> *(Though for a moment I was walking on the porch and heard cars over there on the road, and thought wildly of going off and getting a ride to town . . . Then what? But that is in me, too, the instinct to suddenly go and not know where or why I am going. But it has been a long time since I have been able to really live like that. The evening at the airport [May 5, 1966, with M., J. Laughlin, and Nicanor Parra] was an exception, a throwback to my natural self, the guy that used to vanish into the heart of France or Germany and just wander.) (LL, 320)*

Dreaming of being a "bum," while eschewing the reality of St. Benedict Joseph Labre's "fleas" (*ES*, 275–76) strongly appealed to

Merton, and in his journals, he coveted for himself at least three modes of being a vagabond: the "tramp" (personified by Humble George [*ES*, 149, 171, 209, 222] and Herman Hanekamp [*ES*, 344, *SS* 242–44]), the "migrating monk" (St. Benedict Joseph Labre) (*ES*, 194, 209, 275–76) and, most ideally for Merton, the "hermit ne'er do well" (Blessed Conrad) (*SS*, 30–31; *CGB*, 134–35; *TTW*, 93). An impromptu wandering around appealed to Merton as the ideal lifestyle for allowing the full mysteries surrounding his truer nature to emerge. A deeper study of this covey of Merton's anti-heroes, which would also include his roving painter father, Owen, and his close friend in actual self-exile, Bob Lax, would disclose the natural horizons in which Merton found himself spiritually freer.

Spiritual freedom for Merton was not only an enthusiastic arrival at and departure from experiences or ideologies without becoming mired in their particular interior states. Freedom was also the ability to incarnate himself in the present moment of his experience so as allow the moment to impinge upon him in its fullness. He became stabilized in what always changed by maintaining an "inner silence" which, at its most anguished, was "a continual seeking, a continual crying in the night, a repeated bending over the abyss" (*TS*, 88). He remained stable by means of this inner silence, even as he changed and flowed forward through time.

Merton alluded to his stability in the present moment in a brief yet comprehensive way in a letter to Helen Wolff, an agent at Pantheon Books, the publishers of Boris Pasternak:

> *Certainly I feel that the Christian poetry and literature of our time must abandon static and outworn concepts and utter their praise of Christ in intuitions that are dynamic and in full movement. Such is Pasternak's vision of reality, a reality which must be caught as it passes, reality which must carry us away with it. If we pause for a moment to formulate abstractions we will have lost life as it goes by.* Timeo Jesum transeuntem et non revertentem *(I fear Jesus will go by and will not come back—as St. Augustine says). This is the very vision of reality we have in the* I Ching. *(CT, 97)*

In a letter to Pablo Antonio Cuadra, Merton spoke of the "logos of the situation": "The fact is that each new situation in life has its own mysterious logos, and that it takes a creative intuition to discover it and act accordingly. There is too much temptation to act not according to this mystery but according to some 'clear idea' which represents only an image of the past. Or a wish for the future, based on an image of the past. The present is in neither of these" (*CT,* 186).

The journals are replete with Merton's reporting on his abandoning himself to the discipline and celebration of the present moment:

> *The grip the present has on me. That is the one thing that has grown most noticeably in the spiritual life—nothing much else has. The rest dims as it should. I am getting older. The reality of now—the unreality of all the rest. The unreality of ideas and explanations and formulas. I am. The unreality of all the rest. The pigs shriek. Butterflies dance together—or danced together a moment ago—against the blue sky at the end of the woodshed. The buzzsaw stands outside there, half covered with dirty and tattered canvas. The trees are fresh and green in the sun (more rain yesterday). Small clouds inexpressibly beautiful and silent and eloquent, over the silent woodlands. What a celebration of light, quietness, and glory! This is my feast, sitting here in the straw! (SS, 214–15)*

Merton's admiration for those who made themselves marginal (indeed even fools) for Christ affected his criticisms of Gethsemani as a stable and culturally approved institution. He called his abbey a "shelter [that is] deceptive" and a "well-kept greenhouse" (*CT,* 165).

An early major crisis for Merton at Gethsemani involved his ordination to the priesthood by which he feared he would become a member of a "caste" in which he might lose his personal integrity by putting on an institutional role. Though Merton accepted his ordination with gratitude once he had been anointed, the priesthood had initially conjured up fears of his potentially becoming trapped (and Trappist?) in a role that was at once public and (especially dangerous for a writer and a spiritual exhibitionist) "anonymous."[30]

Merton's conversion to an interiorly migrant life by which he depended on the mercy of God alone, his need to "return to the Father"[31] by enduring a dark transiency, and his voiced hope to disappear and become a "no one" who has "no place," are symptomatic more of a deep spirituality than they are of psychological pathology or of an hyperbolic literary style.

As a young monk, Merton had disliked the Cistercian hermits because their lives "never seemed to get anywhere." Later, however, the erratic Blessed Conrad became his ideal. In reflecting on Conrad, Merton was writing an apology for his own blessed deviance:

Now I know there is something important about the very incompleteness of Bl. Conrad: hermit in Palestine, by St. Bernard's permission. Starts home for Clairvaux when he hears St. Bernard is dying. Gets to Italy and hears St. Bernard is dead. Settles in a wayside chapel outside Bari and dies there. What an untidily unplanned life! No order, no sense, no system, no climax. Like a book without punctuation that suddenly ends in the middle of a sentence.

Yet I know that those are the books I really like!

Bl. Conrad cannot possibly be solidified or ossified in history. He can perhaps be caught and held in a picture, but he is like a photograph of a bird in flight—too accurate to look the way a flying bird seems to appear to us. We never saw the wings in that position. Such is the solitary vocation. For of all men, the solitary knows least where he is going, and yet is more sure, for there is one thing he cannot doubt: he travels where God is leading him. That is precisely why he doesn't know the way. And that too is why, to most other men, the way is something of a scandal. (SS, 31)

Love's Voice Heard in an Inner Silence Beyond Geography: No One Else to Meet, No Place Else to Go

September 13, 1968: A journey is a bad death if you ingeniously grasp or remove all that you had and were before you started, so that in the end you do not change in the least. The stimulation enables you to grasp more raffishly at the same, familiar, distorted illusions. You come home only confirmed in greater greed—with new skills (real or imaginary) for satisfying it.

I am not going "home." The purpose of this death is to become truly homeless.

Bardo of small bad hermitage, empty smell, quiet musty, a cobweb, some cardboard boxes. Very quiet. Good river. Good cliffs. Blue clouds arising after noon. Silence! The big red dog, wet ears full of burrs, his stomach roaring with some grass he had eaten while I was swimming.

Go on! Go on! There is no place left. (OSM, 174–75)

By writing journals, Thomas Merton gradually learned, as we all gradually learn, that at life's banquet he ate the same food as everyone else. He learned that, like everyone else, he needed to take his place at the table, receive the sacrament of his life's particular moments, and participate in a banquet liturgy of shared days among those with whom he found himself enfleshed. He learned that our human vocation to receive together the sacrament of time-sharing is always precarious: We eat together, sometimes celebrating, sometimes in tears. For evil often nestles its head in the shoulder of the good. The weeds grow as strongly as the wheat. What appears to us warm and embraceable by day is often transformed by night into a cold, stained-glass face with a mouth that cannot kiss. We are hot, then cold. We are present, then withdrawn. Today everything is clear, but tomorrow contradicted. Paying our dues in vain to Wisdom's unloving stepbrother, Perfection, we all gradually learn, as Merton did, that no dish on the human menu is cooked without the seasonings of contradiction and vicissitude.

Merton's journals document, deeply below everything, his thirst for the face of God in his human experience. They document how he was drawn forward by a Presence which partially disclosed itself to him but hid its full name. They document how he listened, through experiences of both presence and absence, for the Voice of Love that called him forward out of self-exile from Love back to Love's garden. While they articulate his yearning for God, his journals also give flesh to the hindrances, the delays, and, most of all, his evasions on his dark path toward Joy. They confide both hope and despair that Love resided but also hid in the stitches of the fabric of his days.

By writing journals, he rendered himself conscious of his being embraced by Love but in ways intricate and only slowly possessive of all his heart. Merton journaled not just to find himself in words but to lose himself in words that exhausted themselves into surrender and attention to Love's voice that called him out, beyond all words, to Love's own Self.

Merton's journals bear witness to his basic education as a human being. He learned that God's face in his experience could only be seen veiled, and that his spiritual eyes would usually be clouded over. He learned that he could hear God's voice only with the ears of faith. He learned that, despite the reality of his sins being always before him, he could still hope in the promise of Mercy. In even the most unpromising of seasons (when his mouth turned mute and his heart turned to stone) he could still learn to "love winter when the plant says nothing."

Merton gradually abandoned hope for a suddenly perfect life in some perfect place always elsewhere than where he actually was. He surrendered himself instead to the slow heart-work of seeking God one day and one night at a time in the place where his eyes opened and shut every morning and evening. He got up and fell down, he got up and fell down, and he got up over and over again.

Merton's journals are a confession of the necessity for us all to move insistently forward though our daily experiences of both absence and presence to that Voice of Love calling each of us to Love's Self. As he acknowledged his road to Joy was as curved as everyone else's, and that, in the face of his life's contradictions, all he might really have had left was prayer and hope in God's mercy,[32] Merton nevertheless recorded his stability in the conviction that our common human destiny is the inner journey forward,[33] through "crisis and mystery" (*TTW*, 152), into the full clarity of the Beloved's voice, finally to arrive directly in front of Love's waiting, welcoming arms.

Thomas Merton might have stumbled home, but he has made it home. No longer an orphan or an exile, no longer solitary or a prodigal, Merton now waits in joyful hope for the complete and final epiphany of his Lord. Together with all the saints, Merton waits and still listens for Love's glorious arrival in the bosom of his mother, that universal and ever virginal *Ecclesia*, still pregnant with longing for the full revelation of her Beloved's face. As each of us stumbles falteringly forward toward the one, true Voice of Love, calling us each by our names, may the Holy Spirit who is searching our hearts for us, hurrying like a mother toward the sound of all our cries, find us quickly.

Werner Heisenberg and Niels Bohr

Photograph by P. Ehrenfest, Jr., courtesy of Niels Bohr Archive, Copenhagen.

On Mind, Matter, and Knowing: Thomas Merton and Quantum Physics

Thomas Del Prete

On May 26, 1963, Thomas Merton records in his journal that he is reading Werner Heisenberg's *Physics and Philosophy*, "an exciting book."[1] He does not say how he came to be reading Heisenberg, a key figure in the development of quantum physics. It was not typical intellectual fare for him, his eclectic and voluminous reading diet notwithstanding. But the new theory of matter clearly intrigued him, warranting attention in one of his reading notebooks.[2] Likewise, he was interested in Heisenberg's thoughts on the impact of technical and scientific knowledge on both traditional cultures and world politics (*TTW*, 324–25).

Merton's next intellectual foray into sub-atomic physics was apparently in May and June of 1967, part of some "light" breakfast reading that he had set aside for himself in the hermitage. He began with a book by physicist and popular science writer George Gamow, in all likelihood *Biography of Physics*, and followed with Ruth Moore's biography of Niels Bohr, Heisenberg's mentor.[3] His response is enthusiastic, although he finds the actual physics involved virtually impenetrable. As he writes, "Quantum Physics . . . dazzles and baffles me—but Niels Bohr & Co. are definitely among my No. 1 culture heroes" (*LL*, 237). He also laments his inability to comprehend it all, and the inadequacy of his educational background in the field—"It is terribly exciting, though I can't grasp any of it due to the fact that I never had even high-school physics, and the equations are just hieroglyphics that represent to me no known answers" (*LL*, 237).

Merton discloses another level of personal response, as he realizes with some astonishment how close the momentous developments which resulted from the effort to resolve the mysteries of matter were to his own life, and to his own sense of foreboding and crisis in the world at the time of his religious conversion (*LL*, 243–44). While he was an undergraduate in Cambridge, England, physicists were nearby in Cavendish Lab exploring the inner world of the atom. While he was completing his master's degree requirements at Columbia University, in January 1939, physicists there split the atom, the first time fission was achieved in the United States.

Though in studying Merton, one learns not to be surprised by his intellectual pursuits his fascination with quantum physics is, at least on the surface, an aberration, not easy to reconcile with his principal interests or with his contemplative and monastic vocation. What drew him to it, even if only as "light" reading? What does it signify in terms of his own intellectual development and educational thought? More broadly, what does it suggest in terms of mind, knowing, culture, contemplation, and the spiritual life?

A Note on Methodology

To address briefly an issue underlying Merton scholarship, is there a methodology for answering these questions? In his role as Master of Scholastics, then Novice Master, Merton distributed study guides to Gethsemani novices, on topics ranging from the monastic vows to mystical theology, that were impressively comprehensive and ordered. They suggest the breadth and depth of his knowledge of monastic and Christian spiritual tradition and represent an important resource in understanding his thought. Unlike these guides, however, he rarely develops in a systematic way the kernels of insight that appear in abundance in his journals or elsewhere. More typically, he choreographs insights to illuminate a central theme, or circles from one insight through others and back again.

In keeping with his nature as a poetic and contemplative rather than purely philosophical thinker, Merton is concerned with the truths and reality within his powers of discernment. His rhetorical strategies reflect this concern. Among the most obvious and familiar, he uses paradox to dissolve seeming opposites in deeper, more unifying insights. He uses himself, that is, his "false" or "ego" self, as a kind of foil to point to deeper realities. He uses "western man" or its variants similarly. There is, perhaps above all, the fresh and honest tone. Overall, his "manner of knowing," as he might say, is much more intuitive and sapiential or wisdom-oriented than it is rationalistic and deductive.[4] In this respect, his writing reflects a contemplative way of knowing, not simply an introspective and personal one.

Rich though they are with penetrating insights and commentary, Merton's journals tease with their incompleteness, fragmentation, and allusiveness. To understand and explain his thought based on them, as well as sources such as letters, notebooks, and essays, becomes therefore a process of both exegesis and inference—of making connections to ideas appearing in different places and taking into account Merton's own intellectual training as well as his teaching. To some extent, one has to trace and be willing to travel some of Merton's own intellectual path. Adopting this process, it is possible to expand outward from his relatively brief references to quantum physics to a consideration of their larger significance in terms of the development and integration of mind, consciousness, and Christian spiritual and contemplative awareness. In doing so, one becomes aware of how his intellectual life and contemplative spirituality worked in tandem in the 1960s, in a complementary and mutually informing, if not integrated and holistic way. He comes to exemplify possibilities for connecting intellectual work and the spiritual life—for integration and wholeness—both within and outside monastic culture.

Merton and Heisenberg's Uncertainty Principle

Abbreviated though it is, Merton's journal commentary provides clues as to why quantum physics excited him. In response to his reading of Heisenberg in 1963, he remarks:

> *The uncertainty principle is oddly like St. John of the Cross. As God in the highest eludes the grasp of concepts, so in the ultimate constitution of matter there is nothing really there. . . . Heisenberg shows that the naive objectivity of conventional physics is on the same plane as the ancient conviction that the sun revolved around the earth. A pragmatic observation . . . but not objective fact. And the Soviets struggle to maintain this naive objectivity. . . . Yet with*

> *great sophistication quantum theory also includes the "factual" concepts of daily life, knowing they are not factual, and yet they are part of the observer's reality. This leads to a fabulous new concept of nature with ourselves in the midst of it, and destroys the simple illusion of ourselves as detached and infallible observers. (TTW, 322–23)*

Merton found in Heisenberg's quantum theory an understanding of the physical world that resonated with spiritual insight and intuition. It opened up a kind of cultural space, in a culture advancing technologically at an alarming pace, for science and spiritual wisdom to meet and have an exchange. He alludes to the possibility of a common ground in the idea of reality as ultimately incalculable, as something beyond our power to see, grasp, or measure though not, however, to apprehend or intuit in some basic sense. Both quantum physics and contemplative Christian wisdom also suggested that the mystery of our own being in the world involves some experience of relatedness, though each comes to know and understand relatedness in fundamentally different ways.

The difference between quantum physics and the modernist scientific worldview spawned by classical or Newtonian physics, which it called into question, was profound.[5] The latter, grounded in the Cartesian duality of self and world which Merton frequently disparaged as false and misleading, presumed, in its most positivistic expression, that reality was material, objective, and empirically verifiable.[6] Reality can be broken, reduced, analyzed, defined, and manipulated in terms of its constituent parts. This is the "naïve objectivity" to which Merton refers.

The twofold effect of this worldview was a false sense of human identity and a false relationship to the world. Set over and against reality, the self (at least the self of the "West," which was Merton's main concern) must rely more or less on itself as a source of identity, seeking identity through what Merton called in his spiritual writing, among other things, "the false drive for self-affirmation." In the effort to affirm itself, if not its godlike status in the cosmos, this separate and individual self relates to reality in a technical and utilitarian if not dominating way. Knowledge-making, by implication, is for the purpose of expanding power; ultimate meaning is not intrinsic but derives from the exercise of external power and control. Put in another way, being was in doing—to be was to do. Action did not spring from but rather defined one's sense of being and identity. Identity was not, in other words, inherent in being. This kind of mindset favored the development of technical know-how for its own sake; the threat of nuclear destruction represented its worst consequence.[7]

Quantum physics sets the classical view on its head, and it is humbling. At the sub-atomic level—in the world of mesons, neutrons, protons, and electrons—matter cannot be seen and controlled and exactly measured. As Gamow describes it,

> *The energies on [the atomic] scale are so small that even the most gently performed measurement may result in substantial disturbances of the phenomenon under observation, and we cannot guarantee that the results of measurements actually describe what would have happened in the absence of the measuring devices. The observer and his instruments become an integral part of the phenomenon under investigation. Even in principle there is no such thing as a physical phenomenon per se. In all cases there is an absolutely unavoidable interaction between the observer and the phenomenon. (Gamow, 255)*

The essence of Heisenberg's uncertainty principle, as Merton suggests, is that matter, in terms of its most minute constituent parts, is not wholly within our grasp, that the more we attempt to attain knowledge of it, the less precisely we can pin it down. In the investigation of this world, the observer discovers that she or he is part of the observed, that the effort to observe itself limits what is observable—the particles move in response to us. There is therefore no inherent separation between us and them. In Heisenberg's words, "Natural science does not simply describe and explain nature; it is part of the interplay between nature and ourselves. . . . This was a possibility of which Descartes could not have thought, but it makes the sharp separation between the world and the I impossible" (Heisenberg, 81). As Merton captures it, we are in the midst of nature. The presumption of objectivity is proven naïve. Since we are implicated in it, knowledge-making is no longer impersonal or depersonalized but subjective. Questions of ultimate meaning and identity must take into account reality as a whole with us in it, not reality as a collection of material parts from which we are detached.

The elusiveness of matter according to the uncertainty principle—a notion startling to the modernist scientific worldview—undoubtedly prompts Merton's comparison to St. John of the Cross. If "in principle," as Gamow says, "there is no such thing as a physical phenomenon per se," then there is perhaps an analogy with the sixteenth-century Spanish Carmelite's dark path to God or "ascent to truth," the *via negativa*. According to St. John, in attaining ultimate truth—the mystical knowing of God—one must travel concept-free, blindly as it were, and enter into a realm of nothingness insofar as human perceptivity is concerned. That quantum physics affirms such a realm at the heart of matter, at the heart of what appears to us normally as a solid world, does suggest an odd coincidence. Matter and spirit are in a sense one reality. We live more on faith than we perhaps realize.

This perspective is completely counterintuitive in a modernist scientific worldview, precisely because it depends on letting go of the presumption of our own separateness and centrality, what Merton sometimes called our "empirical" or "ego-self," in knowing reality. It relies on a consciousness of wholeness alien to a modern consciousness of self and the modern perception of mind. Merton certainly saw the irony of the new understanding of matter vis-à-vis the nineteenth-century belief in dialectical materialism on which the worldview of Soviet communism depended, noting, "the joke is that this materialism is now unmasked *as a faith*" (*TTW*, 322).

There are other spiritual analogies that Merton does not make at the time, but which his understanding of quantum physics supports. His awakening experience at Polonnaruwa, for instance, is suggestive. In recounting his aesthetic and spiritual experience upon viewing the reclining Buddhas there, he writes, "All problems are resolved and everything is clear, simply because what matters is clear. The rock, all matter, all life, is charged with *dharmakaya*—everything is emptiness and everything is compassion."[8] All matter is emptiness—no longer an object of one's self-conscious mind. Here is an instance in which Merton's awareness of reality, a contemplative spiritual awareness, breaks through the Cartesian duality of self and world and finds common ground with his understanding of the uncertainty principle and its implications. It should be emphasized, however, that Merton would not equate the Buddhist perception of emptiness and compassion with the darkness of John of the Cross. While there is a sense in which one can speak of reality in terms of emptiness from both a Buddhist and Christian spiritual point of view, Christian spiritual theology is fundamentally different in that it is personal, centered on the Person of Christ as the center of our personal lives.[9]

From Heisenberg and Bohr to Herakleitos

The interrelationship of observer and observed in quantum investigation has an analogy in the attributes and connectedness of sub-atomic particles. Classical or Newtonian physics presumes that one can separate where something is (its location) and how fast it is going (its speed) and measure each definitively. Heisenberg's uncertainty principle evolved partly from the evident impossibility of making such measurement. These attributes (and others—energy, direction, momentum) are not, in fact, entirely discrete and unrelated in matter's component parts; one influences the other. Like the relationship of particle to human investigator, they exist, apparent differences aside, in an intimate mutuality.

It seems likely that this mutuality caused Merton to think of Herakleitos when he was reading about "Niels Bohr & Co." in 1967. He refers in his journal to "This magnificent instrument of thought [quantum mechanics] they developed to understand what is happening in matter, what energy really is about—with their confirmation of the kind of thing Herakleitos was reaching for by intuition" (*LL*, 237). There are, in fact, intriguing parallels among Merton's reading of the fifth-century B.C.E. Greek philosopher, contemplative themes in his own writing, and the fundamental indeterminateness and interrelatedness of matter established by the pioneers of quantum physics.

According to Merton in "Herakleitos: A Study," Herakleitos is a philosopher with an intuitive ability to cut "through apparent multiplicity to grasp underlying reality as *one*."[10] Herakleitos' intuitive manner of knowing, as much as what he discerns, struck a responsive chord in Merton's contemplative spirituality. In both his writing and his teaching, he emphasized the importance of cultivating an intuitive way of knowing—in contrast to speculative knowledge or knowledge arrived at by deductive reasoning—as a basis for becoming aware of and ultimately experiencing the presence and reality of God. In *New Seeds of Contemplation*, for instance, he writes of contemplation as "awakening, enlightenment and the amazing intuitive grasp by which love gains certitude of God's creative and dynamic intervention in our daily life."[11]

To his novices, Merton explained the importance of recognizing one's capacity for an interior, intuitive way of knowing amidst the noise and confusion of modern life, and cultivating it as a basis for opening to our inherent relationship to God. As he expressed it,

> *The natural knowledge of God is not purely that which you arrive to by reasoning . . . we in the West tend to think that reasoning is the whole shooting match. . . . There is such a thing as intuitive natural knowledge of God. . . . And there is this intuition of being, and not only a sense of one's own existence but a sense that everything exists; . . . the whole thing is . . . this very strong experience of isness. . . . If you deepen that . . . all that is, so to speak, becomes completely transparent . . . and you see . . . somehow or other beyond all this being is Infinite Being. And very simply one sees that this Infinite Being is our Father, a person; so this kind of realization . . . should be part of everybody's normal equipment.*[12]

There is clearly no comparison between this understanding of intuition and the popular idea of intuition as mere hunch. For Merton, intuition is a vital epistemological concern. Intuition paves the way for a deeper or interior knowing. An "intuitive grasp" suggests openness and awareness on a deep level, on a level of being, what Merton referred to in a discussion of Christian consciousness as "ontological openness" (*ZBA,* 25). As a matter of experience and consciousness rather than speculation or deduction, this way of knowing leads to what Merton called a "qualitative perception of reality," a recognition of reality "as a thing full of value . . . shining with the light of God" ("*CCL*" tape).

From the point of view of epistemology, an intuitive manner of knowing and the empirical, investigative, and experimental means of the quantum physicist would seem diametrically opposed. But it does not follow that the understanding of reality that results would also have to be in opposition, as the connection Merton sensed between Herakleitos and "Niels Bohr & Co." suggests. While there might not be agreement that reality is "one," the idea of the mutuality and interrelationship of elementary particles and their human observer does recast the reality implied by "multiplicity" or individual, separate, and discrete elements into something more connected, if not whole. A more elaborate explanation of Herakleitean thought will help make this possibility clearer.

Where his contemporaries saw movement, conflict, and separateness, Herakleitos discerns harmony and connectivity. In Merton's words,

> *The heart of Herakleitean epistemology is an implicit contrast between man's wisdom, which fails to grasp the concrete reality of unity-in-multiplicity and harmony-in-conflict, but which instead seizes upon one or other of the conflicting elements and tries to build on this a static and one-sided truth which cannot help but be an artificial fiction. The wisdom of man cannot follow the divine wisdom "one and manifold" in its infinitely varied movement. Yet it aspires to a universal grasp of all reality. In order to "see" our minds seize upon the movement around them and within them, and reduce it to immobility. (BT, 82)*

For Herakleitos, God is "all things." God's energy "works, shows itself and hides in nature" (*BT*, 79).

In conceptual terms, this idea is strikingly compatible with what the quantum physics pioneers learned. When they accepted a reality in which all movement could not be reduced to immobility, in which energy could show itself and hide in nature, then the possibility of reality as interrelated, dynamic, and changing, with movement "infinitely varied" and not wholly determinable, also became real.

It seems likely that Merton drew another important parallel between quantum theory and the Herakleitean view of the world, based on a theory worked out by Bohr. As Moore relates in her biography of Bohr, physicists in the 1920s pressed eagerly forward in the quest to identify, explain, and predict the behavior of sub-atomic particles. They did so believing that the mystery of this hidden world could be unraveled to reveal the ultimate order of reality. Heisenberg's uncertainty principle shook this confidence to its core. Though disconcerted by the new view of reality (Heisenberg evidently spoke of his "despair" [Moore, 155]), Heisenberg and Bohr together determined that if matter could not be known in an ultimate sense, all was still not completely lost (Moore, 155). For example, although one could not know both the position and speed of a particle at any one time, as in the human-scale world, one could determine each of those quantities independently.

But there was yet another dilemma. Prevailing theory held that the movement of an atomic particle (such as an electron) around its nucleus was orbital, analogous to how planets move around the sun. This planetary model was not fully satisfactory, however, in explaining particle behavior. The explanation that was eventually accepted astounded most physicists when it was first proposed. Particles, the presumed discrete units of matter, could also behave like a wave. The idea that matter could be both particle and wave seemed self-contradictory; it would have to be one or the other. After intense investigation, and in the face of all the assumptions that physics had heretofore made about matter and reality, Bohr concluded that particles did, in fact, have this dual nature. The atom enclosed a "strange kind of reality" (Moore, 159).

To explain a reality in which position and velocity could only be known separately, and the smallest components of matter could be both particle and wave, Bohr used the concept of complementarity. As he put it, "However contrasting such phenomena may at first sight appear, it must be realized that they are complementary" (quoted in Moore, 159). A world in which everything has a cause and an effect—the worldview of Einstein among others—became one in which there was indeterminacy and complementarity of seeming opposites.

In explaining, in a way that classical physics could not accept, both the paradox that set limits on what humans can determine (the more one tries to know, the less accurately one can know) and the seeming contradiction of a dual particle-wave nature, Bohr's concept of complementarity reached backward in time to touch Herakleitean intuition. Bohr's illumination of the sub-atomic world is compatible with the Herakleitean one of "harmony-in-conflict" that Merton described—"The real order of the cosmos is an apparent disorder, the 'conflict' of opposites which is in fact a stable and dynamic harmony" (*BT*, 82).

The conceptual link between the fifth-century pre-Christian philosopher and quantum physics is not at all improbable, and exemplifies Merton's capacity to intuit and understand, if not demonstrate, the fundamental relationship between seemingly disparate ideas, cultures, and times in terms of their basic human significance.[13] More importantly, it shows the value he placed on making such connections. He consciously developed this capacity in the belief that the modern Western world needed the perspective of ancient, archaic, non-Western or non-Christian sources of wisdom, as well as Christian spiritual tradition, to recover its slowly eroding sense of inner human depth and meaning.

Consciousness and Knowing in an Interconnected World

In debunking the modernist myth of pure objectivity, quantum physics raised an important epistemological issue. How are we to know when we are part of and affect what we seek to know? This question in some version, in addition to others, no doubt occurred to Merton. Having finished Ruth Moore's biography of Bohr, he comments that he would like "to go further into some of Bohr's notions of epistemology in his last years" (*CT*, 252). He perhaps sensed the possibility for fruitful dialogue on the ways of knowing of the scientist and the contemplative. What are the implications of the breakdown of the subject-object relationship in quantum investigation for an understanding of mind, consciousness, and knowing, and how do they compare to the more intuitive and holistic mode of knowing of the contemplative? Where does the effort to obtain a quantitative description of reality meet with the effort to obtain a qualitative view? Can a physicist escape the paradox that the more we try to know the less accurately we can know? If one cannot measure precisely, can one still, based on the experience of interconnectedness itself, apprehend and, in some profound sense, "know"?

Certainly the formal scientific quest for knowledge has not been stymied by recognition of the apparent relationship between observer and the behavior of sub-atomic particles suggested by quantum theory; much can still be learned through direct observation, investigation, and experimentation in formal science, among other means. Gamow pointed out that although the sub-atomic world resisted human attempts to measure it definitively, accurate measurement "in the realm of ordinary experience" could still be accomplished with some confidence (Gamow, 258).

But acknowledgement that we exist in a responsive relationship with matter at its most basic level can be profoundly important in orienting one's sense of purpose and meaning in learning, and one's sense of mind and consciousness of reality. It makes a difference if one lives with a Cartesian or dualistic view of the world or with a sense of interconnectedness and mutuality, if not with a Herakleitean sense of unity. To repeat Merton's words, "it leads to a fabulous new concept in nature, *with ourselves in the midst of it.*" Bohr said simply, "We ourselves are part of Nature"[14] (quoted in Moore, 181). For Bohr, what follows is that we cannot fully know what we are part of, that life had to be accepted as a basic fact; we cannot reduce our existence to its constituent parts by analysis (Moore, 183). One wonders what Bohr might say in an age of genetic code-breaking and engineering. In any event, his understanding of epistemology in 1932 led him to the border of ontology and what later became complex ecology, familiar terrain for Merton. It is understandable why Merton would have liked to know more.

It seems clear that Merton saw some basic affinity with or complementarity between his own contemplative awareness of life and Bohr's realization of our embeddedness in the world and the limitation thus placed on our ability to know it in an ultimate sense. The affinity is a matter of epistemology but also of the "qualitative perception of reality" of which Merton spoke. There is no longer any "outside" ourselves; when we explore the world, we are in some sense, in a reciprocal way, coming to know ourselves. This idea was fully compatible with Merton's contemplative awareness of "world": "The first place in which to go looking for the world is not outside us but in ourselves. We *are* the world. In the deepest ground of our being we remain in metaphysical contact with the whole of that creation in which we are only small parts."[15]

Sounding a note that a quantum physicist might recognize, he adds, "Through our senses and our minds, our loves, needs, and desires, we are implicated, without possibility of evasion, in this world of matter and of men, of things and of persons, which not only affect us and change our lives but are also affected and changed by us" (*L&L,* 120). What Merton expressed variously as the "deepest ground of our being" or "the hidden ground of love" put in contemplative perspective and gave rich meaning to what Bohr saw as the irreducible "fact" of our existence. It also reflected a "knowing" possible at the newly delineated limit of science—yet one based on the notion of interrelationship that science itself had discovered.

In coming to "know" the natural world as a contemplative, Merton strove to see things whole and to identify wholly with what he was seeing. To cite but one example, taken from a journal entry (April 5, 1958):

> *[One] can know all about God's creation by examining its phenomena, by dissecting and experimenting and this is all good. But it is misleading, because with this kind of knowledge you do not really know the beings you know. You only know* about *them. That is to say you create for yourself a knowledge based on your*

> *observations. What you observe is really as much the product of your knowledge as its cause. You take the thing not as it is, but as you want to investigate it. . . . There is something you cannot know about a wren by cutting it up in a laboratory and which you can only know if it remains fully and completely a wren, itself, and hops on your shoulder if it feels like it. . . . I want not only to observe but to know living things, and this implies a dimension of primordial familiarity which is simple and primitive and religious and poor.*[16]

Merton concludes his epistemological reflection by saying that the reality he needs is "the vestige of God in His creatures . . . [and] in man's history and culture" (*SS*, 190). And indeed he remains true to fulfilling this need in his study of both the natural world and its human counterpart.

If we accept our basic though not fully explainable connectedness to matter, and a spiritual reality in which we are connected in and through the deepest ground of our being, in love, then our consciousness of self and our orientation in learning must change accordingly. Our identity exists in mysterious relationship. Learning in the broadest sense becomes a matter of understanding and deepening a relationship that we cannot fully fathom, and of expanding consciousness of a reality in which God is present rather than seeking to control or manipulate it. To extend this idea fully, we might say one studies in order to love and needs to love in order to learn. This idea is, in fact, rooted in monastic tradition. "We study in order to love," according to Merton's interpretation of St. Bernard (*TMSB*, 127). As Merton notes, monastic theology is not anti-intellectual but aspires "to a kind of understanding rooted in love."[17]

In applying these ideas more broadly to secular learning, one thinks of the Nobel prize–winning biologist Barbara McClintock and Pulitzer prize–winning naturalist Edward O. Wilson. Both McClintock and Wilson approached knowing with a respectful sense of mutuality and relationship. In response to a question on how she conducted her lifelong study of the genetics of corn, McClintock replied, "You have to have a feeling for the organism."[18] Describing the path of his own scientific discoveries, Wilson remarked in a similar vein, "Nature first, then theory. . . . Love the organisms for themselves first, then strain for general explanations, and, with good fortune, discoveries will follow."[19]

The Contemplative and Scientist in Dialogue

Beyond raising questions concerned with Western culture, philosophy, science, and epistemology, Merton's study of Heisenberg and Bohr demonstrated for him the necessity and importance of a prophetic way of addressing the human ramifications of scientific work. Bohr and colleagues were "prophetic," embodying a "truly modern kind of prophetism," to the extent that they understood and articulated the ramifications of their work in profoundly human terms. As Merton put it, men like Bohr "grasped all the consequences of their discoveries in a widely human way. As opposed to this kind of narrow scientism which sees only a short range and purely technical consequence" (*LL,* 244). Bohr in particular "had the ability to translate his discoveries into a language relevant to everybody, to all humanity, and to the deepest and most critical problems of man then and there—here and now" (*LL,* 244). Merton was responding to Bohr's effort, after escaping from Denmark during the Nazi occupation, to convince both Churchill in Britain and Roosevelt in the United States, as well as his fellow scientists, of the advisability of making the secrets of the atomic world a shared knowledge and international responsibility.[20] In this way, Bohr hoped to prevent the terrible arms race which he foresaw as otherwise inevitable.

Bohr was a "culture hero" for Merton precisely because he embodied the possibility of dialogue on critical issues in the modern scientific and technological culture grounded in deep human concern and wisdom. Bohr was one of the "truly wise," a *sapiente.* In the modern world, it was imperative to have such perspective, and possible that a contemplative monastery could play a role in fostering it. Merton outlined this possibility, citing Bohr explicitly, as part of his vision for renewal in monastic education. It was a vision fortified perhaps by the parallelism he had discovered between his life and the development of quantum physics, and emboldened by his own commitment and experience as a learner, a teacher, and, paradoxically, a social critic speaking from monastic silence in the 1960s.

Among other priorities for monastic education, he asserts the importance of developing a capacity to engage intellectual and social developments in the world from the perspective of the interior and qualitative values cultivated in the contemplative life. The prophetic and eschatological witness of the monastery, which was also a witness to solitude and silence, did not in itself have to be silent. The modern world, in fact, needed dialogue based on that witness and from an informed perspective. As he articulated it,

> *The monk must be able to understand the crucial problems of our time and see his own monastic vocation in the light of these problems: race, war, genocide, starvation, injustice, revolution. . . . Finally, it is most important to relate the sapiential theology of the monk to the technological culture of our century. . . . A contemplative monastery should ideally be able to play a significant part in the development of scientific culture. The qualitative, experiential and personal values developed in monastic life should complement the objective, quantitative and experimental discoveries of science and their exploitation by technology and business. . . . We need to form monks . . . who are capable of embracing in their contemplative awareness not only the theological dimensions of the Mystery of Christ but also the possibilities of new understanding offered by non-Christian traditions and by the modern world of science and revolution. (CWA, 203–204)*

It is not hard to speculate, given his ongoing concern for the threat of nuclear catastrophe and the role of science and technology in the world, that Merton was led to this educational vision in part by his study of Heisenberg and Bohr. It was Bohr who helped Merton to understand that the quantitative values of science and the scientific way of knowing could find common ground with the "qualitative, experiential and personal values developed in monastic life." He no doubt realized as well that his own outspokenness on matters of peace, war, and destructive human technology would have been that much more engaging had he had more scientific knowledge, and, better yet, been able to initiate an informed dialogue with Bohr's successors.

Beyond dialogue, Merton clearly sensed the potential for the development of a sapiential culture, for a collaboration of intellect, mind, and contemplative awareness in addressing questions of the development and uses of knowledge, of knowing, and spiritual wisdom. To the extent that we are inspired by this possibility, we owe some gratitude for Bohr and for some "light" reading in the hermitage.

Photograph by Thomas Merton

Used with the permission of the Thomas Merton Legacy Trust.

Dancing with the Raven: Thomas Merton's Evolving View of Nature

Monica Weis, SSJ

In his introduction to Volume 5 of Thomas Merton's journal, the late Robert Daggy reprints an Edward Lear limerick about a raven that Merton had copied into his notebook. Dr. Daggy then explains the multi-layered meaning of the raven: its appearance in Christian scripture to feed Elijah in the wilderness; its symbolism as a companion of St. Benedict and special protector of Benedictines; and its role as a bird of prey, feasting on carrion.[1] The raven, with both its positive and negative overtones, is an apt symbol for Thomas Merton, the man of paradox, especially when we examine his evolving attitude toward nature and explore the ways in which nature supported and deepened Merton's journey to God.

As a child, Thomas Merton reflected his family values, just as each of us does. His New Zealand father, Owen, was a landscape painter who awakened in Tom an attention to detail and color. Tom's mother, Ruth Jenkins Merton, records in the baby book she was keeping to send to the New Zealand grandparents[2] that at three months of age, Tom "watched and talked to a flower" (*TB,* 1), that at eight months, he "stood up in his pram, especially to see the river when we went on the bridge" (*TB,* 3), and that before they left Prades, Tom "had already begun to wave his arms toward the landscape, crying

'Oh color!'" (*TB*, 7). This early habit of noticing, of being attentive to his surroundings, was useful to Merton throughout his life: as a cartoonist at Columbia, as a writer of letters, essays, and books, and as a contemplative monk, especially in the later years when Merton became more and more interested in Zen with its emphasis on awareness.

It is perhaps this same attention to detail, color, and symmetry that drew the college-age Merton to study the avant-garde engraver/poet William Blake whose drawing and poetry became a new poetic genre, and the language-experimenting poet Gerard Manley Hopkins who delighted in lists of words and a world "charged with the grandeur of God." It is perhaps this same fascination that attracted Merton to European cathedrals and icons, and later to taking photographs of textures, movement, and light.

But if we look at the Catholic convert Merton and his enthusiasm for this world, its colors, its breezes, its creatures, we have to acknowledge his sense of separation from them—a certain *contemptus mundi* that overshadowed his newfound religious fervor. His early religious poetry, for example, mentions nature, but, as Bonnie Bowman (Thurston) and others have argued, these references quickly fall into abstractions and speculative thinking.[3] Nature for the young Merton represents gifts from God to be used only as stepping stones to the Transcendent Godhead. Creatures can be appreciated, celebrated even, but not settled on. Matter is one thing; spirit another. Such a dualistic view—that splits the natural and the supernatural, subject and object—is evident also in *The Seven Storey Mountain* as Merton struggles to renounce his previous wild and undisciplined life and enclose himself in the "four walls of my new freedom."[4] Even Merton's attraction to the Trappist Abbey at Gethsemani reveals a dichotomy in this thinking. In Volume 1 of the journals, for example, Merton reveals how nature seems to be an opposing force pulling him away from God. Could he as a Trappist love nature? Would he have to abandon his Franciscan inclinations? No, Merton concludes, nature could help him find God as long as he does not love nature for itself, only "loving it in God's creation, and a sign of His goodness and Love."[5]

This is not the Merton we have come to know in later works such as *Day of a Stranger* or *The Asian Journal*, a Merton who claims to know the fifteen pairs of birds who live near his hermitage and with whom he is in ecological balance;[6] the Merton who is aware of a deep sense of compassion bursting from the very rocks themselves at the Great

Buddhas at Polonnaruwa.[7] For this more mature Merton, nature is one vast sacrament, revealing God's immanence and inviting us into community and communion with it—and, therefore, with God.

Such significant change does not ordinarily occur in one dramatic moment. Just as the mountain and riverbeds are gradually shaped and reshaped by the elements over time, many events and experiences gradually shaped Merton's thinking. Certainly an attraction to nature was evident in his love for Blake and Hopkins. Once he entered the monastery, sacred scripture offered him more nourishment. Seven times a day, he chanted Hebrew psalms praising the God who feeds us with the finest wheat (Ps 81), who leads us to green pastures (Ps 23), who gives the sparrow a home and builds a nest for the swallow in which to place her young (Ps 84), who makes springs gush forth in the valley (Ps 104), and who brings forth grass on the mountains (Ps 147). And Psalm 150 reminds Merton—and us—"Let everything that has breath praise the Lord."

Merton also studied the writings of the Fathers and Doctors of the church, especially Thomas Aquinas, who emphasized the holiness of all creation. As a contemplative monk, Merton steeped himself in Benedictine tradition with its reverence for a rhythm of work and prayer, a rhythm that acknowledges the power of the seed and its interdependence with the soil. Merton also read deeply and widely, not just theological treatises and spiritual mystics like Meister Eckhart, who describes creation as an act of God's passion, but also philosophy, literature, poetry, anthropology. He paid attention to current events and to the stirrings of his own heart. The more Merton immersed himself in solitude, the more he was drawn toward solidarity with and compassion for his world—with all its spiritual and cultural tensions. Indeed, Merton's contemplative vocation was not an experience of separation or alienation *from* the world, but—as he discovered during his twenty-seven years in the monastery—an invitation to community *with* the world, that is, all things on this planet.

I want to suggest—and suggest strongly—that another significant influence on Merton's thinking was his contact with nature at Gethsemani. By nature, I mean non-human creation: the elements (sun, wind, rain), landscape (woods, knobs, rocks), and critters (snakes, deer, birds). If we look at the seven volumes of his recently published journals, it is clear that this move from a dualistic view of nature that sees the world as separate from God to a sacramental view of nature begins early in his monastic life. Merton's journals reveal a seeker drawn more and more to a God whom he perceived as not only transcendent but also immanent, a God who lives within all creation and who desires human beings to dwell in community with all God's expressions of Creative Love.

From a young academic who in 1941 wonders if he can love nature as a Trappist (*RM*, 399), Merton becomes a vowed Cistercian who by 1948 seems to have made peace with this wonderful gift from God. In his entry for the Feast of the Visitation, Merton describes not only the liturgical ceremonies of the Vigil the previous evening, but also the way the "low-slanting rays [of the setting sun] picked out the foliage of the trees and high-lighted a new wheatfield against the dark curtain of woods on the knobs that were in shadow. It was very beautiful. Deep peace," comments Merton. "I looked at all this in great tranquility, with my soul and spirit quiet. For me landscape seems to be important for contemplation . . . anyway, I have no scruples about loving it" (July 2, 1948).[8]

Even experiences of spiritual ecstasy are intertwined with an exuberance toward nature. In September of that same year, Merton writes with uncharacteristic emotion: "Love carries me around. Love sails me around the house. Love, love, love lifts me around the cloister. I walk two steps on the ground and four steps in the air. It is love. It is consolation. . . . I don't want to *do* anything but love. . . . That was the way it was up in the apple trees yesterday morning with all that blue sky. The bulls in their pens were rumbling like old men . . . . That was the way it was after Communion . . . and that was the way it was going into the refectory . . . and that is the way it is writing this, too. I feel all clean inside because I am full of You, O God, and You are love, love, Love!" (*ES*, 234).

Less than a year later, Merton was given permission to go outside the confines of the cloister and walk alone in the surrounding woods. As Jonathan Montaldo notes, June 27, 1949, is a pivotal moment in Merton's vocation after which the "expansiveness and depth" of his prose "breaks out beyond a past mental and spiritual confinement" (*ES*, 328, n. 43). This writer couldn't agree more. Without trying to play the role of psychobiographer, I believe there is another important resonance to this permission to wander in the woods. At the end of Merton's baby book, his mother Ruth includes the daily horarium for her child. After the 7:30 a.m. breakfast, she writes, "Outdoors as soon as possible to stay until bath time"; again after the 2 p.m. dinner: "Outdoors afterward until sunset" (*TB*, 15). It appears that much of Merton's infant experience occurred outside and that his early cognitive and aesthetic development was connected to stimuli from nature. It's easy to conjecture that at least some of this outdoor time might have been spent near his father's painting sites and that patterns of light and color—from nature and from the canvas—might have become part of Merton's informal schooling. "When we go out," writes his mother, "he seems conscious of everything. Sometimes he puts up his arms and cries out 'Oh Sui! Oh joli!' Often it is to the birds or trees that he makes these pagan hymns of joy. Sometimes he throws himself on the ground to see the 'cunnin' little ants' (where he learned that expression, I do not know!)" (*TB*, 6–7).

Although Merton never connects his delight in the woods to these very early experiences—most likely because he doesn't even remember them—I wonder if his sense of being "at home" in the woods isn't a deeply rooted connection with parents now long dead and an emotional link to early nurturing and happier days. Other orphaned writers, such as William Wordsworth, have acknowledged the nurturing and chiding influence of nature on their interior growth.[9]

If we look at the complete journals as a mirror of the interior changes in Merton's attitude toward nature and his growth in contemplation, we can see the clear and strong impact nature has on this development. The increasing frequency of nature references and their connection to prayer indicate how intensely being in the woods nourishes Merton's vocation and how unswervingly and urgently the God of Creation draws him toward the hermitage in his final years. For example, in the first section of Volume 2, "The Novitiate Journal" (December 1941–April 1942), I found only three references to nature in the prose, as well as several scattered references in the poems included; in the memoir of Dom Frederic Dunne (October 1946–August 1948), there are two references to nature; but in the major portion of this journal entitled "The Whale and the Ivy" (December 1946–July 1952)—much of which was published as *The Sign of Jonas*—I counted 180 separate entries that celebrate nature, ending with the rhapsodic Fire watch passage in which Merton celebrates the natural and spiritual rhythms of the night with its "huge chorus of living beings" (*ES*, 486).

By way of contrast, in Volume 5, which details Merton's gradual move to the hermitage full-time, I found 225 separate entries (not counting the four full pages that constitute the core of *Day of a*

Stranger) in which Merton dialogues with his surroundings (*DWL,* 48) or celebrates his harmony with the sun (*DWL,* 146) or articulates how he and the warblers share the same nature—namely, love (*DWL,* 162), or how being in the woods, being in unity with the woods, reaffirms his vocation to solitude (*DWL,* 177–78, 229).

How wonderful to have this chronicle of Merton's spiritual journey—this Emersonian "savings bank of thoughts" in which we can see the growing influence of nature on Merton's thought, prayer, theology, and inner peace. How wonderful that we can delight in his picturesque language, for indeed there is always the touch of the verbal landscape artist about Merton's writing.

After an admittedly cursory look at more than 1,400 references to nature in the almost 3,000 pages of Merton's journals, it seems that nature functions in Merton's writing—and thought—in several distinct ways: as weather report, as trigger for memory, as analogy to explain the conundrums of life, as vehicle for his poetic eye, as language to mediate the ineffable experience of prayer, and finally, as healing influence to provide Merton with a sense of coming home. Surely, these diverse uses of nature intertwine and exert a reciprocal influence on each other; nevertheless, for the sake of clarity and this brief examination, I will look at each use of nature separately.

Weather Report

Perhaps the most frequent references to nature in the seven volumes of Merton's journals are notations about the sun, the wind, the rain, the light—what we might call simple weather data. They appear at the beginning of entries, sometimes in the middle between two longer discussions of events in the monastery or notations on his reading; occasionally they provide the finale for his musings that day. A few examples will illustrate this use of nature: "All day it has been dark and hot and wet. Sweat rolls down your back in church" (*ES,* 217); "Another of the beautiful, cool days we have been having all year. We did not work this afternoon" (*ES,* 86); "It is grey outside, and snow falls lightly" (*ES,* 34); "Hot, murky afternoon."[10] Such notations remind me of how my mother would often begin phone conversations or letters. They resemble, too, the calendars or daybooks kept by Midwestern farmers which record weather data that shape their field activities for the day and provide, over time, a log of climatic patterns and community responses to them.

At first I believed that this was what Merton was up to—this same way of grounding his cognitive/imaginative wanderings in the reality of the moment. That is, until I read his entry for Ash Wednesday, February 27, 1963. Merton writes:

> *Our mentioning of the weather . . . [is] perhaps not idle. Perhaps we have a deep and legitimate need to know in our entire being what the day is like, to see it and feel it, to know how the sky is grey, paler in the south, with patches of blue in the southwest, with snow on the ground, the thermometer at 18, and cold wind making your ears ache. I have a real need to know these things because I myself am part of the weather and part of the climate and part of the place, and a day in which I have not shared truly in all this is no day at all. It is certainly part of my life of prayer. (TTW, 299–300)*

Suddenly I realized how profoundly this exercise had been shaping Merton's whole development. Weather data were not just a guide to how to *act,* but a guide to how to *be.* What might have begun as an exercise to get the writing juices flowing had become an experience of profound integration. Nature was no longer "Other" to be enjoyed, ignored, or adapted to; rather, nature was somehow infused into Merton's being. What was external was affecting the internal. *Habitat*—the landscape—had become interlaced with *habitus*—Merton's way of living.[11]

Memory Triggers

A second way that nature affected Merton was by acting as a catalyst for memory—usually remembrances of places in Europe or Cuba that represent earlier happy times in his life. In the Perry Street journal, for example, he describes the view outside his apartment window: "Water drips on the stones. . . . Over beyond the church, the houses on Eleventh Street—their roofs shine with rain. . . . It does not make me feel sad, particularly. I remember walking along a road towards Caylus with my father. . . ." And so Merton records in the next four paragraphs the rain in the village that Sunday morning long ago, the castles he had seen and how they looked "camouflaged" for protection against ancient marauders; he then concludes with a page-long reflection on why people, including himself, make a habit of going places to look (*RM,* 139–40).

The smell of his hotel room in Miami Beach reminds him of the Savoy Hotel overlooking the English channel and his love for a girl named Diane (*RM,* 162); the rushing waters of Four Mile Valley near St. Bonaventure University remind him of Murat and Le Puy and the statue of the Virgin that often appeared in his father's pictures, and the house that his father built (*RM,* 327); raking leaves in October 1952 reminds him of his first Lent in the Novitiate. "I even think that we raked leaves there my first afternoon in the community as a postulant," he writes;[12] at the hermitage in October 1964, his reading and the night sky remind him of Gethsemani twenty-three years ago: "the stars, the cold, the smell of night, the wonder, the *Verlassenheit* [abandonment] (which is something else again than despondency) and above all the melody of the *Rorate coeli* [Drop down dew, heavens]. That entire first Advent bore in it all the stamp of my vocation's peculiar character. The solitude inhabited and pervaded by cold and mystery and woods and Latin liturgy" (*DWL,* 160).

Poetic Eye

Even the casual reader of Merton's journals cannot miss his talent as a poet. His lyric touch is everywhere. Remembering that Merton thought of himself primarily as a poet (although critics admit an uneven one) I am not surprised that many passages in his writing are either brief lyric descriptions or longer rhapsodic tributes to the elements. Rain—because of the Kentucky climate and the companionship it provides in the woods—seems to merit frequent praise.

But Merton's poetic eye is also able to draw for us visions of nature that enchant. "[T]hree crows . . . flew by in the sun with light flashing on their rubber wings" (*SS,* 14); "A red shouldered hawk wheels slowly over Newton's farm as if making his own special silence in the air—as if tracing out a circle of silence in the sky" (*SS,* 181); "Lovely blue and mauve shadows on the snow, and the indescribably delicate color of the sunlit patches of snow. All the life of color is in the snow and the sky" (*SS,* 171); "Crows swear pleasantly in the distance, and in the depths of my soul sits God" (*ES,* 311); "An indigo bunting flies down and grasps the long, swinging stem of a tiger lily and reaches out, from them, to eat the dry seed on top of a stalk of grass. A Chinese painting!" (*TTW,* 228); "And outside the door, a double bloom on one large violet iris, standing out of the green spears of the daylilies. And on the tongue of one bloom walks a great black-gold bee, the largest honeybee I ever saw. To be part of all this is to be infinitely rich" (*TTW*, 316); "Dead dry weather! The leaves tinkle like flakes of copper when the breeze passes over them. Haze" (*DWL*, 26).

Nature as Analogy

That same poetic eye allows Merton to use imaginative nature imagery to work his way through some of the frustrations and conundrums of life. It offers him a vehicle to describe the unknown and imagery to capture his ambivalent, often depressed, spirit. Perhaps the most well-known and touching analogy Merton uses is comparing himself to a caged bird. After discovering that a meeting of American abbots will take place at Gethsemani the next year (1964) and that he is expected to give them some conferences, Merton vents his bitterness toward the Abbot at not being allowed to give conferences and retreats at other monasteries:

> *[W]hen the canary is asked to sing, well, he is expected to sing merrily and with spontaneity. It is true that I have a nicer cage than any other canary in the Order . . . But this upsets me so that I cannot sleep. . . . Today I feel hateful, and miserable, exhausted, and I would gladly die. Everyone can come and see me in my cage, and Dom James can modestly rejoice in the fact that he is in absolute control of a bird that everyone wants to hear sing. This is the way birds stop singing—at least those songs that everyone wants to hear because they are comforting and they declare that all things are good just as they are. One's song is forced at times to become scandalous and even incomprehensible." (TTW, 320–21)*

Thankfully, there are some less spiteful examples of analogy. In January 1948, after reading the proofs of *The Seven Storey Mountain*, Merton speaks of the need to cut 8,000 words as pruning a "big, frowsy, disheveled tree. . . . St. Paul, help me out, sharpen all my scissors" (*ES*, 160). Just before Passion Sunday in 1949, Merton ponders his faults and imperfections that "grow out of me like weeds. Their leaves are waving all over me. They grow out of my hands like tobacco. And still I am not unhappy" (*ES*, 296–97). After reading Guerric of Igny's Fourth Advent sermon in December 1964, Merton comments on the necessity of Christ's grace to help us overcome the Evil One. "The desert is given us to get the evil unnested from the crannies of our own hearts. . . . After twenty-three years all the nests are well established. But in solitude and open air they are revealed and the wind blows on them and I know they must go!" (*DWL,* 177).

A few entries later, on his fiftieth birthday, as he delights in Sophia and waking in his hermitage, Merton confides: "Last night, before going to bed, realized momentarily what solitude really means: When the ropes are cast off and the skiff is no longer tied to land, but heads out to sea without ties, without restraints! Not the sea of passion, on the contrary, the sea of purity and love that is without care" (*DWL,* 200).

Inner/Outer Landscape

Perhaps the most interesting relationship between nature and Merton, the writer, is the way he uses nature to describe—and therefore to mediate—his ineffable experience of God. The elements of nature and their interaction offer Merton a language to articulate the shifts and movements of grace within his soul. Sometimes woodland observations flow naturally into prayer; sometimes inner experience overflows into an observation of a sacramental world; and sometimes—especially as Merton's understanding and practice of Zen grow, inner and outer landscapes merge. One might say that Merton's nature awareness was training for prayer awareness (Lane, 83).

On the feast of St. Bernard in 1947, for example, Merton comments on his evening meditation, the value of the Cistercian life and its crosses, but then laments: "There was too much emotion in it. After Night Office I stood in the door by the kitchen and looked at the stars and the sky paling out behind Rohan's knob, and the barns and the water tower. How fierce and efficient that tank makes this place look—geared for battle. My God, lock me in Your will, imprison me in Your Love and Your Wisdom, and draw me to Yourself" (*ES,* 101). This movement from chapel experience to details of nature slips easily into an earnest prayer of two paragraphs imploring God to use every means available to bring him into union with God; Merton, in return, abandons himself totally to being possessed: "I will belong to You. I will not be afraid of anything for I shall remain in Your hands and never leave You" (*ES,* 101).

Beginnings and endings of a year are important seasons of reflection for Merton. Often his late December journal entries list the struggles and the graces of the past twelve months as they emerge in his thinking; early January entries look ahead with speculation and great hope. In 1950, Merton describes his walk in the rainy woods on New Year's Day, only to find himself "climbing the steepest of the knobs. . . . Bare woods and driving rain. . . . When I reached the top," he writes,

> *I found there was something terrible about the landscape. But it was marvelous. . . . I said, "Now you are indeed alone. Be prepared to fight the devil." But it was not the time of combat. I started down the hill again feeling that perhaps after all I had climbed it uselessly. Half way down . . . I found a bower God had prepared for me like Jonas' ivy. It had been designed especially for this moment. There was a tree stump, in an even place. It was dry and a small cedar arched over it, like a green tent, forming an alcove. There I sat in silence and loved the wind in the forest and listened for a good while to God. (ES, 393–94)*

Merton concludes this passage: "The peace of the woods steals over me when I am at prayer."

On a day of recollection in November 1958, Merton records his Zen experience in the woods: "My Zen is in the slow swinging tops of sixteen pine trees. One long thin pole of a tree fifty feet high swings in a wider arc than all the others and swings even when they are still. . . . My watch lies among oak leaves. My tee shirt hangs on the barbed wire fence, and the wind sings in the bare wood" (*SS*, 232).

This reciprocal influence of nature and prayer is so pervasive—the sacramental power of nature and the experience of God so intense—that subject/object distinctions dissolve. Merton experiences only communion. He writes:

> *When your tongue is silent, you can rest in the silence of the forest. When your imagination is silent, the forest speaks to you, tells you of its unreality and of the Reality of God. But when your mind is silent, then the forest suddenly becomes magnificently real and blazes transparently with the Reality of God. For now I know that the Creation, which first seems to reveal Him in concepts, then seems to hide Him by the same concepts, finally is revealed in Him, in the Holy Spirit. And we who are in God find ourselves united in Him with all that springs from Him. This is prayer, and this is glory! (ES, 471)*

This kind of contemplative experience is further supported by Merton's reading. Merton is quick to recognize the similarity between the French philosopher Merleau-Ponty and Zen—especially Merleau-Ponty's position that complete separation from environment is a delusion. On the Fourth Sunday of Advent, 1963, Merton writes: "I am inevitably a dialogue with my surroundings, and have no choice, though I can perhaps change the surroundings." Notice that he writes "a dialogue with" not "in dialogue with"; Merton knows he himself is a dialogue. Then he adds a passage in French that sounds strikingly like an Eastern koan: "'*L'intérieur et l'extérieur sont inseparables. Le monde est fait au dedans et je suis tous hors de moi*' ['The interior and the exterior are inseparable. The world is created from within and I am always outside myself.']" (*DWL*, 48).

You may have noticed that all the passages quoted so far celebrate the uniqueness, the goodness, the sacramental aspect of nature. If you are a reader of Annie Dillard or Barry Lopez, you may be asking: what about the horror of nature, the brutality of some species' mating rituals and eating habits? Doesn't Merton acknowledge the other, cruel side of "red in tooth and claw"? This is precisely the tack taken by Czeslaw Milosz, the Polish poet and writer with whom Merton began a ten-year correspondence in 1958. In a letter dated February 28, 1960, Milosz chides Merton: "Every time you speak of Nature, it appears to you as soothing, rich in symbols, as a veil or a curtain. You do not pay much attention to torture and suffering in Nature."[13] Merton's response to this critique is clear; while he admits to many resentments in his life, Merton insists:

> *it is not resentment against nature, only against people, institutions and myself. . . . I am in complete and deep complicity with nature . . . nature and I are very good friends, and console one another for the stupidity and the infamy of the human race and its civilization. We at least get along, I say to the trees, and though I am perfectly aware that the spider eats the fly, that the singing of the birds may perhaps have something to do with hatred or pain of which I know nothing, still I can't make much of it. . . . I don't find it in myself to generate any horror for nature or a feeling of evil in it. (STB, 69–70)*

Merton refuses to take a Manichean approach to nature possibly because his experience with nature has developed in him such a deep sense of belonging, a sense of home. During the previous year when Merton was struggling for several months over an invitation to join a monastery in Mexico, he lists as one of the points in his discernment process the realization of how much he loves "*these woods*" (*SS*, 278) and how his doubts about going elsewhere occur especially when he is in the woods or heading toward the woodshed to read (*SS*, 300). Leaving, he writes, would be a struggle to "not let myself be held prisoner emotionally by the soft embrace of this 'mother'—this silent, gentle, circle of hills that has comforted me for eighteen years and whose secrets I have come to know perhaps better than anyone here" (*SS*, 347). In a December entry for 1960, he celebrates the silence of his hermitage: "the tall pines, the silence, the moon and stars above the pines as dark falls, the patterns of shadow, the vast valley and hills everything speaks of a more mature and more complete solitude. . . . *Haec requies mea in saeculum saeculi* [This is my resting place forever]—the sense of a journey ended, of wandering at an end. *The first time in my life* I ever really felt I had come home and that my waiting and looking were ended" (*TTW*, 79–80).

Nature as Healer

But even more than a sense of home, nature affirms Merton's vocation and heals many of the inner struggles he experiences in the monastery. Making his way from the hermitage to the monastery early on a December 1964 morning, Merton notes: "Seeing the multitude of stars above the bare branches of the wood, I was suddenly hit, as it were, with the whole package of meaning of everything: that the immense mercy of God was upon me, that the Lord in infinite kindness had looked down on me and given me this vocation out of love" (*DWL*, 177). And a few months later: "There is no question for me that my one job as monk is to live the hermit life in simple direct contact with nature, primitively, quietly, doing some writing, maintaining such contacts as are willed by God, and bearing witness to the value and goodness of simple things and ways, and loving God in it all" (*DWL*, 229).

Merton can say confidently, with his fellow Kentuckian and poet friend Wendell Berry: "Passion has brought me to this clearing of the ground. . . . Desire and circumstance are one."[14] Like the eighteenth-century Puritan theologian Jonathan Edwards, Merton understands that where things interface, there is God. Where things interface for Merton—in the woods—locates him precisely in what theologians call liminal space: that wilderness place where God speaks; it locates him precisely in what ecologists call the ecotone: that margin or boundary between two separate and distinct environments which shares some of the attributes of each. Living life on the ecotone, says nature writer John Elder, "is a risky opportunity." The edge offers new sources of nourishment for those venturing beyond the "safety of familiar ground," but it also makes them "potential sources of nourishment" for "opportunists creeping in from the opposite side."[15] Although Elder is referring primarily to animals as opportunists, many of us know how God is also an opportunist. If we allow ourselves to be vulnerable to God, we will be swallowed up in overwhelming and transforming grace. Merton committed himself to just such vulnerability; he allowed himself to be, as Jonathan Montaldo puts it, "God's bait" (*ES*, xiv). Merton, the man of paradox, is both pursuer and pursued—a monk journeying toward God and simultaneously waiting to be caught by the great Fisher-King.

In the spiritual sense of Hosea, Merton allows himself to be lured into the wilderness so that God can possess his heart; in a physical sense, he is lured into the woods so that, like Thoreau, he can learn to live deliberately and reflectively. In this solitude, Merton learns how to live on the ecotone, the margin. Merton is both inside the monastic community and apart from it in his hermitage; he is committed to silence and solitude, yet extends his compassion to the world by writing on controversial contemporary issues such as peace, racism, war, nuclear power, technology, and non-violence; he is both bystander by choice, and central participant in the dialogue of the sixties; a monk of the Western tradition, but through his study of Eastern spirituality—especially Zen—able to contain within himself both East and West; he is both contemplative and practical: sitting quietly in prayer in the woods, and clearing brush and fighting forest fires; Merton is trained in *lectio divina,* yet adept also at reading nature and contemplating God in the unfolding of grace we call Creation; he can write eloquently of the lyricism of nature, yet embrace the daily, prosaic ritual of heralding the king snake curled on the rafters of his outhouse: "Are you in there, you bastard?" (*DS,* 53).

Further, living on the ecotone not only becomes the basis of Merton's spirituality, but actually impels him toward a more public stance on ecological concerns. Just as Merton's silence and solitude compelled him to speak out on contemporary issues as an act of compassion for his world, so too, his growing appreciation for nature as sacrament—as sign pointing to the Creative Spark that is God—drew Merton into public dialogue on environmental issues. As early as the 1950s, Merton engaged in some limited conservation activism. Merton requested from the federal government hundreds of loblolly pine seedlings, and directed the novices, over whom he had charge, where and how to plant them to replace older trees and prevent creek erosion. Such initiative indicates Merton's awareness of responsibility to the earth before environmental consciousness became widespread and trendy. Brother Patrick Hart, one of those tree-planters and later Merton's secretary, remarks that Merton regarded the woods as a "sacrament of God's presence and was concerned about preserving it not only for our generation, but for the generations to come." Merton also saw in the growth of these seedlings, comments Hart, a symbolic parallelism with the young novices entrusted to his care.[16] But Merton goes beyond this local gesture with three public activities: a letter written to a public figure and two published book reviews.

A few months after the publication of Rachel Carson's controversial book, *Silent Spring,* Merton wrote to the author, commending her not only for her text, but also for her "diagnosis of the ills of our civilization" which Merton identified as the "awful irresponsibility with which we scorn the smallest values . . . [and] dare to use our titanic power in a way that threatens not only civilization but life itself."[17] Religious thinkers, Merton writes to Carson, have always understood that God's love is "manifested in all His creatures, down to the tiniest, and in the most wonderful interrelationship between them. Man's vocation was to be in this cosmic creation, so to speak, as the eye in the body. What I say now is a religious, not a scientific statement. That is to say, man is at once a part of nature and he transcends it. In maintaining this delicate balance, he must make use of nature wisely, and understand his position, ultimately relating both himself and visible nature to the invisible—in my terms, to the Creator, in any case, to the source and exemplar of all being and all life" *(WF,* 71). Here Merton is anticipating a central theme of today's creation spirituality, articulated by Thomas Berry and others, namely, that an extreme anthropocentric or egocentric position is no longer tenable. Our vocation is not to dominate the earth, but to discover community with it.

Three years later, Merton again ponders the challenge of ecology. After reading George H. Williams's book, *Wilderness and Paradise in Christian Thought,*[18] Merton comments on the "great richness" he finds in this book: "So many new areas open up. . . . Moved by his deep sense of importance, spiritually, of conservationism. So many things click. Strongly tempted to write to him."[19] Although Merton apparently did not write to Williams, he did write a review of Williams' book (along with Ulrich W. Mauser's text, *Christ in the Wilderness*[20]) which was first published in 1967 in *Cistercian Studies*.[21] Merton concentrates his response to these Protestant writers on the biblical themes of desert and wilderness as prerequisite for the experience of contemplation. He then comments on the texts' usefulness to understand North American culture from New England Puritanism to the wilderness of Gethsemani, Kentucky, highlighting in Williams' book "the criminal wastefulness with which commercial interests in the last two centuries have ravaged and despoiled the 'paradise-wilderness' of the North American mountains, forests and plains" (*MJ*, 150). Merton then uses the opportunity of this book review to go beyond Williams' critique of this "age of the bulldozer" to draw a practical lesson for his readers. "If," writes Merton,

> *the monk is a man whose whole life is built around a deeply religious appreciation of his call to wilderness and paradise, and thereby to a special kind of kinship with God's creatures . . . and if technological society is constantly encroaching upon and destroying the remaining "wildernesses" which it nevertheless needs in order to remain human, then . . . the monk, of all people, should be concerned with staying in the "wilderness" and helping to keep it a true "wilderness and paradise." The monk should be anxious to preserve the wilderness in order to share it . . . . [Monks] would seem to be destined by God, in our time, to be not only dwellers in the wilderness but also its protectors. (MJ, 150)*

Merton adds a footnote to this sentence in which he muses that it "would be interesting to develop this idea" because hermits have a natural opportunity to act as forest rangers or fire guards in our vast North American forests (*MJ*, 184).

Although this book review seems to be directed specifically to a monastic audience, Merton's public stance on ecology assumes even broader scope the year of his death. In February of 1968 Merton wrote a lengthy book review of the first edition of Roderick Nash's *Wilderness and the American Mind*.[22] In this review, published first in *The Catholic Worker* in June 1968, and in *The Center Magazine* a month later, Merton dutifully traces our American attitudes toward the wilderness over three and a half centuries from the Puritan impulse to subdue the wilderness, to Thoreau and the Transcendentalists who see nature as healing, to John Muir who first worked for wilderness preservation, to Theodore Roosevelt and his cult of virility maintained through hunting, and finally to Aldo Leopold who, in the 1940s, offered us ethical principles for land use.

Merton again uses this opportunity of the book review to discuss issues that are bothering him. Roderick Nash is concerned with the historical evolution of our attitudes toward wilderness and with what he sees as the central irony of our American experience, namely, that pioneering destroys the primitive setting that made the pioneer possible. But Merton goes beyond summarizing the book to criticize Nash for remaining in the historical mode and refusing to recognize what Merton regards as the crucial issue of the sixties, namely, that the savagery the Puritans projected "out there" onto the wilderness has turned out to be savagery within the human heart. Merton calls on the reader to recognize the ways we continue to honor the wilderness myth while continuing to destroy the wilderness. He challenges us to come to terms with a deep conflict imposed by our culture—that is, the tension between the wilderness mystique and the mystique of exploitation and power in the name of freedom and creativity. "The ideal of freedom and creativity," writes Merton,

> *that has been celebrated with such optimism and self-assurance runs the risk of being turned completely inside out if the natural ecological balance, on which it depends for its vitality, is destroyed. Take away the space, the freshness, the rich spontaneity of a wildly flourishing nature, and what will become of the creative pioneer mystique? A pioneer in a suburb is a sick man tormenting himself with projects of virile conquest. In a ghetto he is a policeman shooting every black man who gives him a dirty look. Obviously, the frontier is a thing of the past, the bison has vanished, and only by some miracle have a few Indians managed to survive. There are still some forests and wilderness areas, but we are firmly established as an urban culture. Nevertheless, the problem of ecology exists in a most acute form. The danger of fallout and atomic waste is only one of the more spectacular ones.*[23]

Merton concludes his review, as does Nash his book, with a section on Aldo Leopold, who well understood, says Merton, "that the erosion of American land was only part of a more drastic erosion of American freedom" (*PAJ*, 105). Leopold knew, continues Merton, that if freedom means simply "uncontrolled power to make money in every possible way, regardless of consequences, then freedom becomes synonymous with ruthless, mindless exploitation" (*PAJ*, 105). It is this understanding that led Leopold to what Merton regards as one of the most important moral discoveries of our time, Leopold's concept of the "ecological conscience"—an "awareness of man's true place as a dependent member of the biotic community." In Leopold's now famous words, "A thing is right when it tends to preserve the integrity, stability, and beauty of the biotic community. It is wrong when it tends otherwise" (quoted by Merton, *PAJ*, 105–106).

The tragedy of our time, as Merton sees it, is our misplaced reverence for goods, money, and property. We "mistake," he says, "the artificial value of [these] inert objects and abstractions . . . for the power of life itself" (*PAJ* 106). The "character of the war in Vietnam—with crop poisoning, the defoliation of forest trees, the incineration of villages and their inhabitants with napalm—presents a stark enough example to remind us of this most urgent moral need" (*PAJ*, 107). Merton ends his review by asking all of us if Aldo Leopold's ecological conscience can become effective in America today.

Conclusion

This public Merton has traveled a far distance from the youthful Merton attracted to landscapes for their color but regarding them as separate from his experience. Like Thoreau, Merton has made a shift from nature "out there" to environment, of which we are a part. Unlike Thoreau who develops from a transcendental naturalist to a practical ecologist, Merton finds his vocation—his "true north"—in becoming another "voice in the wilderness," reminding us of the sacramentality of nature and our responsibility to act on ecological principles.

Were Merton alive today, I have no doubt he would be in the vanguard of contemporary nature writers and environmentalists—not simply because creation is holy, but because we humans have a moral obligation to be the voice for the voiceless. This is a man who, in the early 1960s, could write in *Conjectures of a Guilty Bystander:* "How absolutely central is the truth that we are first of all *part of nature,*

though we are a very special part, that which is conscious of God";[24] a man who writes in *Thoughts in Solitude*: "Let me seek, then, the gift of silence, and poverty, and solitude, where everything I touch is turned into prayer: where the sky is my prayer, the birds are my prayer, the wind in the trees is my prayer, for God is all in all."[25]

Picturing Merton as a raven—perhaps even dancing with the raven of Elijah, of Benedict, of Buddhist lore, is not mere poetic fancy, but a workable symbol of the intense and changing relationship Merton enjoyed with nature. Both the private voice of his journals and the public voice of his letters, books, and essays testify to the continuing and growing influence of nature on his experience of God and his budding sense of ecology. His insights about our responsibility for creation are not only concurrent with the initial surge of ecological sensitivity, but are well-grounded in Cistercian spirituality and the advice of twelfth-century Bernard of Clairvaux: "You will find something more in woods than in books. Trees and stones will teach you that which you can never learn from masters."[26] I think we can agree that the trees and stones—and all the other elements and critters—taught Thomas Merton well.

Vineyard on Lake Erie

Photograph by Bron Miller, courtesy of Modern-Ad, Butler, Pennsylvania.

Sacrament and Sacramentality in Thomas Merton's *Thirty Poems*

Patrick F. O'Connell

In late November 1944, a copy of Thomas Merton's first published volume arrived at the Abbey of Gethsemani.[1] The slim collection of verse entitled *Thirty Poems* remained a favorite of its author throughout his life. When he drew up a chart evaluating his books in 1967, the year before his death, he ranked *Thirty Poems* in the "better" category, the highest any of his works received.[2] *Thirty Poems* deserves our attention, I would suggest, for at least three reasons. First, it provides insights on Merton's religious and artistic preoccupations in the crucial period leading up to, and into, the monastery: Though published in 1944, most of the poems included in the book were the products of Merton's time teaching at St. Bonaventure College in 1940 and 1941, or of his earliest period of monastic life in the Gethsemani novitiate; thus they provide us with a unique perception of the transition from life in the world to life in the monastery.[3] Second, *Thirty Poems* contains seeds of ideas and themes that will flower much later in Merton's mature works, in both verse and prose; while many of Merton's most significant reflections on the spiritual life—for example, the notion of the true and false self, or the focus on wordless, imageless contemplation—are not to be found here, it is rather startling to discover foreshadowings of later concerns for participating in the paschal mystery, for the revelatory aspects of creation, even for issues of war and peace and of social justice, already present in these early poems. Finally, many of the poems are worth a careful reading for themselves, because of their intrinsic merit as poems; though Merton's achievement in *Thirty Poems* is inconsistent, as it would continue to be throughout his career as poet, the best of these poems provide the reader with a rich and rewarding aesthetic, and perhaps even religious, experience.

Discussing *Thirty Poems* as a whole is rather difficult, because it is a diverse selection, drawn from a considerably larger body of verse written during the same period.[4] As Merton himself noted in the brief preface to his second volume, *A Man in the Divided Sea*, in which *Thirty Poems* was reprinted, they "are not arranged in any special sequence."[5] Nevertheless, there are a number of topics and motifs that recur throughout the volume. Perhaps the most pervasive and most important of these reflects Merton's deeply sacramental consciousness, his intrinsically Catholic recognition of the capacity of material creation to mediate the presence of God. Such an awareness can be found first of all in poems explicitly focused on the sacraments, specifically the eucharist, but also flows out into other poems more generally concerned with the natural world as an epiphany of the divine: these early explorations of both the possibilities and the difficulties of what Merton will later call *theoria physiké*, or natural contemplation,[6] are perhaps the most characteristic, most intensely felt, and most completely realized poems in this first collection. I would like, then, to focus first on some of the poems reflecting Merton's sacramentalism, his consideration of the mystery of the eucharist, and then to examine some of the poems of sacramentality, which envision creation as a manifestation of the love and wisdom of the Creator.

The most logical place[7] to begin an investigation of the sacramental aspects of *Thirty Poems* is with the piece entitled "The Holy Sacrament of the Altar," which is the most explicit and most fully elaborated presentation in the volume of the meaning of the eucharist. The initial focus of the poem's reflections, the exposition of the consecrated host for the worship of the faithful, may not be particularly congenial to a post-conciliar audience, but this point of departure is part of a carefully thought-out pattern of structural and thematic development:

You senses, never still, but shrill as children,
Become more humble and more low:

Learn adoration, where our secret life,
Our Corpus Christi,
Here lives uplifted in His golden window. (ll. 1–5)

The comparison of the senses to restless children (perhaps to be envisioned squirming in the pews) is a vivid opening image, but the instruction that follows is to become not less but more childlike, in the sense intended by Jesus when he said, "Whoever humbles himself as this little child is the greatest in the kingdom of heaven" (Mt 18:4; cf. also 11:25). The senses are to be aware of their creaturely condition, of human beings' absolute dependence upon God. Yet as the second part of the directive makes clear, lowliness is not to be equated with ignorance. The command to "Learn adoration" seems to be not only in dialectical tension with the previous command, but also paradoxical in itself; yet it articulates well the convergence of dogma and devotion which the eucharistic mystery demands. Thus the opening stanza both validates and restricts the role of the senses in acknowledging the presence of God, specifically the presence of Christ in the Blessed Sacrament. They are to recognize and worship the God who makes himself available to human perceptions, but the predominant impression here is of the distance between creatures and Creator: at this point in the poem, a suitable response to the eucharist seems to be confined to reverent, passive observation of the host through the "golden window" of the monstrance. But already there is a hint of a deeper, more intimate connection with the sacrament in the description of the eucharist as "our secret life." The full implications of this phrase remain to be worked out in subsequent sections of the poem, since it describes a relationship which transcends the capacities of the unaided senses.

The two sections which immediately follow, however, still addressed to the senses, seem to be little more than an elaboration of the two imperatives of the opening stanza. The first of these particularizes and specifies what humility and lowliness entail:

Eyes, in your murky night, know new simplicity.
You ears and iron voices, leave your wars.
Hands, have one action more: wash yourselves clean, and then be
still. (ll. 6–8)[8]

Each of the instructions enjoins a movement toward purification and unification. Simplicity of vision is attained by focusing on an single object, the consecrated host: to adore "Our Corpus Christi" is to discover clarity in the midst of confusion, as "in your murky night" is juxtaposed with "in His golden window." Conflict between listening and speaking, particularly the misuse of language as a weapon (hence "iron voices"), is to give way to a new peace, evidenced particularly by silence in the presence of the Lord. The stillness of folded hands provides not only an appropriate reminiscence of Psalm 46:10, "Be still, and know that I am God," but a contrast to the description of the senses as "never still" in the opening line. It may seem, then, that these lines are simply intended to repeat, with greater concreteness, the initial command to the senses, but subtle indications of development are evident. The fact that only three senses are addressed here, that smell and taste are omitted, is suggestive in itself, since they, particularly the latter, are associated not with observing but with eating. Likewise, the instruction to wash the hands is not only related generally with purification, but refers to the usual preparations for a meal (being customarily directed to children), and recalls as well the "*Lavabo*" prayer of the offertory of the Mass, preceding the consecration and communion. Thus, by indirection, these lines imply that while recognition of the Real Presence is a necessary first step, a complete response to the gift of the eucharist will go beyond what has been discussed to this point.

A similar development can be noticed in the next section, which plays variations on the earlier instruction to "Learn adoration":

And all you senses, waiting here, reborn by water,
Stay wakeful in these joyful attitudes,
Attentive to the wheat our holy Stranger:
He is bright heaven's open door. (ll. 9–12)

Each of these lines includes a significant scriptural allusion. The continuation of the water imagery from the previous line links the two sections together, but the reference here is clearly baptismal (cf. Jn 3:5), thus indicating the relation and progression between the two sacraments. The command to "Stay wakeful" initiates a series of allusions to the parable of the wise and foolish virgins (cf. Mt 25:13), which will be important not only for the light imagery of the following sections of the poem, but in its implicit introduction of the figure of the Bridegroom, a key link to the images of the wedding banquet to follow. The epithet "the wheat our holy Stranger," a description of the presence of Christ not immediately perceived in the form of bread, recalls both the story of Abraham at Mamre welcoming the three strangers without at first realizing their identity (Gn 18:1–15), and the incident of the disciples on the road to Emmaus, who recognize their companion only in the breaking of the bread (Lk 24:30–31, 35). Both episodes, which exemplify the scriptural command to "entertain strangers" (Heb 13:2) and do so in the context of a meal, suggest the association of the eucharist with eating, as does the word "wheat" itself. But the final line reverses the participants' roles, at least for the time being. Rather than receiving the guest within their own doors, the senses are to recognize the sacramental presence of Christ as the entranceway to eternal life: the image of the "golden window" has been transmuted into that of the "open door" (cf. Jn 10:7, 9) to "bright heaven," an indication that we are called not merely to gaze at "Our Corpus Christi" but to pass through him into the presence of God.

At this point, however, the door still seems to be intended for looking through rather than walking through, as we are offered a vision reminiscent of the Book of Revelation (cf. Rv 5:6 ff.), the heavenly liturgy of the Lamb:

Look where the Lamb bends all His brightness
Low as our dim and puny lights
Although His fleece is full of sun.
Not all the universe can comprehend
His glory's equal, nor His light's,
Who loves us so, He won't outshine our winking candles! (ll. 13–18)

The focus here is clearly on the Incarnation, and the predominance of light imagery indicates that interest is still centered on perception rather than communion. Attention is directed to the gracious condescension of the Son of God, the sun of righteousness (Mal 3:20), who tempers the surpassing glory of his divinity to the capacity of the human senses by himself assuming human nature: here the "kenosis" passage of the Philippians hymn ("Though he was in the form of God, he did not count equality with God a thing to be grasped, but emptied himself, taking the form of a slave, coming in human likeness" [Phil 2:6–7]) is rephrased in terms of the light imagery of the Johannine

Prologue (cf. Jn 1:4–5, as well as the reference to seeing his glory in vs. 14, the key expression of the doctrine of the Incarnation in the entire New Testament). The eucharist serves as a "door" through which this mystery can be seen because the presence of the glorified Jesus under the form of bread provides a kind of analogy to the Incarnation (though not a perfect one, since only the "accidents" of the bread remain, while the full humanity of Jesus coexists with his divinity). The eucharist is the primary way in which the presence of Christ continues to be available and accessible to the "dim and puny lights" of the human senses. The image of "the Lamb" is a particularly appropriate one here because in the final chapters of the Book of Revelation the Lamb is presented as the Bridegroom of the New Jerusalem, redeemed humanity, so that there is a link with the parable of the wise virgins (numbering five, appropriately), who await the coming of the Bridegroom with their lamps. But the opening words also recall the liturgical summons as host and chalice are raised, "*Ecce Agnus Dei*" ("Behold the Lamb of God"), which concludes with a blessing on those called to the banquet table (also obliquely suggested by the final image of the senses as "winking candles," like those on the altar). Once again, a reference to the eucharist as communion is hidden just below the surface of the doctrinal presentation.

The section which follows continues the light imagery, but now transfers it from the senses to the intellect:

> *Be kindled, intellect, although your strongest lamps are night-lights*
> *By the beams of this wonderful Sun!*
> *Created wisdom makes at best a metal monstrance for His crown,*
> *And those stiff rays look like no living light:*
> *They are no more than golden spikes, and golden thorns! (ll. 19–23)*[9]

The opening lines here can be read in two distinct ways: understanding "By" in terms of agency, they say that the lamp of the intellect (the clearest allusion to the parable of the wise virgins) can be kindled by the light of the Sun, that the human mind is capable of being enlightened to comprehend the mystery of Christ; but when "By" is interpreted as "next to," they say that in comparison with the divine light, the light of the mind remains a dim ray in the midst of darkness. As with the senses earlier, both the capabilities and the limitations of the intellect to respond to the meaning of the Blessed

Sacrament are affirmed, simultaneously. A similar point is made, though in more critical terms, about "[c]reated wisdom" in the following lines. The comparison of human wisdom to a monstrance suggests that it has a legitimate function, to manifest divine wisdom as the monstrance reveals the host, but that when it attempts to usurp a role beyond its capacity, when it tries to substitute the "stiff rays" of its own artificial light for the "living light" of Christ and thus confuses the container with the reality it holds, it acts not as a crown of honor but a crown of thorns; it becomes merely the wisdom of this world (1 Cor 1:20), a barren rationalism which rejects and indeed persecutes the Lord of Glory, which scorns the mystery of the eucharist because it fails to comprehend it. Here the dangerous propensities of the human mind to claim autonomy from the divine source of true wisdom threaten to undermine any fruitful relation to the eucharist.

This negative response to the eucharist is continued in the next section of the poem:

> *But where is reason at the Lamb's bright feast?*
> *Reason and knowledge have bought oxen and they cannot come.*
> *Thrift and prudence give their own excuses,*
> *And justice has a wife, and must stay home. (ll. 24–27)*

Here at last, the imagery of the sacrament as a meal becomes explicit, expressed in terms of the parable of the wedding banquet in Matthew 22:1–14 (though the specific images come from the parallel passage in Luke 14:15–23, where the dinner is not described as a wedding feast). These lines continue the device of personifying the human faculties, here exposing the failure of the natural powers to respond positively to the Lamb's invitation to communion with himself. The oxen (Lk 14:19) of "Reason and knowledge" perhaps represent the sterility of the human mind detached from its divine ground; the excuses of thrift (perhaps a stand-in for temperance among the traditional cardinal virtues) and prudence represent the "safe" response of the worldly wise to the risk of contact with the divine, while it is appropriately justice, the virtue ensuring that each receives what is due, who claims his duties toward his wife keep him away. Thus the irony is that when the long-awaited, frequently adumbrated revelation of the sacrament as food is finally made, there seem to be no takers. The eucharist holds no attraction to natural human capacities by themselves.

But just as the master sends his servants out into the highways and byways to bring in the poor to his feast, so here there remains another guest to be invited:

To the cold corners of the earth rise up and go:
Find beggar Faith, and bring him to the holy table.
He shall sit down among the good Apostles,
And weep with Peter at the washing of the feet. (ll. 28–31)[10]

The allegory, obvious enough on one level, is perhaps puzzling on another: it is Faith alone which is able to recognize and respond to the mystery of the eucharist, and is able to do so precisely because it is a "beggar," claiming nothing as its own and receiving all as a gift. The eyes of Faith see what the eyes of reason cannot: the divine presence in the most ordinary of forms. Thus far, the contrast is clear, but the reference to the footwashing episode (Jn 13:1–20) might seem to be an extraneous distraction from a focus on the eucharistic meal. Its presence might well be due to the custom of the monks at Gethsemani of washing the feet of the poor—of "beggars"—on Holy Thursday, which Merton had observed during his Holy Week retreat there,[11] but its point doesn't depend on its biographical context. On one level, the footwashing, like the handwashing above, represents a rite of repentance and purification preceding the reception of communion, symbolized by the weeping of Peter (borrowed, scripturally, from the later scene following his denial [Lk 22:62 and par.], and poetically, from Merton's earlier poem, "The Trappist Abbey: Matins"[12]). But there is a deeper significance: what this scene does is to place Faith not only at the "bright feast" of the Lamb, a foreshadowing of the eschatological banquet, but at the Last Supper itself, the original eucharist. For the believer, past and future, foundation and fulfillment, become present at each celebration of the Mass. It is not merely a remembrance but a re-presentation, a participation in the once-for-all event of the paschal mystery which redeems the world.

The full meaning of this belief is revealed in the poem's final quatrain, in which the reception of Holy Communion finally takes place:

His bread shall be the smiles of Pity's human face:
He'll eat, and live with God, at least in longing, ever after:
His wine shall be the mortal blood of Mercy, Love and Peace:
And, having drunk, he'll hear the martyr's joyful laughter. (ll. 32–35)

The terminology here, which completes the series of personifications but now associates them with divine rather than human reality, is borrowed, as Merton surely intended the reader to notice, from William Blake's poem "The Divine Image,"[13] one of the "Songs of Innocence." There, "Mercy, Pity, Peace, and Love" (ll. 1, 5) are identified as divine attributes to be incarnated in "the human form divine" (ll. 11, 15), implicitly identified with Jesus and potentially with all who share the divine image. These terms function here as a reminder that Jesus is the incarnation of the divine compassion, shown above all in the salvific death which the gift of his body and blood at the Last Supper prefigured. The eucharist has a profoundly paschal significance: To receive communion is to be united with Jesus in his passion; it is to accept the gift of salvation, to be nourished by "the smiles of Pity's human face" (cf. Blake, l. 10), that is, to experience the tender forgiveness of God embodied in the crucified Lord; it is to "live with God" by denying the self, to share in the heavenly banquet, eternal life, now, even while "longing" for its definitive fulfillment. But the full meaning of communion has further implications: It is to become what one receives, to enflesh the "Mercy, Love and Peace" revealed and received in the sacrificial blood of Jesus: "the martyr's joyful laughter" is a communion in, an expression of, "the smiles" of the divine Pity, for the martyr is the one who enters fully into union with Christ's sacrifice, who understands that "the cup of blessing is a participation in the blood of Christ" (1 Cor 10:16), who answers with the affirmation of his very life the question of Jesus, "Can you drink of the cup of which I drink?" (Mk 10:38). The poem concludes, then, if not by sharing that laughter, at least by hearing it, that is, recognizing the ultimate promise and challenge that partaking of "The Holy Sacrament of the Altar" entails. This culminating reference to martyrdom explains the painstaking care which was shown through the course of the poem that one be fully aware of what, who, was to be received, for "anyone who eats and drinks without discerning the body, eats and drinks judgment on himself" (1 Cor 11:29). For the recent convert Thomas Merton, such a danger was not to be taken lightly, and his poem is evidence of his own concern to "discern the body" humbly, perceptively, and faithfully.

Impressive as it is in its own way, "The Holy Sacrament of the Altar" is not typical of Merton's sacramental consciousness. Though it escapes being versified catechesis by its skillful synthesis of scriptural allusions and the tension inherent in its gradual disclosure of the "communion" dimension of the sacrament, it retains a certain formality and impersonality, evidenced particularly by the consistent use of personification, which gives the poem a decidedly allegorical cast. While it provides a useful framework for appreciating the young Merton's understanding of the eucharist, other poems in the volume will develop aspects of that understanding in more dramatic fashion and with a more personal voice. Perhaps the poem which best incorporates these characteristics is "The Sponge Full of Vinegar,"[14] though with its anguished tone and hypersensitive awareness of human failings, it, too, is far from a "typical" poem of sacramentalism. Its eucharistic imagery and liturgical setting accentuate by contrast the speaker's still unsatisfied longing for full communion with Christ. The effectiveness of the poem arises precisely from its acute depiction of the unresolved conflict between that desire and its continued frustration.

The structure of the poem recalls that developed by the religious poets of the seventeenth century, in which a concrete description of a scriptural scene is followed by personal reflection and application, often, as in this case, in the form of a prayer. The setting here is Golgotha, and the focus is on the agonizing thirst of the crucified Jesus:

When Romans gambled in the clash of lancelight,
Dicing amid the lightnings for the unsewn mantle,
Thirst burned crimson, like a crosswise firebird
Even in the eyes of dying Christ.
But the world's gall, and all its rotten vinegar
Reeked in the sponge, flamed on His swollen mouth,
And all was paid in poison, in the taste of our feasts! (ll. 1–7)[15]

What is perhaps most immediately apparent here is the patterning of sounds, the insistent reiteration of alliteration and assonance, as in: "gambled . . . clash . . . lance-" (l. 1); "Dicing . . . lightnings" (l. 2); the linking of "gambled" and "mantle" (ll. 1, 2); "Thirst burned . . . -bird" (l. 3); "crimson . . . crosswise" (l. 3); "-wise fire- . . . / . . . eyes . . . dying Christ" (ll. 3, 4); "gall . . . all" (l. 4); "rotten . . . / Reeked" (ll. 5, 6); "paid . . . poison" (l. 7); "flamed . . . / . . . paid . . . taste. . . feasts" (ll. 6, 7). The effect of having virtually every important word linked by sound to at least one other (a technique which, like much else in the poem, suggests the influence of Gerard Manley Hopkins) is to make the entire description more emphatic, while avoiding the danger of inflated rhetoric by using quite ordinary language, made up almost exclusively of one- and two-syllable words. The approach taken to the scene is essentially that of the "composition of place" and "application of the senses" recommended by the Ignatian *Spiritual Exercises*,[16] in which a biblical event is imaginatively recreated as vividly as possible, so that its general significance and personal application can be recognized and accepted. Here, except for the detail of the seamless garment, borrowed from John 19:23–24, the account is dependent on Matthew's Passion narrative, particularly chapter 27, vv. 34 and 48: "They offered him wine to drink, mingled with gall"; and "one of them at once ran and took a sponge, filled with vinegar, and put it on a reed, and gave it to him to drink."[17]

The speaker develops the information provided by these verses in two successive ways. First, he finds images which will enlist the aid of the senses in making the scene present to the mind—and heart. Thus the phrase "clash of lancelight" combines sensations of sight and sound: Figuratively, the light reflecting off the soldiers' weapons has a harsh, dissonant cast, comparable to the sounds of the lances themselves striking against one another in battle, a reminder that this is a scene of violent conflict even though the soldiers are gambling rather than fighting; on a more literal level, it may indeed seem that the light can be heard, since its source is the bolts of lightning that pierce the unnatural darkness of the afternoon, accompanied, of course, by thunderclaps (the word "clash" itself combines the "crash" of the thunder with the "flash" of the lightning). The overall effect of this juxtaposition of sound and sight imagery is to exemplify the discordance it describes. This synaesthesia is also used in the main clause, "Thirst burned crimson," as the torment of Christ's thirst is so intense that it becomes visible, to him and to us: the color of fire and of blood; it virtually assumes a concrete shape as the "firebird,"[18] an image which combines two attributes associated with the Holy Spirit, but reverses their significance, thus appearing as contrary, "crosswise," a term which suggests as well the pain slashing across his field of vision, and perhaps also the idea that the "firebird" is already familiar with the agonies of those undergoing crucifixion.

The intent of this opening sentence is to describe the scene at the cross, and the sufferings of Jesus, as graphically as possible, so that the reality of the Passion will be vividly perceived and deeply felt. As the focus shifts in the succeeding lines from Christ's thirst to the drink offered him, the purpose likewise moves toward interpretation, an attempt to understand the significance of this response to Christ's agony. For the gall and vinegar, far from relieving the thirst of Jesus, make his pains worse, intensifying the burning sensation "on His swollen mouth." This fact is recognized as having not only a literal but a moral application: It is not merely "gall" but "the world's gall" which is given to Jesus, not simply "vinegar" but "all its rotten vinegar": Christ is being forced to taste all the bitterness, the sour, spoiled decoctions of a fallen world. Rather than repaying the debt of gratitude to the Redeemer in some beneficial, if inadequate, fashion, all that sinful humanity has to offer is more of the same poison that brought Christ to Calvary in the first place. Moreover, by referring to "our feasts," the speaker personalizes the situation, drawing himself and his audience into the drama: we are no longer just observers of the crucifixion, but are implicated in the events, since Christ's lips are now burned not just by "the world's gall" but by "the taste of our feasts." But the full ironic implications of this phrase are to be found in its placement, in parallelism with "in poison." That is, what is being given here to Christ is what, in fact, we ourselves feast on, as though it were a delicacy, fare for a banquet—but is actually poison. The fruits of human sin which are now raised to Christ's lips have already, whether we realized it or not, been poisoning us.

This awareness of personal responsibility for the sufferings of Christ becomes the predominant focus of the second part of the poem, the speaker's prayer, which begins:

O Lord! When I lie breathless in Thy churches
Knowing it is Thy glory goes again
Torn from the wise world in the daily thundercrack of Massbells,
I drink new fear from the four clean prayers I ever gave Thee!
(ll. 8–11)[19]

The scene has shifted to the present, to "Thy churches" during the celebration of Mass. The connection with the event it commemorates is suggested by the image of "the daily thundercrack of Massbells," which recalls the lightning flashes on Golgotha. There is even a grammatical parallelism between the opening sentences of the two sections, in each case a temporal clause preceding a main clause focused on thirst or drinking. But the effect of the liturgy on the speaker is not an experience of consolation or communion with

Christ, but of unworthiness, separation, abandonment. It is not the continued presence of Christ in the eucharist that holds the speaker's attention, but the sacrifice of the Mass as a recapitulation of Christ's return to the Father: The language recalls the prophet Ezekiel's vision of the divine Glory deserting the Jerusalem Temple before the Babylonian conquest (cf. Ez 10:1–23); it is a memorial of the death of Christ, "[t]orn from the wise world," that is, from a world impressed with its own wisdom and thus unable to recognize the true significance of the "folly" of the cross (cf. 1 Cor 1:18 ff.). The consequence of this viewpoint is that the speaker is left with a profound mistrust of self, a suspicion that even his best efforts to love and honor God, his "four clean prayers," are unworthy and worthless. (The specific number, besides being low, seems to have been chosen not for any specific reference but for its consonance with "fear," which is also linked by assonance to "clean" and by a near-rhyme to "prayers.")

Such an attitude seems excessive, illogical, even irrational, but is given an explanation in the concluding lines of the poem:

For even the Word of Thy Name, caught from Thy grace
And offered up out of my deepest terror,
Goes back gallsavored of flesh.
Even the one good sacrifice,
The thirst of heaven, comes to Thee: vinegar!
Reeks of the death-thirst manlife found in the forbidden apple.
(ll. 12–17)

The connection between the pair of offerings here, "the Word of Thy Name" and "The thirst of heaven," is not immediately evident, but it is almost certainly intended to recall the prayer before reception of the cup in the communion rite of the Roman Mass: "What return shall I make to the Lord for all that he hath given me? I will take the chalice of salvation, and I will call upon the Name of the Lord." Thus the first offering becomes a kind of grotesque parody of the doctrine of the Word made flesh, here not an affirmation of the humanity of Christ, but the speaker's horrified recognition that even the name of Jesus, a divine gift "caught from Thy grace," is defiled by his own impure motives. The phrase "gallsavored of flesh" is reminiscent of the cry, "I am gall! I am heartburn!" from Hopkins' sonnet "I wake to feel the fell of dark" (l. 9),[20] but even more the description of "the spider love" in Donne's "Twicknam Garden," which "transubstantiates all, / And can convert Manna to gall" (ll. 6–7);[21] as in that poem, there is here a kind of inversion of the words of consecration over the bread: this is not "my flesh for the life of the world" (Jn 6:51), but "the works of the flesh" which merit condemnation (Gal 5:19–22). A parallel development vitiates "the one good sacrifice" of the following lines, in which "The thirst of heaven" is adulterated by its opposite, "the death-thirst" caused by original sin, and in a sort of reversal of transubstantiation, is compared not to the wine transformed into Christ's blood, the cup of salvation, but to spoiled wine, the vinegar given him on the cross. Despite his best attempts, the speaker remains aligned with Christ's persecutors; there is no "communion in the blood of Christ" (1 Cor 10:16), but only a solidarity in sin, a profane communion in "the forbidden apple." The speaker identifies so completely with the first Adam that he is unable to share the passage from death to life of the second, as the powerful but despondent final line implies.

With its acute awareness that all human efforts are tainted by self-interest, this could be described as the most "Protestant" of the *Thirty Poems*. It depends for its effectiveness on its sacramental imagery, yet the speaker's own desire for communion with the divine remains unslaked. But perhaps this is precisely the point: in his own utter destitution he, too, thirsts, but drinks only "new fear"; overwhelmed by "deepest terror," he is perhaps much closer to the figure on the cross than he realizes. Such a response, then, may be considered appropriate to the scene of Christ's thirst, but it is certainly not adequate to the Passion as a whole. But, of course, this is not the final incident of the drama, and there is at least a hint of a deeper and more satisfying response still to come. At the beginning of the prayer, the speaker describes himself as "breathless," a condition which may be associated with adoration, awe, or fear, but which should perhaps be considered here in a more explicitly paschal context: to be "breathless" is to be dead, deprived of the "pneuma" which means both "breath" and "spirit"; but before the cross, it is also to be awaiting the gift of new life, the divine Pneuma to be poured out on the world in Jesus' last breath (cf. Mt 27:50; Lk 23:46; and especially Jn 19:30). There is at least a hope, then, that subsequent meditation on the climactic event of the Passion will restore the divine Breath to the speaker, will lead to awareness not just of sin but of redemption, and that the "communion" in gall and vinegar will give way to a saving participation in the body and blood of the Lord.

The power of the eucharist to renew and transform is recognized as having not only an individual but a social dimension in a third poem of sacramentalism, entitled "Holy Communion: The City,"[22] which reflects Merton's experiences working in Harlem during the summer of 1941 at Catherine de Hueck's Friendship House.[23] The poem begins with a question, to which the rest of the poem will serve as a reply:

> *"What light will, in your eyes, like an archangel,*
> *Soon stand armed,*
> *O you who come with looks more lowly than the dewy valleys,*
> *And kneel like lepers on the step of Bethlehem?"* (ll. 1–4)[24]

The two pairs of lines are filled with contrasts between future and present: "lowly" looks are soon to give way to the boldness and brilliance of an "armed" light in the eyes of those being addressed. Now they "kneel like lepers," but soon that light is to "stand" "like an archangel." The explicit question concerning the light thus suggests further questions about the occasion and the cause of this anticipated transformation. The final line of the stanza contains oblique hints of an explanation, though initially it may seem to be a rather confused jumble of scriptural allusions, since there are no lepers in the infancy narratives, nor do we know of any step to kneel on at the stable. But Merton intends the reader to recall the etymology of "Bethlehem" as "House of Bread," so that the scene takes on a eucharistic significance: The figures approaching the communion rail to receive their Lord are comparable both to despised lepers, coming to be healed of their affliction and restored to fellowship with the wider community, and to the humble shepherds, likewise poor and insignificant in the eyes of the world, who come to adore their King. Thus the light which will shine from their eyes is the light of Christ who is received in the eucharist. It is a light described in militant terms, as "armed," "like an archangel," perhaps reminiscent of the "glory of the Lord," which shone when the "multitude of the heavenly host" (Lk 2:9, 13) appeared to the shepherds, but which will now be coming from within themselves. The eucharist is being envisioned as an empowerment, and those who enter into communion with Christ are enlisted in the cosmic conflict against evil: To receive "the Light of the world" (Jn 8:12) is to become "light for the world" (Mt 5:14), shining amid the surrounding darkness. Such, at least, are the implications of these opening lines, which will become more explicit in the response of the participants themselves that makes up the rest of the poem.

The first part of their answer, in its implicit contrast between the pastoral associations of Bethlehem and the harsh inner-city environment in which they themselves live, seems to cast doubt on, but ultimately confirms, the aptness of their being likened to the shepherds:

"Although we know no hills, no country rivers,
Here in the jungles of our waterpipes and iron ladders,
Our thoughts are quieter than rivers,
Our lives are simpler than the trees,
Our prayers deeper than the sea. (ll. 5–9)

The initial contrast between rural and urban settings, in which the "iron ladders" of tenement fire escapes replace hills, and "the jungles of our waterpipes" substitute for "country rivers," gives way to an inner landscape marked by stillness, simplicity, and peace. While the comparisons are almost banal in their plainness, the words actually exemplify the qualities they describe. The comparisons reveal, with no rhetorical elaboration whatever, that the calm and beauty of the speakers' inner lives more than compensate for their external circumstances.

But the following stanza makes clear that such interior composure and harmony cannot be presumed or taken for granted. Spiritual fruitfulness is the result of a process of healing:

"What wounds had furrowed up our dry and fearful spirit
Until the Massbells came like rain to make them vineyards?
"Now, brighter on our minds' bright mountains
Than the towns of Israel,
Shall shine desire! (ll. 10–14)[25]

The wounded spirit had been like a parched and barren field before being made to flourish, renewed by the power of the eucharist. Here the Massbells are compared not to thunder but to the gentle rain which slakes the thirst of the "dry and fearful spirit." United sacramentally with the passion of Christ, the archetypal pattern of death transformed into life, the speakers discover that their injuries themselves become meaningful: the furrows of pain and perplexity can now be recognized as the preliminary ploughing which is a necessary prelude to planting and harvesting; wounds become vineyards, by analogy with the wounds of Jesus the true vine (cf. Jn 15:1), whose blood is received sacramentally under the form of wine; in communion with the crucified Lord, they themselves are enabled to bear fruit, fruit that will last (cf. Jn 15:16). Even the topography of the spiritual landscape is radically altered: the "dewy valleys" of the first stanza are replaced by "bright mountains," whose light surpasses that of "the towns of Israel." They become, not merely residents of a dreary and oppressive city, but themselves that "city set on a hill" which "cannot be hid" (Mt 5:14), a sign to the world around them of the redeeming power of Christ. It is the light of desire for union with the Beloved, the divine glory which illuminates the New Jerusalem, the City of God, "a light by which the nations shall walk" (Rv 21:24), which shines from their eyes.

This glory is identified explicitly with the eucharist in the prayer which follows:

> *"O Glory, be not swift to vanish like the wine's slight savor,*
> *And still lie lightly, Truth, upon our tongues,*
> *For Grace moves, like the wind,*
> *The armies of the wheat our secret hero!*
> *And Faith sits in our hearts like fire,*
> *And makes them smile like suns, . . . (ll. 15–20)*

The speaker's request is that the visible, tangible presence of Christ in the sacrament will not disappear as the "accidents," like the taste of the wine, quickly do: they are to continue to manifest the divine glory themselves. Truth is to remain, like the host, upon the tongue, because the Truth who is Christ (Jn 14:6) is to be proclaimed as it has been received. Holy Communion enables its recipients to become what they have been given, the Body of Christ, "sacraments" of the continuing presence of the risen Lord in space and time. They are to become active, dynamic witnesses to Christ's Good News. As the wind moves over the fields of grain, so Grace, the presence in humanity of God's Spirit who "blows where it wills" (Jn 3:8), moves the "armies" of those who follow "the wheat our secret hero," Christ hidden in the form of bread. Here the opening image of the "armed" light is developed further: those who receive Christ in Holy Communion are empowered to speak and do the truth, to be faithful to the Gospel in a hostile world, to confront and overcome evil armed only with the light of Christ. But this light of Truth in the mind is simultaneously experienced as the fire of Faith in the heart, which both provides warmth for the spirit within and shines "like suns" to enlighten and enkindle and encourage others.

But the effects of this sun of Justice (Mal 3:20), as the concluding lines indicate, are not only personal but social:

> *"While we come back from lovely Bethlehem*
> *To burn down Harlem with the glad Word of Our Saviour."*
> *(ll. 21–22)*

The Augustinian distinction between the two cities, the city of God and the city of man, is represented by the contrast between "lovely Bethlehem" and Harlem. The shock of the final line is a powerful one, even when the image of burning down Harlem is seen to refer not to literal fire but to the fire of the Word of God, the fire which Jesus came to cast upon the earth (cf. Lk 12:49). It is a purifying flame which is to consume all that is incompatible with God's reign, specifically the evils of poverty and disease and segregation and oppression and racism symbolized by Harlem, that "huge cauldron" of "misery and degradation" as Merton described it in his autobiography (*SSM*, 345). But it is ultimately less a word of judgment than a "glad Word," a message of hope, of liberation, of re-creation. It is a promise that the power of the sacrament which brings communion with Christ, and which has changed the speakers' own lives, can transform others as well, and will renew the face of the earth. But the poem is also, implicitly, a word of challenge to all those who receive the same eucharist, who are incorporated into the same Body of Christ, to hear what the "Word of Our Saviour" is saying about and through the brothers and sisters of "the city," and to respond to Grace with a Faith equal in commitment to theirs.

If "Holy Communion: The City" uses landscape images to describe the reality and impact of the eucharist, that is, depicts the sacrament in terms of a broader sacramentality, a number of the other poems in the volume use the converse approach, linking eucharistic images to a broader vision of creation as a sign and instrument of divine love.[26] For Merton, there is a congruency between sacramentalism and sacramentality, between the divine self-disclosures in the outward signs of the sacraments, preeminently the eucharist, and the more general revelation of the Creator and Redeemer in the beauty and mystery of the natural world. This link is particularly evident in one of the most beautiful poems in this first collection, entitled simply "Evening."[27]

The poem begins with a pair of personifications that convey a sense of cosmic unity and complementarity:

Now, in the middle of the limpid evening,
The moon speaks clearly to the hill.
The wheatfields make their simple music,
Praise the quiet sky. (ll. 1–4)

The clarity of the moonlight is imaged as speech, yet comes forth from a "quiet sky," a coincidence of opposites in which apparent antitheses are transcended; its message is not one which can be confined to words, less a matter of communication than of communion. In the transparency of the evening air, there is no barrier keeping moon and hill apart: they share a common universe. The "simple music" of the evening breeze moving across the wheatfields suggests that earth and heavens are in harmony, and its identification as praise makes the exchange a kind of paradigm of revelation and response. Even the sound of the lines contributes to the impression of creation as an orderly, integrated whole, as the alliteration of "middle," "moon," "make," and "music," and the repeated short "i" of "middle," "limpid," "hill," and "simple," are woven through the successive long-vowel pairs of "evening" and "speaks," "wheatfields," "make" and "praise," "quiet" and "sky." The four modifiers—"limpid," "clearly," "simple," "quiet"—distributed one to a line, echo and reinforce one another to intimate an atmosphere of gentleness and stillness reminiscent of paradise, the world as the Creator intended it to be.

The second stanza attempts to integrate the human element into this vision of wholeness and mutuality, with mixed results:

And down the road, the way the stars come home,
The cries of children
Play on the empty air, a mile or more,
And fall on our deserted hearing,
Clear as water. (ll. 5–9)

There is an implicit alignment here between the human and the cosmic, a suggestion that the children are spontaneously conformed to the pattern of the universe, as the road that carries the sound of their cries "a mile or more" is also identified as "the way the stars come home." The children seem to belong to the edenic world of the first stanza, an impression supported by the continued interweaving of long-vowel pairs in these lines, with "road" and "home," "way" and "Play," "cries" and "mile." But the concluding verses of this second section indicate that the adult world, as represented by the speaker and his audience, is less attuned to the speech and music of nature. The contrast is epitomized in the parallel phrases "Play on the empty air" and "fall on our deserted hearing"; "Play on" carries connotations of joy, lightness, and unselfconsciousness, while "fall on" conveys notions of heaviness and an unreceptiveness, or at least a certain passivity, in the listener; "empty," regarded as part of the series of modifiers already noted, has favorable associations of "unobstructed" or "unhindering"; but linked with "deserted" in the following line, it suggests vacancy and lack of fulfillment, a projection of the speaker's sense of alienation from the scene he has been describing, for to be "deserted" is to be abandoned, relegated to being an observer of cosmic order rather than a participant in it. Yet this contrast between children's experience and that of adults contains the elements of its own reconciliation: The simile "Clear as water" not only links the cries of the children to the speech of the moon, but suggests that they may have a revelatory function for the speaker, as they "fall" on a "deserted," or desertified, consciousness like life-giving, refreshing rain. But at this point in the poem, it is not clear whether this positive interpretation can be sustained.

In the central section of "Evening," the content of the children's cries is reported. On one level, their words are childish prattle, but on another, they express a profound wisdom which recognizes and responds to creation as a manifestation of God:

They say the sky is made of glass,
They say the smiling moon's a bride.
They say they love the orchards and apple trees,
The trees, their innocent sisters, dressed in blossoms,
Still wearing, in the blurring dusk,
White dresses from that morning's first communion. (ll. 10–15)

The first image, the sky made of glass,[28] witnesses to the children's sacramental intuition of the transparency of the created world, their ability to see the transcendent through the material. The second, the moon as bride,[29] further personalizes the complementary relation of earth and sky from the opening quatrain, and expresses it in terms of a love leading to total union. This focus on love becomes explicit in the children's third statement, which voices their own love for "the orchards and apple trees," not only a declaration of their own intimacy with the natural world, but a reminder of the unfallen paradise that the innocent children can still perceive in the beauty of the spring. The imagery describing the trees is at once Franciscan, as they are "innocent sisters" of the children; edenic, as they are clothed only "in blossoms"; and explicitly eucharistic, as they are still wearing their communion dresses: The flowering of the trees, a sign of renewal, is indeed a communion with the creative Lord who gives form and life to all creatures. But the specificity of the reference to "that morning's first communion" suggests that the image is not only metaphorical but literal, that it refers not only to the orchard but to the children, whose entrance into sacramental union with their Lord earlier that day is not only an analogy with but the cause of their experience of unity with all that the Lord has made, still clear to them even "in the blurring dusk."

The fourth stanza brings the poem to the climactic moment of sunset, the border between day and night:

And, where blue heaven's fading fire last shines
They name the new come planets
With words that flower
On little voices, light as stems of lilies. (ll. 16–19)

Once again, sound patterns bind the lines closely together, with the assonance of "fire" and "shines," the consonance of "name" and "new come," the alliteration of "fading fire" and "flower," and of "little," "light" and "lilies." Here the children engage in the task of naming the planets, itself an edenic activity, and as the words they use are said to "flower," there is a further correspondence between celestial and terrestrial planes. The words are compared specifically to lilies, emblems of innocence and purity, lifted up on their "little voices" like the blooms on their fragile yet efficient stems. Clearly the children belong to the world they respond to with such wonder; they are fully integrated into the larger whole. There is also at least the possibility, in the structural similarity between "words that flower / On little voices" and the earlier "cries" that "fall on our deserted hearing" that the words of the children have had a beneficial effect on the listening adults, have been able to mediate a renewed experience of the sacramentality of nature, so that the desert has bloomed.

This supposition receives further support from the final stanza of the poem, in which the human element apparently disappears:

And where blue heaven's fading fire last shines,
Reflected in the poplar's ripple,
One little, wakeful bird
Sings like a shower. (ll. 20–23)

The parallelism established by the repetition of the opening line from the previous stanza is continued throughout the quatrain: The setting sun reflected in "the poplar's ripple" (note how the rearrangement of the same consonants in the two words virtually exemplifies in sound the meaning of what is said) is another instance of the correlation between upper and lower worlds, while the "little, wakeful bird" echoes the "little voices" of the earlier description. Thus the song of the bird, "wakeful" in its immediate awareness of and response to its surroundings, has an analogous role to the children's words; moreover, it "Sings like a shower," reminiscent of the cries "Clear as water" earlier in the poem. The implication is that through the instrumentality of the children's vision and voices, the speaker is now enabled to respond directly to the sacramentality of the natural world represented by the bird's song, that children and bird alike are experienced, by ears no longer "deserted," as revelatory of the divinely instilled harmony of creation.

"Aubade: Lake Erie"[30] shares with "Evening" a focus on the revelatory dimension of the natural world, and it, too, pivots on the contrast between the receptivity of children and the insensibility of adults, but it is somewhat more complex in tone and structure. The opening four lines present the speaker's own response to the scene he observes along the lakefront:

When sun, light handed, sows this Indian water
With a crop of cockles,
The vines arrange their tender shadows
In the sweet leafage of an artificial France. (ll. 1–4)

The attitude of the speaker toward what he sees is initially somewhat puzzling. He appears to be comparing the sun to the figure who sows weeds among the wheat in the parable of Matthew 13:24–30, until we realize that there is a play on "cockle" as weeds and "cockle" as mollusk, or perhaps more specifically on cockle-shell boats on the lake, glinting in the early morning sunlight. But the wordplay seems to have little point beyond calling attention to its own cleverness. There is likewise a certain sterility in the description which follows of the vineyards as "an artificial France," a second-rate imitation of French wine country. Not only do the speaker's rather jaded perceptions fail to appreciate the landscape for itself, as it is compared, unfavorably, to what is presumably a more impressive or more authentic scene; but juxtaposed to the allusive reference to the weeds among the wheat parable, the vineyard image suggests a failure of sacramental vision. These opening lines, then, are a kind of aesthetic deadend, a failure to respond with immediacy and spontaneity to the experience being offered. Read biographically, the reference to "an artificial France" may also be a nostalgic recollection of Merton's own childhood, a reminiscence of a time of innocence now lost both for himself and for the country of his birth, in the throes of a cataclysmic war. In any case, the problem is not with the vineyards but with the speaker himself, and the solution is not a return to France but a return, vicariously, to childhood.

These opening lines serve as a framing device, setting off by contrast the visionary awareness of the children in the central section of the poem. The speaker's call for the children to awaken signals his recognition of the need for a response different from his own; the children are summoned, in a sense, to come to the speaker's rescue, to mediate the revelatory vision which he knows is there, but which is no longer available to him directly. The juxtaposition implies both a loss of vision and the simultaneous recognition of its validity and continued availability to those whose innocence enables them to see as he, perhaps, once saw, with uncontrived appreciation and delight:

Awake, in the frames of windows, innocent children,
Loving the blue, sprayed leaves of childish life,
Applaud the bearded corn, the bleeding grape,
And cry. . . . (ll. 5–8)

In calling the children to appear in the windows, he wishes them both to see and to be seen: as they look out at the world, he is enabled to see them and so to see the world anew mirrored through their eyes, to participate imaginatively in their enjoyment and enthusiasm. Unlike his, their response is an immediate intuition of relatedness, love for the leaves which share their own vitality, their "childish life," and a sense of wonder and admiration for the natural process of growth.

The personification begun with the image of "the bearded corn, the bleeding grape" is heightened in the actual words of the children:

> *"Here is the hay-colored sun, our marvelous cousin,*
> *Walking in the barley,*
> *Turning the harrowed earth to growing bread,*
> *And splicing the sweet, wounded vine. (ll. 9–12)*

On one level, of course, the scene described could be dismissed as a childish fantasy, but its literal impossibility does not conflict with the truth of its symbolism: The sense of correspondence between celestial and terrestrial dimensions is indicated in the epithet "hay-colored sun," which suggests not only the similarity in color but the cause-and-effect relationship between yellow sun and yellow hay. The Franciscan awareness of the unity of all creation, of kinship with "our marvelous cousin" the sun, is deeply sacramental and authentically contemplative and contains resonances of both creation and redemption: The sun "Walking in the barley" is a sort of typological counterpart to the Lord God walking in the Garden of Eden, while the transformation of "harrowed earth" to "growing bread," and the healing and restoration of the "sweet, wounded vine" (which picks up the earlier image of "the bleeding grape") point to a prereflective acknowledgement of the salvific effects of suffering. The ultimate fruitfulness of a painful growth process, particularly as referred to the eucharistic elements, bread and wine, suggests of course an analogy with the Passion of Jesus, a correspondence between the natural and supernatural dimensions. The pattern of nature points beyond itself to the events of faith for its full explanation and justification; creation is a sign of the Creator's designs.

But the children's words are not merely a general announcement of the sun's arrival; they appeal to others to recognize and respond to the new day as they have:

> *Lift up your hitch-hiking heads*
> *And no more fear the fever,*
> *You fugitives, and sleepers in the fields,*
> *Here is the hay-colored sun!" (ll. 13–16)*

The vagrants addressed here represent the opposite pole from the children: They are transient, rootless, without any sense of relatedness to the landscape they presently happen to occupy. They are invited to pass from fear to trust, from sickness to wholeness, from alienation to accepting and being accepted by their world. The circularity of the children's speech, which repeats its opening words at its conclusion, is an invitation to share the sacramental vision that has been expressed.

But the final section of the poem suggests how difficult it is to respond positively to such a summons:

And when their shining voices, clean as summer,
Play, like churchbells over the field,
A hundred dusty Luthers rise from the dead, unheeding,
Search the horizon for the gap-toothed grin of factories,
And grope, in the green wheat,
Toward the wood winds of the western freight. (ll. 17–22)

The voices of the children call the listeners to a kind of cosmic liturgy, to worship the Creator with and in and through creation (the trochaic rhythms of the first two lines here are perhaps intended to echo the pealing of the bells). But this call is unheeded by the busy but aimless adults who miss the signs of salvation all around them. Perhaps awakened, but definitely not enlightened, by the children, the tramps "rise from the dead" not in the sense of rebirth or regeneration, but to a kind of death-in-life, a return to the meaningless round of pointless activities: They are "dusty Luthers" (definitely a pre-ecumenical image!) come back from the grave, who "[s]earch the horizon" for new possibilities, for their own revelation, but settle for the soulless urban world of factories with their "gap-toothed grin" of specious welcome (the internal rhyme of "Luth-" and "tooth-" reinforcing the connection between the searchers and the object of their quest). Their blindness to the beauty and harmony in which they find themselves is suggested by the verb "grope," as they leave behind the "green wheat," emblem of physical and spiritual nourishment, in their restless urge to move on. In preference to the "shining" and "clean" voices, they listen to the seductive music of "the wood winds of the western freight" (an image which suggests as well the sooty smoke pouring from the train's engine) drawing them to the grim, fruitless world of materialism.

The poem appears, then, to end on a pessimistic "note," with a negation of the revelatory message offered by creation and mediated by the children. But it is essential to recognize that the poem is a triptych, not a diptych, containing three "panels" rather than two. The entire poem, after all, is presented from the perspective of the original speaker, who has given us in the children an alternative not only to the obliviousness of the "fugitives, and sleepers in the fields," but to the strained frigidities, the aborted sacramentality, of his own initial response to the scene. The poem itself represents the possibility of a response different from that of the "dusty Luthers," one that is able to recapture, or be recaptured by, the spontaneous joy and love and reverence toward creation of the innocent, and is an act of faith in the power of words to articulate and communicate that vision. The challenge is now presented to the poem's audience to choose which response to make their own.

One of the finest poems in the collection, "The Trappist Abbey: Matins," written shortly after Merton's first visit to Gethsemani during Holy Week, 1941, begins by presenting the alternatives of a sacramental and nonsacramental worldview, embodied in the monastic and urban settings, respectively; it then confronts the speaker with a choice between the two, expressed in scriptural terms appropriate to the abbey's name.

The opening stanza depicts a predawn landscape of order and harmony, within which the monastery is fully integrated:

When the full fields begin to smell of sunrise
And the valleys sing in their sleep,
The pilgrim moon pours over the solemn darkness
Her waterfalls of silence,
And then departs, up the long avenue of trees. (ll. 1–5)

A sense of balance pervades the scene, at that unique moment when light and darkness, sound and silence are not opposed but complementary: The singing valleys and the moon's "waterfalls of silence" do not conflict but fulfill one another, as the light of the moon bathes the landscape without destroying the "solemn darkness." Above all, the image of the moon as a pilgrim who has stopped at the abbey and now leaves before daybreak to continue her journey, proceeding up the road leading from the gatehouse, suggests a perfect conformation of the human presence to the natural setting. The initial focus on the senses of smell and hearing emphasizes an awareness within the darkness, particularly appropriate to the contemplative atmosphere of the monastery. Even the intricate patterning of sounds, particularly the variations using "l" at the end of accented syllables ("full," "fields," "smell"; "val-"; "pil-," "sol-"; "-falls," "sil-"), the sibilance of "smell," "sun-," "sing," "sleep," "solemn," "silence," and the frequent "s" endings of words (including all the line endings except l. 2, where "sleep" begins with "s"), reinforces the impression of quiet harmony.

The following stanza describes exactly the opposite situation, a lack of order, of pattern, of integration between the human and the natural:

The stars hide, in the glade, their light, like tears,
And tremble where some train runs, lost,
Baying in eastward mysteries of distance,
Where fire flares, somewhere, over a sink of cities. (ll. 6–9)

In contrast to the moon's passage up the "avenue of trees," the stars are presented as hiding "in the glade," and the moon's waterfall is replaced by their light imaged as tears (a reminiscence, perhaps, of the stars, which "water heaven with their tears" in Blake's "Tyger" [ll. 17–18]). The reason for the concealment and for the tears is indicated by the rest of the quatrain: the natural world weeps for human misery and perversity and trembles for the fate of the passengers on the lost train, likened to a dog hunting without a scent, with no clear sense of purpose or direction, in implicit contrast with the stately journey of the pilgrim moon. The train's only destination is the "sink of cities," the antithesis of the singing valleys, a repository of waste water (negative counterpart of the moon's waterfall) and marked by flares of fire, a destructive image of light amid the darkness. The entire scene exemplifies disorder and alienation from the rest of creation. (The contrast is made more marked by the ironic echo in line 9 of the sound pattern of the opening verse, with its substitution of "fire flares" for "full fields," of "somewhere, over a sink of cities" for "smell of sunrise.")

Thus the two initial sections starkly juxtapose two irreconcilable scenarios for the relationship between human beings and the rest of creation. The remainder of the poem will personalize this opposition by requiring the speaker to decide which alternative to identify with and participate in, the environment of disorder he has known in the past or the newly revealed harmony he has experienced at the abbey. In the first and longest of the three final stanzas, he considers the summons to the monastic service of matins, the early morning portion of the liturgy of the hours, in terms of the gospel parable of the wise and foolish virgins:

Now kindle in the windows of this ladyhouse, my soul,
Your childish, clear awakeness:
Burn in the country night
Your wise and sleepless lamp.
For, from the frowning tower, the windy belfry,
Sudden the bells come, bridegrooms,
And fill the echoing dark with love and fear. (ll. 10–17)

There is an implicit contrast here between the fires of the cities in the previous line and the "wise . . . lamp" which is to "Burn in the country night." On the literal level, the light will be used to guide the speaker from the monastery guesthouse ("this ladyhouse") into the church for matins, but it also represents the inner light which should shine forth from the windows of his body, that should likewise be a ladyhouse, dedicated to the Virgin Mary, model for the wise virgins who await the arrival of the Bridegroom (Mt 25:1–13). The instruction to "kindle . . . / Your childish, clear awakeness" recalls the closing words of that parable, "Therefore, stay awake" (Mt 25:13); it also suggests that this spiritual light represents the vision characteristic of an innocent child, a sacramental awareness of the world as a sign of divine love. This call to full consciousness is addressed to the speaker's soul, traditionally imaged in mystical literature as feminine and therefore readily identified with the figure of the wise virgin; but the distinction between self and soul (itself a traditional poetic image[31]) may also signal a lack of complete personal integration between the empirical self (the speaker) and the true self (the soul, the image of God)—to use Merton's later terminology.[32] Thus the bells drawing worshippers to the church, imaged as "bridegrooms" representing Christ who calls the soul to himself, are said to ring out from "the frowning tower," a description more appropriate for a summons to judgment than an invitation to a wedding, an indication of the speaker's own ambivalence and lack of assurance. Likewise the final statement that the tolling of the bells (well represented by the predominantly trochaic rhythms of the feminine endings in "frowning towers," "windy belfry," and the echoing "bells come, bridegrooms") fill the early morning "with love and fear," the fitting reactions of the two groups of virgins, wise and foolish, prepared and unprepared, counters any premature expectation that the speaker is already included among the former group, despite what he has said to his soul.

That such apprehension is not ungrounded is evident from the following stanza, which begins by repeating the counsel of line 10, but goes on to point out potential problems:

Wake in the windows of Gethsemani, my soul, my sister,
For the past years, with smokey torches, come,
Bringing betrayal from the burning world
And bloodying the glade with pitch flame. (ll. 17–20)

The location is now specified as Gethsemani, which in the context refers both to the abbey and to the garden of the agony, and the scene which now unfolds reveals the reasons for the speaker's conflicted feelings of love and fear. The call to stay awake to meet the Bridegroom has now become the call to the disciples in the garden to "stay awake, and not fall into temptation" (Mt 26:41), which they failed to obey; as they were left unprepared to meet the crisis which was about to come upon them, so the speaker finds himself unprepared to deal with his own confrontation at Gethsemani. The contrast is no longer merely between the lit and unlit lamps of the two groups of virgins, but between the bridesmaids' lamps and the torches of the mob coming to seize Jesus, bringing with them the fires from "the burning world" described earlier. The reference to "the glade" here likewise recalls the stars hidden in the glade in the second stanza, and makes clear that the principal reason for their weeping is because of the betrayal of Christ. Worse still, these traitors are recognized as "the past years," that is, the speaker's own past, the sins that have betrayed not only Christ but his own true identity, and that now threaten to align him with the enemies of the Lord. While his soul may have been renewed by baptism and restored to childlike innocence, he remains overwhelmed by a sense of guilt for past transgressions, which he fears may disqualify him for the roles of disciple and spouse of Christ.

But the introduction of the figures of the disciples, even the sleeping disciples, represents a way out of the dilemma, a realization that he is not inevitably to be classed with the treacherous betrayers. As the disciples failed and fled, yet were restored, so the opportunity for repentance and regeneration is available for the speaker as well:

Wake in the cloisters of the lonely night, my soul, my sister,
Where the apostles gather, who were, one time, scattered,
And mourn God's blood in the place of His betrayal,
And weep with Peter at the triple cock-crow. (ll. 21–24)

By joining with the apostles, represented here by the community of monks, the speaker is able to identify not with Judas but with Peter, to conclude not with despair but with redemption. Like Peter, he is led by "the triple cock-crow" to mourn the death of Christ and to repent his own denials, but also to rejoice in the resurrection symbolized by the new day about to dawn, heralded of course by the very same sound. As he participates in the pattern of the liturgy of the hours, the speaker is both drawn into the rhythms of the daily round, the alternation of darkness and daylight, and becomes a participant in the paschal drama of death and resurrection. For someone imbued with a sacramental sensibility, these two patterns mutually illuminate one another, each deepening an appreciation for both.

In his poems on sacraments and sacramentality, Merton has demonstrated that such a sensibility is indeed central to his own spiritual vision and has offered his readers an opportunity to deepen and sharpen their own recognition of the presence of the Creator in and through the gift of creation. As he himself would later write, "To the true Christian poet, the whole world and all the incidents of life tend to be sacraments—signs of God, signs of His love working in the world."[33] The evidence of *Thirty Poems* provides strong support for finding in Merton "the true Christian poet" which he describes.

Photograph by Maryke Kolenousky

Courtesy of the photographer

Wrestling with Angels: Some Mature Poems of Thomas Merton

Bonnie Thurston

Twenty years ago, I wrote a doctoral dissertation on Thomas Merton's later poetry in which I argued that Merton's studies in theology and religion, particularly the religious traditions of the East, drastically affected his voice and technique as a poet.[1] Both as a student of the East and as director of the Thomas Merton Studies Center at Bellarmine College, Bob Daggy was an immense—indeed, invaluable—help to me in the project. This essay, by which I hope to do Bob honor, takes a slightly different, although related, tack. It is an attempt to examine Merton's understanding of the spiritual life as it is reflected in his mature poetry. All but two of the poems treated here[2] appeared in *Emblems of a Season of Fury* (1963), the last collection of lyrics which Merton himself prepared for publication.[3]

One of the things I find attractive about this mature poetry is that Merton didn't need to speak about religious experience in explicitly "religious language." (And in this, there is an affinity with Bob Daggy, who never, to my knowledge, spoke directly about his faith but whose life bespoke volumes about it.) In his study of Merton's poetry, George Woodcock called the early body of work "poetry of the choir," by which he meant explicitly religious verse and noted the world-denying stance of its persona.[4] After Merton "outgrew" this narrowly devotional verse of the 1940s and early '50s, his poetic voice assumed a greater range and depth precisely because he was able to speak obliquely of profoundly religious experience. Merton came to approach the mystery of God-with-us not in the language of church, of liturgy, of theology, but in the language of the natural world with imagery drawn from plants, seasonal change, and the daily cycles of light and darkness.

This is poetry that has affinity with the work of R. S. Thomas and Mary Oliver, who both write poetry which is theological in content without being traditionally religious in subject matter.[5] George Kilcourse has called this aspect of Merton's work "poetry of the forest," noting that it has the "paradisal consciousness reminiscent of the best 'poetry of the choir'" as well as the "austere, ironic absences reminiscent of the best 'poetry of the desert'"[6] (Woodcock's other category for Merton's later poetry). Some years after the young monk (whom Merton himself parodied[7]) stormed out of the world, the mature monk "returned" to love it; his mature poet's eye rested lovingly on the created world, and his mature poetic voice bespoke a deeply incarnational, immanent, theology.

Merton did not reflect a facile understanding of the relationship between God and human beings (what I take to be the essence of spirituality). In fact, I think as much as any single Biblical account would do so, the narrative of Jacob wrestling with the "angel" in Genesis 32:22–32[8] is paradigmatic of Merton's understanding of the human encounter with God. This encounter often occurs in darkness (at night, Gn 32:22) and in solitude ("Jacob was left alone," Gn 32:23–24a). It may involve terrible struggle ("a man wrestled with him until the break of day," Gn 32:24b) and possibly wounding ("Jacob's thigh was put out of joint," Gn 32:25, 31), but also revelation ("I have seen God face to face," Gn 32:30), blessing (Gn 32:26–28), change—often profound change—of identity ("your name shall no more be called Jacob, but Israel," Gn 32:28), and "enlightenment" ("the sun rose upon him," Gn 32:31). This pattern of spiritual experience is evident in poems which suggest that one who wishes to encounter God must come to accept darkness, solitude, silence, "winter." In so doing, one learns the positive value of struggle and its inherent blessing (what we might call the "wound that leads to unity") and is, thereby, changed. Merton's mature poetry expresses profound moments of awareness of the presence of God, of the timeless in the temporal, of the clean cut of vertical love, and of how "ordinary" that moment is. The encounter with God is "ordinary" in the sense that it is always available to the one who is ready to invite, accept and receive it, to "send the relatives away" and sit silently in darkness and solitude.

Two quotations from *Conjectures of a Guilty Bystander*, a collection of Merton's personal reflections from the late 1950s and early 1960s (and thus written at roughly the same time as the poems treated here), express two pivotal insights on the spiritual life which are evident in the poems and which frame my discussion of them. The first is Merton's understanding that human beings are part of, even at one with, the natural world:

> *How absolutely central is the truth that we are first of all part of nature, though we are a very special part, that which is conscious of God. In solitude, one is entirely surrounded by beings which perfectly obey God. This leaves only one place open for me, and if I occupy that place then I, too, am fulfilling His will. The place nature "leaves open" belongs to the conscious one, the one who is aware, who sees all this as a unity, who offers it all to God in praise, joy, thanks.*[9]

In the mature poems, the "dividing wall of hostility" (Eph 2:14) between humans and nature is down. "We" are not the subject, and "it" is not our object. Self and world are two aspects of creation which interpenetrate and are unified. This is evident in the fact that in some of Merton's poems the persona (or speaker) is not human. In "Night-Flowering Cactus"[10] the speaker is a plant. In "O Sweet Irrational Worship" (*CP*, 344–45) the "I" of the poems has become "light / Bird and wind" (ll. 4–5). No human appears in "Love Winter When the Plant Says Nothing" (*CP*, 353).

The second insight is related to the first. God is directly present to human beings, and since all that is originates in God, reality (that which is) reflects God and is an entry to God's presence:

> *For God is present to me in the act of my own being, an act which proceeds directly from His will and is His gift. My act of being is a direct participation in the Being of God. God is pure Being, this is to say He is the pure and infinite Act of total Reality. All other realities are simply reflections of His pure Act of Being, and participations in it granted by His free gift. (CGB, 201)*

All of the poems treated below attempt to express concretely the insight that God is directly present in Being itself. In fact, poetry was Merton's most effective means of communicating this insight.

If we do not experience God in the present, in the words of Genesis 32, experience being "face to face" with God, Merton suggests that it is because we have not come to terms with the three things that facilitate the encounter: solitude, silence, and "winter." Although many of his prose works deal with solitude and silence, the slim 1958 volume *Thoughts in Solitude* is an extended meditation on both. There Merton writes, "Actual solitude has, as one of its integral elements, the dissatisfaction and uncertainty that come from being face to face with an unrealized possibility."[11] Merton suggests we avoid solitude because it forces us to confront our shortcomings, our "unrealized possibilities."

In the poem "Song: If You Seek . . ." (*CP,* 340–41) Merton writes explicitly that "If you seek a heavenly light / I, Solitude, am your professor!" (ll. 1–2). Solitude is personified as a sort of Beatrice figure who goes before, raises "strange suns for your new mornings" (l. 4) and opens "the windows / Of your innermost apartment" (ll. 5–6). In its silence, Solitude is an "angel" (l. 11) who announces:

I am the appointed hour,
The "now" that cuts
Time like a blade.
I am the unexpected flash
Beyond "yes," beyond "no,"
The forerunner of the Word of God.
Follow my ways and I will lead you
To golden-haired suns,
Logos and music, blameless joys,
Innocent of questions
And beyond answers:
For I, Solitude, am thine own self:
I, Nothingness, am thy All.
I, Silence, am thy Amen! (ll. 15–28)

Solitude will lead beyond duality ("yes" and "no"). It is solitude that precedes the coming of "the Word of God," both the literal Christ event and a metaphor for direct encounter with the Divine. At the end of the poem, Solitude is equated with the true self (an important concept in Merton's thought[12]), with Nothingness (undoubtedly to be understood in its Zen connotation[13]), and with Silence.

But the tendency is to avoid silence as well as solitude. Merton notes, "We put words between ourselves and things" but "[t]he solitary life, being silent, clears away the smoke-screen of words. . . . In solitude we remain face to face with the naked being of things" (*TS*, 85). Solitude and silence go hand-in-hand because, together, they provide the "place" where the true Word is spoken. "When we have really met and known the world in silence, words do not separate us from the world nor from other men, nor from God. . . . Truth rises from the silence" (*TS*, 86).[14]

Merton makes just this point in the poem, "In Silence" (*CP*, 280–81). It is cast as a sort of dialogue as the voice of the poem offers directives and a hearer (whose words are indicated by quotation marks) responds:

Be still
Listen to the stones of the wall.
Be silent, they try
To speak your
Name.
Listen
To the living walls.
Who are you?
Who
Are you? Whose
Silence are you? (ll. 1–11)

The poem asks the hearer to be silent in order to discover both his/her identity and "ownership." Not only our silence, but our very selves belong to God; we must be what God "speaks." As Merton writes in *New Seeds of Contemplation*, "God utters me like a word containing a partial thought of Himself" (*NSC*, 37). Furthermore, the poem goes on to point out, everything speaks to us because *all* is spoken by God. All creation shares the same origin which is our ultimate point of unity.[15] (Recall the quotations from *Conjectures* above.)

And all things live around you
Speaking (I do not hear)
To your own being,

Speaking by the Unknown
That is in you and in themselves.
"I will try, like them
To be my own silence:
And this is difficult. The whole
World is secretly on fire. The stones
Burn, even the stones
They burn me. How can a man be still or
Listen to all things burning? How can he dare
To sit with them when
All their silence
Is on fire?"[16] *(ll. 24–38)*

In this last stanza of the poem, the one spoken to realizes the difficulty of really remaining in the solitude of silence. It is the experience of perpetual Pentecost, the experience of the *mysterium tremendum*[17] which both attracts and repels, which elicits both awe and fear. And, as Merton wrote in *Conjectures of a Guilty Bystander*, silence, also, "is a response. It can at times be the response of a greater love, and of a love that does not endanger truth or sacrifice reason" (*CGB*, 86).

Merton suggests that if we, like Jacob, are to receive blessing, it will only be when we have not only faced, but embraced solitude and silence. And that experience is often for us "winter," a time of darkness, apparent death, sterility. We must love this "nothing" as the very place from which all else springs. "To really know our 'nothingness' we must also love it. And we cannot love it unless we see that it is good. And we cannot see that it is good unless we accept it" (*TS*, 43). This process is described in "Love Winter When the Plant Says Nothing" (*CP*, 353), which depicts a moment of deep and spontaneous prayer:

O little forests, meekly
Touch the snow with low branches!
O covered stones
Hide the house of growth!

Secret
Vegetal words,
Unlettered water,
Daily zero.

Pray undistracted
Curled tree
Carved in steel—
Buried zenith!

Fire, turn inward
To your weak fort,
To a burly infant spot,
A house of nothing.
O peace, bless this mad place:
Silence, love this growth.

O silence, golden zero
Unsetting sun

Love winter when the plant says nothing.

"Winter" is an image of *apparent* death and fruitlessness, when it *seems* as if nothing is going on, when the "house of growth" (literally, of course, the snow-covered ground) is hidden. But, ironically, the winterscape described in the first three stanzas is an image of prayer. The snow-laden branches of the trees are bending in prayer. Theirs is a "secret," "vegetal," "unlettered" language of prayer. They pray by being what they are. *New Seeds of Contemplation* provides an interesting gloss on the poem. There Merton writes, "A tree gives glory to God by being a tree. For in being what God means it to be it is obeying Him. . . . [A] tree imitates God by being a tree" (*NSC,* 29). (Similarly, on October 2, 1958, Merton notes, "I am coming to the conclusion that my highest ambition is to be what I already am" [*SS,* 220]).

This, in part, is what the poet calls forth from the reader. "Fire," Merton's image of God's inherence in all created things which also is found in "In Silence," reappears here with the same connotation. "Fire" is directly addressed, asked to "turn inward" (l. 13), to come within the speaker who is a "house of nothing" (l. 16). It is this internal place, this "mad place" (l. 17) which is indwelt by God's fire, that peace and silence must love. The last line, "Love winter when the plant says nothing" (l. 21), is a reminder that the "house of growth" (l. 4) is hidden, secret, inward; it is apparently a "house of nothing," but in reality it is the place where "growth" occurs, and for this reason is to be "loved," not just passively accepted, but embraced. The time of apparent coldness and death, winter, is, in fact, the time of fire and growth. The poem ends with an image of the "Unsetting sun" (l. 20) (a pun on Son?), which loves this silent winter, this time of growth and expectancy.

The poem can be read on many levels, of course. "Love Winter When the Plant Says Nothing" is a poem about expectancy and resurrection. It bespeaks the very Biblical truth that "unless a grain of wheat falls into the earth and dies, it remains alone; but if it dies, it bears much fruit" (Jn 12:24). The life of the spirit needs "down time," time for germination. Merton's March 1966 preface to the Japanese edition of *Thoughts in Solitude* articulates the notion of solitude as "germination time" in an interesting way. He writes, "one goes into solitude to 'get at the root of existence' . . . . He lives, then, as a seed planted in the ground. As Christ said, the seed in the ground must die. To be as a seed in the ground of one's life is to dissolve in that ground in order to become fruitful."[18] This idea of life melting into the Life-Giver, becoming One, is, as noted above, prominent in Merton's mature poems on spiritual life. But ironically, in "Love Winter When the Plant Says Nothing," under their weight of snow, the trees of the forest are bowed down, almost "forced" to pray. They are like human beings who only "bend the knee" (pray) when facing crises—personal "winters." The point is that these "winters" must be embraced, not just endured, when they arrive. Human beings must come to accept winter as naturally as the created world does.

Merton knew that, like the stranger with whom Jacob wrestled, the things with which we struggle, our "winters," often turn out to have positive value; the struggle itself gives meaning. The "angels" of solitude, silence, and winter, then, are "the forerunners of the Word of God," which, as "A Messenger from the Horizon" (*CP,* 349–51) explains, come suddenly and without warning:

Look, a naked runner
A messenger,
Following the wind
From budding hills.

By sweet sunstroke
Wounded and signed,
(He is therefore sacred)
Silence is his way. (ll.1–8)

Note that, once again, the messenger is solitary, single, alone, and that his "way" is silence. He is "Wounded and signed"; he has struggled and been "marked." This messenger, we are told, is Adam who has been "Born of one word" (l. 18) (cf. Gn 1:26–27; 2:7). He comes "without warning /A friend of hurricanes, / Lightning in your bones!" (ll. 24–26). This messenger comes unannounced, and thus the poet says:

Pardon all runners,
All speechless, alien winds,
All mad waters.

Pardon their impulses,
Their wild attitudes,
Their young flights, their reticence.

When a message has no clothes on
How can it be spoken? (ll. 35-42)

We experience Merton's sense of humor when the moment of divine encounter is framed by a reference to the children's story of "The Emperor's New Clothes" or is even compared to seeing a streaker. But the point is serious: The messenger who brings God's Word/Presence is unadorned and wounded. One must be ready to receive God in this mad, impulsive, wild, naked way or miss the experience altogether. The message which arrives is stripped bare and strips bare. Again, it brings internal fire, "Lightning in your bones."

The experience of the Divine of which Merton writes is momentary, sudden, and unexpected. Jacob prepares for such an experience by entering solitude and silence, but there is no indication in Genesis 32 that he *expected* the experience which followed or that he caused it. In "Night-Flowering Cactus" (*CP*, 351–52) Merton compares the experience of revelation (enlightenment?) to that of the night-flowering cactus, which, from silence and darkness, bursts forth with the Word of God. Interestingly, in this poem the "voice" is that of the plant, which says, "I know my time, which is obscure, silent and brief / For I am present without warning one night only" (ll. 1–2) and "I show my true self only in the dark"[19] (l. 4). As in "Messenger," here, too, God comes unannounced in an experience that is sudden and brief. This is, in fact, the reality of the night-flowering cactus, which blooms only once, during the night, and which emits an exquisite, almost unearthly perfume during that brief blossoming. The flowering is described in the poem as a "sudden Eucharist" (l. 10), as "a white cavern without explanation" (l. 20). It continues:

He who sees my purity
Dares not speak of it.
When I open once for all my impeccable bell
No one questions my silence:
The all-knowing bird of night flies out of my mouth.

Have you seen it? Then though my mirth has quickly ended
You live forever in its echo:
You will never be the same again. (ll. 21–28)

The experience of the God-moment changes the one who experiences it.[20] It completely re-orders the manner in which the one who receives it understands life. It is entirely a gift. As Jacob could not have compelled the "angel" to appear, one cannot force the God-encounter. The response to such a gift, even when it comes with struggle, must be praise and worship. It is at this point, when "wrestling" becomes praise, that the "sun rises" and blessing is given. The result is joy, exuberance, a sense of being one with creation and Creator. This cosmic unity is expressed in "O Sweet Irrational Worship" (*CP*, 344–45):

Wind and a bobwhite
And the afternoon sun.
By ceasing to question the sun
I have become light,

Bird and wind.

My leaves sing.

I am earth, earth

All these lighted things

Grow from my heart. (ll. 1–9)

The physical circumstances of the experience are, on the surface, unremarkable, an "ordinary" sunny afternoon. But the God-encounter changes everything in the twinkling of an eye. In Merton's terms, one "ceas[es] to question," to rationalize, to bring the objectifying force of the intellect to bear on experience.[21] Thus the speaker of the poem becomes one with the surroundings. The speaker realizes he is "earth," the very dust from which Adam, and everything else, was created.

When I had a spirit,
When I was on fire
When this valley was
Made out of fresh air
You spoke my name
In naming Your silence:
O sweet, irrational worship! (ll. 13–19)

Note that, again, the image of fire appears in the context of encounter with the Divine. In naming the Divine silence, God speaks the poet's name (as in Genesis 32:27–28 the "man" is renamed Israel), and thus "creates" him in exactly the same way that all else was created, by God's speaking, God's word. As a result, the poet sees himself as part of elemental nature, not in essence different from it. This awareness of unity causes an explosion of love which issues forth in praise. Earth bursts with hay and flowers, that which is useful and that which is ornamental; there is a metaphorical return to Eden.

I am earth, earth

My heart's love
Bursts with hay and flowers.
I am a lake of blue air
In which my own appointed place
Field and valley
Stand reflected.

I am earth, earth

Out of my grass heart
Rises the bobwhite.

Out of my nameless weeds
His foolish worship. (ll. 20–31)

The speaker of the poem is pure spirit ("blue air") in his own appointed place. He has come to know *whose* he is. Out of his "grass heart" (perhaps an allusion to Isaiah's assertion that all flesh is grass [40:6]), his "nameless weeds" (the anonymity of silence and solitude, or perhaps an allusion to the speaker's depressed state before the experience since "weeds" are mourning clothes) rises the bobwhite. The bird rising is an image of praise as the speaker takes his proper place in creation. As Sheila Hempstead notes in her essay "Emblems of Birds: Birds as Symbols of Grace in Three Poems of Thomas Merton," by this means the poet "is mystically joined with 'All these lighted things' and all the things of the earth."[22] His worship may be foolish—that is, pointless or without measurable value in society's terms—but it is what the creature was created to do, to worship and glorify its Creator, to "enjoy God" and "praise Him forever" in the words of the old catechism. In *Conjectures of a Guilty Bystander,* Merton writes of the "primary usefulness of the useless," which is the "capacity to live for the sake of living and praising God," having a "'Eucharistic' spirit" (*CGB,* 282).

In these poems, Merton communicates not only a great sense of the regularity of the created world but of its natural praise. It, like the tree, gives glory to God by being what it is. Merton encourages oneness with the created world, because for him God Incarnate means that God is mysteriously *in* the creation, more immanent than transcendent. Merton suggests that those who have wrestled with angels can no longer be subjects watching the object "nature," because those who have so wrestled have learned that they are both part of the one great object, the creation which God (the subject) is continually speaking.

In Merton's mature poetic depiction of the spiritual life, a series of elements recur. In them, the matrix of identity and of enlightenment is solitude and silence; their locus is internal. Solitude is the "professor," the teacher of enlightenment in "Song: If You Seek . . ." In "Stranger" (*CP,* 289–90) "no one" (ll. 1, 3, 5) is apparently present but the "inward Stranger / Whom I have never seen" (ll. 26–27). The night-flowering cactus is alone in darkness, and no human appears in "Love Winter When the Plant Says Nothing." All of these poems presume silence, and each is really about an "internal landscape," what is happening in the life of the spirit. As John F. Teahan correctly observed, "monks and mystics often understand solitude as the climate and silence as the language of liberation, enlightenment, or union with God. Silence and solitude then become sacred metaphors, often more than metaphors, to express the experience of ultimate transformation."[23]

Merton's mature spiritual poetry is perhaps his most profound (and certainly his most concentrated) attempt to express "the experience of ultimate transformation." While his is a poetics of internality, the repeated images which are used to depict this "internal landscape" are simple, "external realities." God or the Divine Presence appears with the traditional images of fire and wind. In "In Silence," the "world is secretly on fire"; all things are burning with God's presence; "their silence / Is on fire" (ll. 37–38). In "O Sweet Irrational Worship" the speaker is "on fire" (l. 14) in his perception of God's presence, and in "Love Winter When the Plant Says Nothing," the speaker prays "Fire, turn inward" (l. 13). Wind, too, bespeaks God's presence or coming. In "Stranger" (discussed below), the unspoken wind, which moves leaves, blossoms, and water on the surface of the pond and clouds in the sky, precipitates the realization that "Our cleanest Light is One" (l. 39). "O Sweet Irrational Worship" begins with wind (l. 1), and "A Messenger from the Horizon" is filled with images of "hurricanes," "somersaulting air," and "alien winds" (ll. 25, 29, 36), suggesting that God's arrival is not always peaceful. In each of these poems, God's presence and/or the speaker's enlightenment is described in terms of sunrise, dawning, or the coming of some sort of light.

As Merton describes the spiritual life in his mature poems, he consistently depicts enlightenment occurring in solitude, silence, and often "winter." The resulting internal transformation is reflected in images of fire, wind, and light. "Stranger," a poem that describes the unity and peace of a world understood to be in the continual process of God's creating, brings these features together and serves as a summary of my suggestions in this essay:

When no one listens
To the quiet trees
When no one notices
The sun in the pool

When no one feels
The first drop of rain
Or sees the last star

Or hails the first morning
Of a giant world
Where peace begins
And rages end:

One bird sits still
Watching the work of God:
One turning leaf,
Two falling blossoms,
Ten circles upon the pond.

One cloud upon the hillside,
Two shadows in the valley
And the light strikes home.
Now dawn commands the capture
Of the tallest fortune,
The surrender
Of no less marvelous prize!

Closer and clearer
Than any wordy master,
Thou inward Stranger
Whom I have never seen,
Deeper and cleaner
Than the clamorous ocean,
Seize up my silence
Hold me in Thy Hand!

Now act is waste
And suffering undone
Laws become prodigals
Limits are torn down
For envy has no property
And passion is none.

Look, the vast Light stands still
Our cleanest Light is One!

The poem depicts a world in which the distinction between subject and object has been obliterated. Here, the "subject" or "perceiver" is not human but "One bird" which Hempstead suggests "symbolizes the gift of grace, . . . the moment of grace in which Merton the poet finds the presence of God within himself" (Hempstead 22). Here, the work of God is the natural "being" of a day: sun on water, a drop of rain, a leaf turning in the wind, falling blossoms, clouds in the sky, and shadows on the earth. This is the world with which the speaker of the poem is one. An experience of or glimpse of the Absolute, the presence of God in the creation, engenders a wholeness and results in a new way of looking at what was previously understood to be "mundane." The "ordinary" gives glimpses of the cosmic, universal, and unifying truth of God (which, paradoxically, is ordinary in its etymological meaning; the Latin *ordo* means "regular arrangement," "usual order," in short, "orderly" as God's creation is). As "Stranger" suggests, this requires no special event or observer. Even if no one is watching, God's work is going on smoothly, in an orderly fashion. The light is striking home. God's enlightenment is dawning and one-making.

In Merton's mature poetry, this dawning, this "vast Light" (l. 38), this truth "Deeper and cleaner" (l. 28) than the noisy movement of the ocean's surface, is available to all willing to receive it. For it is an internal reality, "Closer and clearer / Than any wordy master" (ll. 24–25), an "inward Stranger" whom most of us "have never seen" (ll. 26–27) because we have not embraced the angels of solitude, silence, and winter. When we are willing to wrestle with them, to admit their truth and be wounded and changed by them, we become not only like the wounded Jacob who received the blessing of seeing God face to face and being made new (re-named, given a new identity), we become like Job after God spoke to him from the whirlwind: "I had heard of thee by the hearing of the ear / but now my eye sees thee" (Jb 42:5). That is, we can experience what before we had only heard about.

Merton probably hoped his poetry would *facilitate* this experience. George Kilcourse is exactly correct when he writes "the real experience of Merton's 'poetry of the forest' is the encounter within the 'true self'—of the poet, of the creature(s) he encounters, of one's own person as awakened by the experience of the poem. It is an immediate . . . ontological intuition recreated by the experience of the poem" (Kilcourse, 104). In other words, what happens to the speaker of the poem (the poet) is what is supposed to happen to us who read the poems: "the light strikes home" (l. 19). To mix a metaphor (something to which Merton was not adverse), we are to "live forever in its echo" and "never be the same again" ("Night-Flowering Cactus," ll. 27, 28).

Ananda and Doña Luisa Coomaraswamy
Courtesy of Dr. Rama Coomaraswamy

Thomas Merton and Ananda Coomaraswamy

Erlinda G. Paguio

Men and women who are able to unite within themselves and experience in their own lives all that is best and most true in the great spiritual traditions are considered by Thomas Merton to be "sacraments" or signs of peace. Ananda Coomaraswamy, the geologist who became one of the most sensitive art historians and critics of the twentieth century, is the Indian writer Merton feels most indebted to for presenting a valid synthesis of Eastern and Western thought.[1] He regrets that Coomaraswamy has been much neglected as a writer even though he had a great deal to say about the meeting of Eastern and Western culture.[2] Merton tells Coomaraswamy's widow, Dona Luisa, that her husband was a model for him in thoroughly uniting in himself the spiritual traditions and attitudes of the Orient and the Christian West.[3]

In studying the philosophies of Merton and Coomaraswamy, several themes develop. The first such motif is the impression of William Blake on each of them. There is also great significance in Coomaraswamy's book *The Transformation of Nature in Art*, both for Merton and for Coomaraswamy himself, including its connection to Meister Eckhart. Finally, two topics in Coomaraswamy's works, taken by Merton on his journey to Asia, become important: *claritas*, or clarity, and *lila*, or the cosmic dance.

The artistic and literary works of William Blake (1787–1827) left a profound impression on both Coomaraswamy and Merton. In *The Seven Storey Mountain*, Merton recalls that his love for Blake had something in it of God's grace because it entered very deeply into the development of his life. When he was ten years old, his father tried to explain to him what was good about Blake's writings and works of art. As a teenager Merton read and thought about Blake a lot, especially when he was at Oakham. As a graduate student at Columbia University, he chose Blake as the subject of his master's thesis. It seemed to him that God's Providence in leading him to Blake awakened some faith and love in his soul that eventually led him to seek Christ and be converted to the Catholic faith.[4]

Coomaraswamy's encounter with Blake as a great spiritual writer and artist also marked him permanently. He was much moved by Blake's energy and ideas and considered Blake's art of illustrated books to be as visionary as Indian art. Blake and his works became a means for Coomaraswamy to make Indian imagination acceptable to the West. He found Blake's theories of imagination and art similar in spirit to Indian aesthetic. In his seminal study of Rajput paintings, he called Blake the "most Indian of modern minds." When Coomaraswamy wrote about a picture cycle in Rajput paintings depicting various moments and movements of love, he was judging them according to Blake's thought that "the soul of sweet delight can never be defiled."[5] He described these paintings as sincerely sensual and sincerely religious.

He admired Blake's insistence on the primacy of the Imagination, his attack on materialism, and his call to fellow men to be creative and free. Blake's *The Marriage of Heaven and Hell* was the work he loved best. He saw in Blake's works the essentials of religion which he read in the Vedas and hieroglyphics, and in the teachings of Jesus, Lao-Tse, Meister Eckhart, and Rumi (Lipsey, 3.108).

Merton followed Coomaraswamy's lead in exploring the resemblance of Blake's art to Indian art. In his master's essay, Merton analyzed the possible contacts Blake may have had with India, through friends or acquaintances who had been there, or through his reading something about it. He noted Blake's reading of the *Bhagavad Gita,* a classic in Sanskrit literature. Item no. X, in Blake's *Descriptive Catalogue* of his paintings, described the subject of the piece in question as "Mr. Wilkin, translating the *Geeta;* an ideal design, suggested by the first publication of that part of the Hindoo scriptures, translated by Mr. Wilkin." Mr. Wilkin is the Orientalist Charles Wilkins, who published the *Geeta* in 1785. Merton also noted that Blake's friend, Osias Humphrey, who had been to India and painted some miniatures of

Indian princes, may have shared Blake's enthusiasm for Indian art.[6] Even if he was not an authority on Indian art, Merton dared state that Blake's *Last Judgement* resembled Hindu art in a remote way.

Both Merton and Coomaraswamy saw that for Blake, art appealed entirely to the intellect. What made him similar to medieval and Oriental artists is his looking at natural objects as they are in God. His technique was to "copy" a "vision" or a mental image just as the traditional artists of the East and the West did (*LE*, 409).

In his book *The Transformation of Nature in Art*, Coomaraswamy's concern was the intellectual work that the artist becomes engaged in before he actually produces a work of art. He stressed the mental visualization of artists, a method that was closely related to one of the practices of Hindu and Buddhist worship. After eliminating the distracting influences of uncontrolled emotions and creature images, self-willing and self-thinking, the maker of an icon in India proceeds to visualize the form or that aspect of God in a given canonical prescription. This undistracted attention or visualization of an image is similar to Blake's thought that "he who does not imagine in clearer and better lineaments than this perishing mortal eye, does not imagine at all."[7] Blake also stated that in art as in life, the more distinct, sharp, and wiry the bounding line, the more perfect the work of art. He stressed the definite and bounding line of form in the artist's mind. He thought that without this line, everything would be chaotic unless the line of the Almighty is drawn upon it. This idea follows his saying that "if the doors of perception were cleansed, everything would appear to man as infinite" (Lipsey, 3.109).

One of the essays in Coomaraswamy's book is "Meister Eckhart's View of Art." Meister Eckhart never wrote a philosophy of art, but in studying his sermons, Coomaraswamy was able to synthesize a theory of art from the examples the preacher used in teaching about the art of knowing God. "Art" for Coomaraswamy means the idea of the theme as it presents itself to the artist. He noted that the artist preserves his art within himself. The art in him is the form of his work, just as the soul is the form of the body (Coomaraswamy 69–76). He found an analogy in Meister Eckhart's sermons on discernment for the kind of "emptying" or "purification" and visualization required of the traditional artist. Meister Eckhart says a man

> *must practice a solitude of the spirit, wherever or with whomever he is. He must learn to break through things and to grasp his God*

> *in them and to form him in himself powerfully in an essential manner. This is like someone who wants to learn to write. If he is to acquire the art, he must certainly practice it hard and long, however disagreeable and difficult this may be for him and however impossible it may seem. If he will practice it industriously and assiduously, he learns it and masters the art. To begin with, he must indeed memorize each single letter and get it firmly into his mind. Then, when he has the art, he . . . can write effortlessly and easily—and it will be the same if he wants to play the fiddle or to learn any other skill.*[8]

Coomaraswamy brings out the other important theme in Meister Eckhart's sermons, which is how God's image is ever present in the ground of the soul, but concealed by veils and hindrances. Meister Eckhart explains that if a craftsman makes figures out of wood or stone, he does not introduce the figure into the wood, but he chips away the fragments that had hidden and concealed the figure. He gives nothing to the wood, rather he takes away from it, cutting away its surface and removing its rough covering so that what is hidden may shine (Eckhart, 243). This is analagous to Chuang Tzu's story of the woodcarver, who contemplated on making a bell stand by emptying himself of all distractions. When he went to the forest, the right tree appeared before his eyes. He said that his own collected thought encountered the hidden potential in the wood, which enabled him to make the bell stand.[9]

Coomaraswamy's editor and biographer, Roger Lipsey, remarks that this essay on "Meister Eckhart's View of Art" is the art critic's first published book on Scholasticism (Lipsey, 3.174). He read the original sources, and in publishing his book, he brought his mature thought on art to the public for the first time. There was no polemic in it. It contained comparative ideas on the Western medieval and Oriental concepts of art, the artist's practice, the spectator's practice, the purposes of art, and some problems of content and style.

For Merton, Coomaraswamy's book was decisive in leading him to take the right turn in life and to set his way upon the spiritual road which led to the monastery and the contemplative life (*HGL,* 126). In the 1960s, he began to compile some of Coomaraswamy's sayings, hoping that one day, he could have them printed in a book. Unfortunately he was not able to finish this project, which was approved by Coomaraswamy's widow. He did, however, continue to read other works by Coomaraswamy. This study and other readings of Indian literature made him well prepared for his trip to Asia in 1968.

At the conclusion of Coomaraswamy's article on "Meister Eckhart's View of Art," he summarized the Meister's understanding of aesthetic experience. It is recollection, illumination, contemplation, the culminating point of vision, rapture, and rest. Man's experience of this is like a flash of lightning—a vision of the world-picture as God sees it, loving all creatures alike, having compassion on all of them, seeing them in their unity as an image of Himself. Meister Eckhart writes: "To have all that has being and is lustily to be desired and brings delight; to have it all at once and whole in the undivided soul and that in God, revealed in its perfection, in its flower, where it first burgeons forth in the ground of its existence . . . that is happiness, a 'peculiar wonder' neither in the intellect nor the will, . . . as happiness and not as intellection, not dialectically but as if one had the knowledge and the power to gather up all time in one eternal now, as God enjoys Himself" (Coomaraswamy, 93–94).

For beauty to delight the mind, it is necessary that integrity, proportion or unity, and brightness or *claritas* are present. Coomaraswamy defines *claritas* as "the radiance, illumination, lucidity, splendor, or glory proper to the object itself, and not the effect of external illumination." He cites examples of *claritas* from the *Summa* of St. Thomas Aquinas: the sun and gold, to which a "glorified" body is commonly compared; and the Transfiguration also as a clarification. In the *Chandogya Upanishad,* this clarity is well expressed in one man's saying to another: "Your face, my dear, shines like that of one who has known God." Another example Coomaraswamy used is Blake's poem, "Tiger, tiger, burning bright." He writes that clarity is the same as intelligibility, whether the beautiful thing referred to is as splendid as a tiger, a poem, or a tree (Lipsey, 3.222).

Merton considered *claritas* as the most important condition of beauty because it is the glory of form shining through matter. He interprets Blake's use of the term "particularizing" and his statement "Distinctness is Particular, not general" as Blake's seeing a thing as it essentially is, and how it is charged with the glory of God. Blake had this direct intuition of beauty (*LE,* 443). During his Asian trip, Merton spoke about William Blake and his fourfold vision to one of the Indian scholars he met, noting that once one has known Brahman, the supreme being, who is the source and end of all, one's life is permanently transformed.[10]

Merton's own experience of *claritas* may be gleaned from his *Asian Journal.* At Polonnaruwa, he was immensely struck by the three colossal figures of the Buddha, carved from the face of the rock. He described the faces of the Buddhas as "[f]illed with every possibility, questioning nothing, knowing everything, rejecting nothing, the peace not of emotional resignation but of Madhyamika, of sunyata, that has seen through every question without trying to discredit anyone or anything—*without refutation*—without establishing some other argument" (*AJ*, 233).

It was such a profound experience that even if Merton tried to talk about it to casual acquaintances at a dinner party, he sensed that he had spoiled it. Only to the Rev. Dr. Walpola Rahula, a Buddhist monk and a leading authority on early Buddhist scriptures of various schools, did he feel comfortable to share his experience. He was pleased to hear Dr. Rahula say that the artists who carved those statues were not ordinary men (*AJ*, 230). Merton described his experience of being knocked over with a rush of relief and thankfulness at the *obvious* clarity of the figures, the clarity and fluidity of shape and line and the sweep of bare rock sloping away on the other side of the hollow, where different aspects of the figures could be seen. He spoke of "an inner clearness, clarity, as if exploding from the rocks themselves." This clarity gave him that certainty that dissolved any puzzles, problem, and mystery. It seemed to him that all that was around him, and all life, was charged with both emptiness and compassion (*AJ*, 233, 235). He wrote: "I don't know when in my life I have ever had such a sense of beauty and spiritual validity running together in one aesthetic illumination. Surely, with Mahabalipuram and Polonnaruwa my Asian pilgrimage has come clear and purified itself. I mean, I know and have seen what I was obscurely looking for. I don't know what else remains but I have now seen and have pierced through the surface and have got beyond the shadow and the disguise" (*AJ*, 235–36). Merton also noted that the whole thing was similar to a Zen garden, which he described as a beautiful and holy vision, "a space of bareness and openness and evidence" in which the lines of the great figures' body and clothing appeared "in full movement" like waves, though they were motionless (*AJ*, 236).

This pure aesthetic experience that Merton describes is also related to Coomaraswamy's other description of an aesthetic experience: it is like "seeing a play played eternally before all creatures, where player and audience, sport and players, are the same, their nature proceeding in itself, in clear conception and delight, or to an operation in which God and I are one, works wrought there being all living" (Coomaraswamy, 94). This is the cosmic dance that Merton writes about in *New Seeds of Contemplation* [11] and in his letter to Latin American poets,[12] the *lila* he refers to in his Introduction to the *Bhagavad Gita* (*AJ*, 348–53), and which Coomaraswamy discusses in several of his works, particularly in *The Dance of Shiva.*

Coomaraswamy says that the clearest image of the activity of God of which any art or religion can boast is the dance of Shiva, who represents the Lord. His dance reflects all the activities He is engaged in this world. The deepest significance of this dance is realized within the heart. Everywhere is God, and that everywhere is the heart. The ego must be destroyed; all illusions must be discarded. Only the thought of God must remain.[13] *Lila* is the Sanskrit term that refers to this divine playing. Meister Eckhart speaks of this play going on in the Father's nature: From the Father's embrace of His own nature comes this eternal playing of the Son. Their playing before all creatures is also the Holy Spirit. This divine activity is a game, in which we all can participate (Lipsey, 2.148–55).

Merton explains that the realization of the Supreme "player" whose divine play, *lila*, is manifested in the million-formed inexhaustible richness of beings and events, is the key to the meaning of life. Life moves in its true and deepest dimension when we live in awareness of the cosmic dance and move in time with the dancer. To learn to live life as a "game," a "play" in union with the Cosmic Player, is to lose one's self-important seriousness. It is God alone whom we must take seriously. If we did that, we would find joy in everything, because we would discover that everything is a gift and a grace. If we could let go of our own obsession with what we think is the meaning of it all, we will be able to hear God calling us to follow Him in His mysterious cosmic dance (*AJ*, 348–50).

Merton tells us that the cosmic dance is everywhere. We are in the midst of it, and it is in our midst. In his letter to Latin American poets, he says, "Come, dervishes: here is the Water of Life. Dance in it" (*RU*, 161). In one of his taped conferences on the mystical life, he says to the monks at Gethsemani: "What do you do when the Shekinah is in front of you? Dance with the Shekinah." Coomaraswamy, on the other hand, says that the best and most God-like way of living is to play God's game (Lipsey, 2.151).

Photograph by Thomas Merton

Used with the permission of the Thomas Merton Legacy Trust.

Thomas Merton in Dialogue with Eastern Religions

William H. Shannon

In March of 1997, Cardinal Joseph Ratzinger, sometimes described as the "Torquemada" of today's Roman Catholic Church, gave an interview to the French magazine, *L'Express*.[1] One of the topics he touched on was the relationship of Catholics to Buddhism. "A Catholic," he said, "cannot renounce his understanding of the truth revealed in Jesus Christ, the unique Son of God. . . . If Buddhism seduces," he claims, "it is because it appears as a way of being in touch with the infinite and with a happiness that brings with it no concrete religious obligations." He describes Buddhism as "a spiritual auto-eroticism of a sort." Then he warns, "Someone rightly predicted in the 1950s that the challenge for the Church in the twentieth century would be not Marxism, but Buddhism."

Thomas Merton and the Dialogue with Buddhists

As a member of the same church to which he belongs, I am embarrassed by these words of this German cardinal at the Vatican. Yet they are public information, and the cardinal from Germany is a powerful man and well known. Still I take solace from the words of a saintly Thai Buddhist monk, Buddhadassa (who died a few years ago). He said, "Whatever foreigners write about Buddhism is usually wrong, especially if the writer is German."[2]

I take solace also from the fact that the Second Vatican Council, which enjoys a much higher authority than the Congregation for the Doctrine of the Faith over which Cardinal Ratzinger presides, speaks of Buddhism in a respectful, even cordial, tone. It simply says, "In Buddhism according to its various forms, the radical inadequacy of this changeable world is acknowledged and a way is taught whereby those with a trustful and devout spirit are able to reach a state of perfect freedom or attain supreme enlightenment either by their own efforts or with the help of a higher source."[3]

There is here no air of condescension, simply an effort to understand. The document goes on to say: "The Catholic Church rejects nothing of those things which are true and holy in [other] religions." On the contrary, it continues, "it regards with sincere respect those ways of acting and living and those precepts and teachings which, though differing in many particulars from what it holds and sets forth, frequently reflect a ray of that truth which enlightens everyone" (*Nostra Aetate,* 2; Tanner, 968).

The document then proceeds to encourage the sons and daughters of the church, "with prudence and charity, through dialogues and collaboration with other religions, bearing witness to the Christian faith and way of life, to recognize, preserve and promote the spiritual and moral good things, as well as the sociocultural values which are to be found among [these religions]" (*Nostra Aetate,* 2; Tanner, 968).

I take solace, then, from the fact that these statements from "The Declaration on Non-Christian Religions" of Vatican II, rather than Cardinal Ratzinger's offensive statement, represent the official attitude that the Catholic Church takes toward Eastern religions. This Council document was approved on October 28, 1965.

I also take solace from the obvious eagerness and delight with which Thomas Merton, the Trappist monk, entered into dialogue with Buddhism and other Eastern religious traditions. Even before the Second Vatican Council met (1962–1965), he had reached a point in his life where he was no longer content to explore his own faith tradition simply from *within;* he needed to enrich that tradition by contact with *outside* traditions: not only those outside the Roman Catholic tradition but still within the context of Christian faith, but even those that were outside the pale of Christian faith. His own growth in this direction anticipated what was beginning to happen in his own church.

The Council's Declaration simply gave him a mandate to do what he was already doing, a mandate to continue his exploration of other faith traditions. Merton accepted that mandate and applauded the direction in which his church was moving. In *Conjectures of a Guilty Bystander,* he writes: "If the Catholic Church is turning to the modern world and to the other Christian Churches, and if she is perhaps for the first time seriously taking note of the non-Christian religions in their own terms, then it becomes necessary for at least a few contemplative and monastic theologians to contribute something of their own to the discussion."[4]

In Their Own Terms

To take note of non-Christian religions in their own terms: this is a new stance for the Catholic Church. Heretofore the only approach to non-Christian religions that the church was willing to take was in its own terms. Non-Christian religions, if they were mentioned at all, were evaluated in terms of how much they might perhaps resemble the Catholic Church. And for the most part, they were found wanting.

Taking note of non-Christian religions in their own terms can be pretty scary for a church that for so long a time considered itself to be in sole possession of all the truth about reality. Taking note of Eastern religions in their own terms calls for the humility to believe that we can learn from others. It demands discipline and openness. It means letting others explain themselves in their own way rather than seeing them as we perceive them through our Catholic lenses. So often we can be so deeply entrenched in our own positions that it becomes threatening to discover that what others say makes much more sense when they say it than when we recall what was our version of their position. Hearing another's position and coming to understand it may even challenge us to possible modifications of our own position that may well enrich it.

The Demands of Dialogue

Dialogue can be uncomfortable, especially dialogue about religion, for such dialogue touches on what is sacred and inviolable to me. It may impinge on realities in which I have made the investment of my whole life. Interreligious dialogue may all too easily appear to be what Paul Tillich called a "shaking of the foundations."[5]

What this suggests, I believe, is that only people equipped with a firm grasp of their own religious tradition are capable of carrying on interreligious dialogue. We can all recall how in the tumultuous '60s many people turned to the East. What they were searching for was not dialogue to enrich their own faith; rather, they were looking for an alternative to the faith which they had inherited from their family or their culture, but which they had never really come to know and understand.

Thomas Merton, when he traveled to the East in October of 1968, was well equipped spiritually and intellectually for fruitful interreligious dialogue. Long years of study, reflection, and prayer had prepared him for his journey to the East, both the spiritual journey and the geographical one. His deep immersion in the richness of his own tradition, his extensive study of the mystical tradition of the West—the desert fathers and mothers, St. Gregory of Nyssa, Pseudo-Dionysius, St. Bernard of Clairvaux, Julian of Norwich, Meister Eckhart, St. John of the Cross, and Teresa of Avila, to name but a few representatives of that tradition—rooted him in his own faith tradition and gave him the spiritual equipment he needed in order to understand and appreciate the way of wisdom that is proper to the East.

That is why I said in my biography of Merton, *Silent Lamp*, that he had to "find the East in the West before he could find the East in itself."[6] Amiya Chakravarty, a Hindu scholar who greatly admired Merton and accompanied him on part of his Asian journey, wrote to him in 1967 that "the absolute rootedness of your faith makes you free to understand other faiths."[7] Dr. John Wu, his Chinese friend, wrote in much the same vein, "You are so deeply Christian that you cannot help touching the vital springs of other religions"—Hinduism, Buddhism (*HGL*, 620).

Five Insights

I would suggest five insights emerging from Merton's study of the Western spiritual classics that find resonance with the spiritual wisdom of the East and enabled him to enter into meaningful dialogue with representatives of Eastern religious traditions. I shall mention them and then discuss each in some detail. They are: (1) the priority of experience over speculation; (2) the inadequacy of words to articulate religious experience; (3) the fundamental oneness of all reality; (4) the realization that the goal of all spiritual discipline is transformation of consciousness; and (5) "purity of heart," a term employed by the desert fathers which meant for them liberation from attachment. This last may be the most difficult to understand; yet it is extremely important in both Eastern and Western spiritual traditions.

1. Experience

Merton came to see very early the importance of experience as a locus for theological reflection. The Greek and Latin Fathers, as well as the great mystics of the twelfth, fourteenth, and sixteenth centuries, were not speculative theologians (as we tend to think of theologians today). They were theologians of experience. When they wrote theology, they were talking about their experience of God. Indeed, for many centuries, the Greek word *theologia* meant contemplation, the contemplative experience of God. The earliest notion of the theologian was that he/she was the saint who had experienced God, but who in addition had the ability (which other holy people may have lacked) to articulate his/her experience for others. Thus it was that, from his own tradition, Merton learned something most congenial to Eastern thought: what really counts in life is experience; and if at times we need to test our experience, we also have to learn to trust it.

Of all the religions of the East Merton was acquainted with, Zen was what he wrote most about. And to him, the meeting ground for Christianity and Zen was the level of experience. *Zen clearly gives priority to experience; but so does Christianity if it is properly understood.* It is true that Christianity, unlike Zen, begins with revelation. But it is a huge mistake to think of this revelation simply as doctrine. It is the self-revelation of God calling the Christian to *experience* God in Christ through the Spirit. Christian theologians, at least in their better moments, have always understood that at the heart of Christianity, there is, in Merton's words, "a *living experience* of unity in Christ which far transcends all conceptual formulations."[8]

This was the understanding of the Apostolic Church. The preaching of the early church (the *kerygma)* was not simply an announcement of certain propositions about Jesus Christ, dead and risen; it was a summons to participate in the reality of his dying and rising. It was a call to taste and experience eternal life. As the first epistle of John says: "[We] proclaim to you the eternal life that was with the Father and was made visible to us—what we have seen and heard we proclaim now to you so that you too may have fellowship with us; for our fellowship is with the Father and with his son, Jesus Christ" (1 Jn 1:2-3). Christianity, like Zen, is first and foremost about experience. The only theologian who can talk about God is one who has walked with God.

2. *Words*

Equally important as experience is the understanding that words cannot adequately capture the religious experience. This leads me to a second insight that grew out of Merton's study of his own religious tradition: namely, his realization of the inadequacy of language to express the experience of ultimate reality. God (or *atman* or *nirvana* or *sunyata*) cannot be captured in the net of our thoughts, images, and words. God is always greater than we can think or imagine or put into words.

In *The Ascent to Truth,* Merton speaks of the way in which we take images and concepts drawn from our experience of created things and apply them to God. "[A]s soon as we light these small matches which are our concepts: 'intelligence,' 'love,' 'power,' the tremendous reality of God Who infinitely exceeds all concepts suddenly bears down upon us like a dark storm and blows out all their flames!"[9] Interestingly, a Zen master (Abbot Zenkei Shibayama) writes in a similar vein: "However great the conceptual knowledge and understanding may be, in the face of real experience, concepts are like flakes of snow fallen on a burning fire."[10] Or, as Merton described the aim of Zen, "[It] is not to make foolproof statements about experience, but to come to direct grips with reality without the mediation of logical verbalizing" (*ZBA*, 37).

The inadequacy of words derives from the very nature of what words are. The only words we have, when we want to talk about God (or whatever term one wants to use to designate ultimate reality), are words which describe finite reality. They are like windows in our homes through which we look out at the reality of the universe. What we see, as we look out a window, shows us so little of the universe that we can say that we are hardly seeing it at all. Even looking out of many windows from many different places is totally inadequate. The astronauts saw the earth from outer space and saw more than we can ever see from our place on this planet, but what they gained in quantity of vision, they lost in "quality," that is to say, they could not see the earth in its details and concreteness. I am not intending to imply that Merton did not use human language to speak about God—in fact, he spilled out a lot of words to demonstrate the inadequacy of human words to "say God," but he understood well the meaning of Meister Eckhart's words: "One who speaks about the Trinity lies."

Zen would go even further. It would say that words are not only inadequate, they are useless, even harmful. It is something of a paradox that there is a Zen literature that uses words to deplore the use of words. There are many stories about Zen masters and the cryptic "non-answers" they often gave to their students. One that comes to mind is that of the Zen master whose students kept insisting that he give them a lecture on Zen. After refusing several times, he appeared to accede to their request. The students gathered, waiting for his lecture. He stood before them and said, "For the scriptures, there are scripture scholars. For the sutras, there are sutra scholars. But I am a Zen master, and you ought to know that." With these words he left the platform and returned to his room, leaving his students confused perhaps, but possibly closer to the Zen experience.

3. Non-Dualism

The intuition of the ultimate unity of all reality is yet a third insight which grew out of Merton's reading of the Christian mystical tradition as well as his own contemplative experience. He would have identified with the words of Meister Eckhart: "The eye with which I see God is the same eye with which God sees me."[11] This vision of reality is not always easy for today's Christians to grasp. Much of Christian theology and spirituality (particularly in the post-Cartesian era) has been unequivocally dualistic in tone: separating God from God's creation, the sacred from the profane. In my book *Silence on Fire,* I have described this dualism as "spiritual apartheid," just as harmful in its own context as political apartheid in its setting.[12] Mystical writers have never made this mistake. The thrust of what they have to say about the experience of God is always in the direction of unity. This is the direction in which Merton's thoughts consistently moved. The world, though distinct from God, is yet not separate from God. Thus, you who are reading this and I who am writing it are distinct from God, for obviously we are not God. But we are not (and cannot be) separate from God, for God is the source and ground of our very being. Both of us can (and must) say: I cannot exist apart from God, for apart from God, I am nothing. To put it another way: God plus me equals, not two, but one. And me minus God equals zero. For if God were to remove the divine presence from me, I would simply cease to be.

And we can go yet a step further. Not only are you and I one with God. Precisely because we are one with God, we are also one with one another. It's a very simple equation: you are one with God. I am one with God. It follows that we are one with one another. This is true not only of us but of all reality. We do not see God and creation aright until we grasp the non-dualism of all reality.

It can safely be said that an implicit non-dualism runs through Merton's writings, even the very earliest: a non-dualism that becomes more and more explicit as he turns to the East. This ripening intuition was given classical expression in what has probably become the best known event in Thomas Merton's life: the so-called "vision" of Louisville that he experienced on March 18, 1958, in a shopping district at the corner of Fourth and Walnut. As he saw people moving in and out of stores, he was overwhelmed with the realization that he loved all these people and that they were neither alien to nor separate from him. He saw that they were all one, as if they were "billions of points of light coming together in the face and blaze of a sun" that could, if they only realized who they really were, "make all the darkness and cruelty of life vanish completely" (*CGB,* 140–42).

I recall this word picture Merton creates coming to my mind on one occasion when I was making a retreat at Merton's hermitage. I was sitting on the porch as dusk was falling. All at once, the fireflies seemed to put on an entertainment for me. There seemed to be hundreds, perhaps thousands of them in the valley. One would light here, another there. They were in so many places. The thought came to me: what if they all lit up at once? The whole valley would be a blaze of fiery light. And I remembered those billions of points of light of which Merton spoke and what they symbolized for him. And I remembered, too, the words he spoke at Calcutta in October of 1968: "[W]e are already one. But we imagine that we are not. And what we have to recover is our original unity. What we have to be is what we are."[13]

This insight was crucial for Merton in his approach to the East. No one will ever make any headway in understanding Eastern religions until she or he has grasped the non-dualism of all reality. Zen, Merton wrote, "is a recognition that the whole world is aware of itself in me, and that 'I' am no longer my individual and limited self, still less a disembodied soul, but that my 'identity' is to be sought not in that *separation* from all that is, but in oneness."[14] Zen is a direct experience of life, with no gloves on (as D. T. Suzuki put it), that is at once an experience of undifferentiated unity and at the same time of existential concreteness.

4. Transformation of Consciousness

The goal of all spiritual discipline is transformation of consciousness. Such transformation leads to a sense of one's own identity. Chuang Tzu, the Taoist philosopher Merton so admired (he wrote a delightful book of poems called *The Way of Chuang Tzu*[15]) raises the problem of what level of consciousness actually identifies who I am. He tells of a dream he had one day: "I, Chuang Tzu, dreamed I was a butterfly fluttering hither and thither, to all intents and purposes a butterfly. . . . Suddenly I awakened. . . . Now I do not know whether I was then a man dreaming that I was a butterfly or whether I am now a butterfly dreaming that I am a man."[16] The question Chuang Tzu proposes is clear: What is the state of consciousness that puts me in touch with what is truly real? We are all aware of the difference between waking consciousness and dream consciousness. Suppose I dreamed last night that I was on the bank overlooking Niagara Falls. I am standing close to the edge. Suddenly the ground gives way beneath me, and I feel myself falling into the rocks and swirling waters below. In the middle of this terrifying dream, I awake and, with a cry of great relief, return to waking consciousness.

What has happened? I have moved from one state of consciousness to another. In the dream, the dream objects were very real. It was only when I awakened that I realized that the dream objects had no substance. To repudiate the reality of the dream objects, I had to move to another level of consciousness. Let me invite you to think of two possibilities. First, suppose a person were to enter into a dream and never awake from the dream. That person would always consider the dream objects as real, for to be aware of their unreality, one has to move to the state of waking consciousness. Second, let me ask you to think of another possibility. Suppose there is another state of consciousness beyond our ordinary state of being awake, which—if you entered it—would give you a new and exciting experience of reality. This new experience would enable you to see that the objects of ordinary waking consciousness—which for so long a time you took as real—are actually as illusory as the objects in a dream. Once you awakened to this new, heightened state of consciousness, you would repudiate the objects of ordinary waking consciousness as not being real in any ultimate sense. In repudiating them, you would at last be fully awake. You would—as Zen would put it—have recovered your original face, or—in Christian terms—you would have discovered your true self, which is one with God.

This discovery of the true self is much more than a change in behavior. It is nothing less than a spiritual revolution that awakens deep levels of consciousness far beyond the surface consciousness of our superficial self (or what Merton would call the *false* self or the *external* self). We would at last be in touch with "the Real within all that is real."[17] In Zen, this is enlightenment; in Christianity, it is the return to paradise.

Yet it is important to realize that enlightenment, transformed consciousness, is to be found in the realities of daily life. As Zen Buddhists might put it: *nirvana is samsara. Samsara* means the flow of the realities of one's daily life. To say *nirvana is samsara* is simply to say that enlightenment is not something that is "not there" and has to be "put there." It is one's everyday mind. This is the meaning of the Zen saying: Going to a monastery to achieve enlightenment is like a person riding on an ass in search of an ass.

In similar fashion, the Christian contemplative would not say that we become contemplatives, but that we are contemplatives at the very root of our being. For at the deepest level we are one with God. Our problem is that we are unaware that we are contemplatives. The contemplative dimension of our being is asleep and needs to be awakened. We have to become aware. Merton's first words about contemplation in *New Seeds* describe contemplation as "the highest expression of man's intellectual and spiritual life. It is that life itself, fully awake, fully active, fully aware that it is alive. . . . It is a vivid realization of the fact that life and being in us proceed from an invisible, transcendent and infinitely abundant Source. Contemplation is, above all, awareness of the reality of that Source" (*NSC*, 1).

5. *Purity of Heart or Non-Attachment*

The way to this state of heightened consciousness is purity of heart (as Christian contemplatives would call it) or liberation from attachment (which I believe would be the term preferred in Zen). The story of the Buddha and the way he achieved enlightenment illustrates the importance of such non-attachment. He came to the realization that all life is suffering and that, at the heart of suffering, is the desire to be a separate self. Letting go of this desire is the way to enlightenment. This understanding of the human dilemma would be quite congenial to the Christian mystical tradition which would say that we achieve a realized union with God only by giving up the false self that so easily dominates our lives and keeps us at the level of superficial consciousness. The false self makes us victims of our selfish desires. The Christian contemplative denies neither the goodness of creatures nor our need to use them. John of the Cross makes clear that it is not creatures but the *desire* for them that impedes our quest for God. In his *Ascent of Mount Carmel,* he says: "In order to have pleasure in everything, desire to have pleasure in nothing. In order to arrive at possessing everything, desire to possess nothing. In order to arrive at being everything, desire to be nothing. In order to arrive at knowing everything, desire to know nothing."[18] Desire is the enemy. The way to freedom is detachment, not from things or people, but from the desire to possess or manipulate them.

Liberation from attachment (or non-attachment) is as difficult to understand as it is to achieve, for a person can easily be attached to good things as well as evil things, to spiritual things as well as material things. Merton writes in *New Seeds*: "Sometimes contemplatives think that the whole end and essence of their life is to be found in recollection and interior peace and the sense of the presence of God." It is easy for would-be contemplatives to be attached to these things. As Merton suggests: "Recollection is just as much a creature as an automobile. The sense of interior peace is no less created than a bottle of wine. The experimental 'awareness' of the presence of God is just as truly a created thing as a glass of beer" (*NSC,* 205). The fact that these realities are spiritual pleasures makes it more difficult to detect that they may well be attachments. Yet, as Merton points out, "You will never be able to have perfect interior peace and recollection unless you are detached even from the desire of peace and recollection" (*NSC,* 208).

In 1967 William Johnston, the Irish Jesuit priest who has taught for many years at Sophia University in Tokyo, wrote to Merton telling him about Father Enomiya Lasalle, another priest at the university who believed that it was possible for a Christian to achieve *satori,* the Zen experience of enlightenment. Moreover, he personally wanted to achieve it. What did Merton think, Johnston asked, about Fr. Lasalle's desire to achieve enlightenment? Merton wrote back that he believed a Christian could have *satori* as well as a Buddhist. And he added: "I am all for Fr. Lasalle getting there. . . . I'm rooting for him!" (*HGL,* 443). But, Merton wondered, might Fr. Lasalle's attachment to his plans to achieve *satori* perhaps prevent him from achieving it? A very perceptive reflection! Merton is very emphatic (and the whole Christian mystical tradition, as well as the traditions of the East, would be in full agreement with him) that the only way to true and perfect freedom is through detachment or, if you prefer the term, non-attachment.

A Summing Up

To sum up, Merton's spiritual outlook, emerging from his reading of the Christian mystical tradition and from his own prayer, is rooted in (1) experience; (2) a keen perception of the limitation of words to articulate experience; (3) a growing intuition of the unity of all reality; (4) an understanding of the crucial importance of a transformation of consciousness; and (5) a realization that the only way to true freedom in life is through non-attachment. These five elements of his thought were the keys that, in the 1960s, opened for him the doors to Eastern religious traditions. Finding the East in the West made it possible for him to discover the East in itself.

Merton's 1968 Trip to the East

In 1968, Merton traveled to the East to honor a commitment he had made to speak at a meeting of Benedictine monks near Bangkok, Thailand (the place where he would die a mysterious and unexpected death). His talk was scheduled for December 10. He arrived in the East on October 16. This meant that he had nearly two months to be in touch with various Eastern monastic orders. He took full advantage of this opportunity which he had longed for over so many years.

Especially memorable were the three days in November (4, 6, 8) when he visited with the Dalai Lama. At Merton's request, the Dalai Lama instructed him in the ways of Dzogchen, the "Great Way of All-Inclusiveness," considered the highest form of Tibetan Buddhism. They talked about many things. Each was impressed with the other. Merton wrote after the third visit: "It was a very warm and cordial discussion and at the end, I felt we had become very good friends and were somehow quite close to one another. I feel a great respect and fondness for him as a person and believe, too, that there is a real spiritual bond between us" (*AJ*, 125).

Some two decades later, in 1990, the Dalai Lama, in his autobiography, spoke movingly of his impressions of Merton: "I could see he was very truly humble and a deeply spiritual man. This was the first time that I had been struck by such a feeling of spirituality in anyone who professed Christianity. Since then, I have come across others with similar qualities, but it was Merton who introduced me to the real meaning of the word 'Christian'." He spoke of their conversation:

"It was a most useful exchange—not least because I discovered from it that there are many similarities between Buddhism and Catholicism."[19] He also speaks of what he feels Buddhism can learn from Christianity. Marveling at the practical works of Christian charitable organizations, with their schools and hospital facilities, he writes: "It would be very useful if Buddhists could make a similar contribution to society. I feel that Buddhist monks and nuns tend to talk a great deal about compassion without doing much about it" (Dalai Lama, 190).

In 1968, Merton had gone to the East, and one of the high points of his trip was the opportunity of paying his respects to the Dalai Lama. Twenty-seven years later, the Dalai Lama came to the West, and one of the high points of his trip was a visit to the Abbey of Gethsemani, where he was taken to Thomas Merton's grave. He sat in prayer for a few moments before the small cross that marks the place where Merton's mortal remains had been buried. After rising from prayer, he said: "I am now in touch with his spirit."[20]

These two men (one from the East and one from the West)—both monks, both committed to serious spiritual discipline, both concerned to involve themselves in the problems and needs of the world in which they lived—can be seen as examples of the kind of paradigm of the encounter that, for the sake of the world and its people, must take place between the religious traditions of the East and the West.

Appendix
Robert E. Daggy: A Bibliography

1977

"Thomas Merton's Writings in Poland." *The Merton Seasonal* 2.3 (Fall 1977) 4–5.

Thomas Merton's Major Writings: A Bibliographical Checklist. Louisville: Thomas Merton Studies Center, 1977.

1978

"Thomas Merton: Journey in Kentucky." *Adena: A Journal of the History & Culture of the Ohio Valley* 3 (Fall 1978) 45–48.

"Introduction." In "Christian Contemplation," by Thomas Merton. *Cimarron Review* 44 (July 1978) 32–36.

"Introduction." In "Christian Contemplation," by Thomas Merton. *Cistercian Studies* 13 (1978) 3–7.

"The Arts & Letters of Thomas Merton": Interview with Robert E. Daggy by Agnes S. Crume. *Louisville Magazine* 29 (February 1978) 28–29, 60.

"Thomas Merton's Writings in Japan." *The Merton Seasonal* 3.1 (Spring 1978) 2–3.

"Thomas Merton: Cosmopolitan in Kentucky." In *The Photography of Thomas Merton: Catalogue of the Exhibition at the Louisville School of Art, Louisville, Kentucky, 10 December 1978–14 January 1979* (Louisville: Louisville School of Art, 1978) [unpaged].

1979

"Thomas Merton's Writings in German." *The Merton Seasonal* 4.2 (Summer 1979) 10–11.

"Thomas Merton and Brazil." *The Merton Seasonal* 4.3 (Autumn 1979) 2–3.

"Thomas Merton's Writings in Portuguese." *The Merton Seasonal* 4.3 (Autumn 1979) 4–6, 15.

"The Works of Merton: Letter to the Editors." With a reply by J. M. Cameron. *New York Review of Books* 26 (November 22, 1979) 51, 53.

"Thomas Merton: A Cosmopolitan in Kentucky." *Olean Times-Herald* 119 (April 18, 1979) 5.

1980

"More Merton 'Storeys'." *The Merton Seasonal* 5.1 (Spring-Summer 1980) 2.

"Thomas Merton's Writings in Slavic Languages: Czech, Polish, Russian, Serbo-Croatian, Slovene." *The Merton Seasonal* 5.1 (Spring-Summer 1980) 11.

"Dan Walsh and Thomas Merton." *The Merton Seasonal* 5.2 (Late Summer 1980) 2.

1981

Editor. *Day of a Stranger* by Thomas Merton. Salt Lake City: Gibbs M. Smith, 1981.

"Introduction." In *Day of a Stranger*, by Thomas Merton. ed. by Robert E. Daggy. Salt Lake City: Gibbs M. Smith, 1981: 7–26.

Editor. *Introductions East & West: The Foreign Prefaces of Thomas Merton.* Foreword by Harry James Cargas. Greensboro, NC: Unicorn Press, 1981.

"Introduction." In *Introductions East & West: The Foreign Prefaces of Thomas Merton*, ed. by Robert E. Daggy. Greensboro, NC: Unicorn Press, 1981: 3–6.

"Thomas Merton—Star and Hero!" *The Merton Seasonal* 6.1 (Winter-Spring 1981) 2–3.

"John Howard Griffin." *The Merton Seasonal* 6.1 (Winter-Spring 1981) 4–5.

"John Jacob Niles." *The Merton Seasonal* 6.1 (Winter-Spring 1981) 6–7.

"Merton as Poet: A Brief Bibliography." *The Merton Seasonal* 6.2 (Summer 1981) 5–7.

"Sr. Therese Lentfoehr, S.D.S.: Custodian of 'Grace's House' and Other Mertoniana." *The Merton Seasonal* 6.3 (Autumn 1981) 2–6.

"A Sister Therese Bibliography." *The Merton Seasonal* 6.3 (Autumn 1981) 6–11.

1982

"Thomas Merton at Bellarmine College." *The Merton Seasonal* 7.3 (Autumn 1982) 2–3.

1983

"Mei Teng, the Silent Lamp: Thomas Merton and China." *The Merton Seasonal* 8.1 (Winter-Spring 1983) 2, 9.

"Journey to Publication: Bringing *Woods, Shore, Desert* into Print." *The Merton Seasonal* 8.2 (Summer 1983) 2–3.

"Merton: The 'Canadian Connection'." *The Merton Seasonal* 8.3 (Autumn 1983) 2–3.

1984

"An Updated Merton Memorial." Comment on *Thomas Merton, Monk: A Monastic Tribute* (new & enlarged edition) ed. Brother Patrick Hart. *Cistercian Studies* 19 (1984) [Bulletin 284] 665–66.

"A Canadian Merton Symposium." Comment on *Thomas Merton: Pilgrim in Process*, ed. Donald Grayston & Michael W. Higgins. *Cistercian Studies* 19 (1984) [Bulletin 289] 669.

"Merton's Early Conversion Experience." Comment on "Conversion: Merton's Early Experience and Psychology's Interpretation," by Walter E. Conn. *Cistercian Studies* 19 (1984) [Bulletin 290] 670.

"Merton on the Contemplative Life." Comment on "Thomas Merton on the Contemplative Life: An Analysis," by Bonnie Bowman Thurston. *Cistercian Studies* 19 (1984) [Bulletin 291] 670.

"Merton and the Desert Vocation." Comment on "Merton and the Desert Experience," by James R. McNerney. *Cistercian Studies* 19 (1984) [Bulletin 292] 671.

"New Merton Bio Coming Out Soon." *The Concord* [Bellarmine College] 35 (November 2, 1984) 3.

"Merton: Views and Re-Views." *The Merton Seasonal* 9.1 (Winter-Spring 1984) 2-3.

"Of Films, Courses and Hostels: Merton Films, Merton Courses and Weeks with Thomas Merton (Naturally)." *The Merton Seasonal* 9.2 (Summer 1984) 4–5.

"Preview: Five Merton Publications." *The Merton Seasonal* 9.3 (Autumn 1984) 2–3.

1985

"Merton's Heritage." Comment on *Getting It All Together: The Heritage of Thomas Merton*, ed. Timothy Mulhearn. *Cistercian Studies* 20 (1985) [Bulletin 310] 690–91.

"Review of *Follow the Ecstasy: Thomas Merton, The Hermitage Years 1965–1968*, by John Howard Griffin." *Epiphany* 5 (Summer 1985) 90–93.

"Seventy Years and Seven Mountains: A Review-Symposium of *The Seven Mountains of Thomas Merton*, by Michael Mott." *The Merton Seasonal* 10.1 (Winter 1985) 2–3.

"An Encomium for Raymond Treece; Reviews by and about Victor Kramer; A *Huzza* from Michael Mott." *The Merton Seasonal* 10.2 (Spring 1985) 8–9.

"William Shannon and the Merton Letters: The First Selection." *The Merton Seasonal* 10.3 (Summer 1985) 2–3.

"Biographer Like Me: John Howard Griffin's *Follow the Ecstasy*." *The Merton Seasonal* 10.4 (Autumn 1985) 6–8.

"Mott's Merton: Letter to the Editors. Re: *The Seven Mountains of Thomas Merton*, by Michael Mott." *National Catholic Reporter* 21 (February 22, 1985) 21.

1986

Editor (with Marquita E. Breit). *Thomas Merton: A Comprehensive Bibliography*. New York & London: Garland Publishing Company, 1986.

"Beatitude Saints Yesterday and Today." Comment on *Beatitude Saints*, by Daniel Morris. *Cistercian Studies* 21 (1986) [Bulletin 21] 22–23.

"Leclercq and Merton: A Monastic Exchange." Comment on "Jean Leclercq and Thomas Merton: A Monastic Exchange of Letters," by Patrick Hart. *Cistercian Studies* 21 (1986) [Bulletin 34] 33–34.

"Merton's Circular Letters." Comment on "The Circular Letters of Thomas Merton," by M. Basil Pennington. *Cistercian Studies* 21 (1986) [Bulletin 35] 34–35.

"Merton on Centering Prayer." Comment on "Thomas Merton and Centering Prayer," by M. Basil Pennington. *Cistercian Studies* 21 (1986) [Bulletin 36] 36.

"Cistercian Scholarship Computerized." Comment on *Guide to Cistercian Scholarship*, ed. E. Rozanne Elder & Benoit Chauvin. *Cistercian Studies* 21 (1986) [Bulletin 82] 76.

"Merton Smorgasbord: A 'Feast' of Merton Projects for 1986." *The Merton Seasonal* 11.1 (Winter 1986) 2–4.

"'A Great Soul': Owen Merton, May 14, 1887-January 18, 1931." *The Merton Seasonal* 11.3 (Summer 1986) 2–4.

"Merton Tapes: Letter to the Editor." *Our Sunday Visitor* 75.8 (June 22, 1986) 22.

1987

"Writings of Merton Purpose of Society": Interview with Robert E. Daggy by Deb Hilliard. *Arkansas Catholic* 76.48 (December 18, 1987) 3.

Editor. *The Alaskan Journal of Thomas Merton*. Preface by David D. Cooper. Isla Vista, CA: Turkey Press, 1988.

"Introduction: Ideal Solitude." In *The Alaskan Journal of Thomas Merton*, ed. Robert E. Daggy. Isla Vista, CA: Turkey Press, 1988: 5–13.

"Review of *Selected Poems, 1935–1985*, by James Laughlin." *The Courier-Journal* [Louisville] (April 5, 1987) 19.

"Review of *Selected Poems, 1935–1985*, by James Laughlin." *kentucky poetry review* 23 (Spring 1987) 56–58.

"Birthday Theology: A Reflection on Thomas Merton and the Bermuda Ménage." *The Kentucky Review* 7 (Summer 1987) 62–89.

"Bridge-Building: Merton Renderings and Renderings of Merton." *The Merton Seasonal* 12.1 (Winter 1987) 2–3.

"The Three Temptations of Thomas Merton." Review of *The Tragedy of Thomas Merton*, tapes by Alice Jordain Von Hildebrand. *The Merton Seasonal* 12.2 (Spring 1987) 13–15.

"Dom James and 'Good Father Louis': A Reminiscence." *The Merton Seasonal* 12.3 (Summer 1987) 6–12.

1988

"'Whatever May Be of Interest': The Merton Center at Bellarmine College." *America* 159.11 (October 22, 1988) 288–91, 299–301.

"Daggy Transcribes Text on Merton's Alaskan Travels": Interview with Robert E. Daggy by Rebecca N. Towles. *Bellarmine Connection* 1.3 (Spring 1988) 1, 7.

"Merton and Hinduism." Comment on "Thomas Merton: A Modern Arjuna," by Paul Veliyathil. *Cistercian Studies* 23 (1988) [Bulletin 259] 236–37.

Editor. *Encounter: Thomas Merton & D. T. Suzuki*. Monterey, KY: Larkspur Press, 1988.

"Introduction." In *Encounter: Thomas Merton & D. T. Suzuki*, ed. Robert E. Daggy. Monterey, KY: Larkspur Press, 1988: xiii-xx.

"Thomas Merton." *kentucky poetry review* 24.2 (Fall 1988) 1, 3–4.

"The Merton Phenomenon in 1987: A Bibliographic Survey." *The Merton Annual* 1 (1988) 321–37.

"Forecast 1988: A Bumper Selection of Merton Books." *The Merton Seasonal* 13.2 (Spring 1988) 21.

"In Pursuit of Thomas Merton." *The Merton Seasonal* 13.3 (Summer 1988) 2–5.

"Thomas Merton (1915–1968): Conferences, Commemorations, Festivals, Books, Articles, and Festschrifts Twenty Years Later." *The Merton Seasonal* 13.4 (Autumn 1988) 2–3.

"The Road to Joy: Thomas Merton's Letters to and about Young People." In *Toward an Integrated Humanity*, ed. M. Basil Pennington. Kalamazoo, MI: Cistercian Publications, 1988: 52–73.

1989

"Thomas Merton: A Biographical Reflection." In *An Easter Anthology: Catalogue of the Exhibit*, February 26–April 9, 1989. Catalogue # 23. Owensboro, KY: Owensboro Museum of Fine Art, 1989: 49–52.

Editor. *"Honorable Reader": Reflections on My Work* by Thomas Merton. Foreword by Harry James Cargas. New York: Crossroad, 1989.

"Introduction." In *"Honorable Reader": Reflections on My Work*, by Thomas Merton, ed. Robert E. Daggy. New York: Crossroad, 1989: 3–6.

Editor. *Monks Pond: Thomas Merton's Little Magazine*. Afterword by Brother Patrick Hart. Lexington: University Press of Kentucky, 1989.

"Introduction: Beyond Cheese and Liturgy." In *Monks Pond: Thomas Merton's "Little Magazine,"* ed. Robert E. Daggy. Lexington: University Press of Kentucky, 1989: ix–xv.

Editor. *The Road to Joy: Letters to New and Old Friends* by Thomas Merton. New York: Farrar, Straus, Giroux, 1989.

"Introduction." In *The Road to Joy: Letters to New and Old Friends*, by Thomas Merton, ed. Robert E. Daggy. New York: Farrar, Straus, Giroux, 1989: ix–xiv.

"Merton and 1988: A Survey of Publications and Commemorations." *The Merton Annual* 2 (1989) 291–308.

"Merton: Islands, *The New Yorker*, and Other Connections." *The Merton Seasonal* 14.1 (Winter 1989) 2–3.

"Merton: Kentucky Writers, Artists & Events." *The Merton Seasonal* 14.2 (Spring 1989) 2–3.

"After the First General Meeting of the ITMS." *The Merton Seasonal* 14.3 (Summer 1989) 2.

"Of Grace, Mystery, & Joy: The Second Volume of *The Merton Letters*." *The Merton Seasonal* 14.4 (Autumn 1989) 2–3.

"Introduction: Ideal Solitude: The Alaskan Journal of Thomas Merton." In *Thomas Merton in Alaska: Prelude to The Asian Journal—The Alaskan Conferences, Journals and Letters*. (New York: New Directions, 1989): xi–xvii.

1990

"Review of *Thomas Merton and the Education of the Whole Person*, by Thomas Del Prete." *America* 163.12 (October 27, 1990) 308.

"The Louis Massignon / Thomas Merton Connection." Comment on *Memoir of a Friend: Louis Massignon*, by Herbert Mason. *Cistercian Studies* 25.2 (1990) [Bulletin 455] 420.

"An Anthology of Spiritual Classics." Comment on *Catholic Spiritual Classics*, by Mitch Finley. *Cistercian Studies* 25.3 (1990) [Bulletin 458] 423.

"A 'Souffle' on Aspects and People of Prayer." Comment on *The Narrow Gate: Aspects of Prayer, People of Prayer*, by Francis Byrne, OSB. *Cistercian Studies* 25.3 (1990) [Bulletin 459] 423–24.

"The Continuing Tsunami: 1989 in Merton Scholarship and Publication." *The Merton Annual* 3 (1990) 277–89.

"Women and Merton & ITMS General Meeting Reflections." *The Merton Seasonal* 15.1 (Winter 1990) 2.

"Thomas Merton's 'Muse of Fire'." *The Merton Seasonal* 15.2 (Spring 1990) 2–3.

"Thomas Merton and the East: A Reflection." *The Merton Seasonal* 15.3 (Summer 1990) 2–3.

"Merton Connections: The Monastery of the Holy Spirit, Bobbie K. Owens, Least Heat Moon, & The Fourteen-Carat Molehill." *The Merton Seasonal* 15.4 (Autumn 1990) 2–3.

"Introduction: Thomas Merton's Practical Norms of Sanctity in St. John of the Cross." *Spiritual Life* 36.4 (Winter 1990) 195–97.

1991

"'A Man of the Whole Hemisphere': Thomas Merton and Latin America." *American Benedictine Review* 42.2 (June 1991) 122–39.

"Reflections on Thomas Merton." *Earth Voices: Journal of Ecology & Spirituality* 3 (Winter 1991) 6–9.

"'What They Say': 1990 in Merton Scholarship and Publication." *The Merton Annual* 4 (1991) 259–71.

"Merton & Initiation: Being 'Educated' and Educating." *The Merton Seasonal* 16.1 (Winter 1991) 2–3.

"Thomas Merton in Belgium: A Report to the ITMS." *The Merton Seasonal* 16.1 (Winter 1991) 24–25.

"Merton: The Desert & the Traveler." *The Merton Seasonal* 16.2 (Spring 1991) 2–3.

"Choirs of Millions: Thomas Merton & God's Creatures—Presidential Address at the Second General Meeting of the ITMS, 13 June 1991." *The Merton Seasonal* 16.3 (Summer 1991) 11–17.

"Merton & His Friends." *The Merton Seasonal* 16.3 (Summer 1991) 2–3.

"Of Merton & Dreams." *The Merton Seasonal* 16.4 (Autumn 1991) 2–3.

"Release of Journals May Debunk Merton Myth": Interview with Robert E. Daggy by Keith Picher. *New World* [Chicago] (May 29, 1991) 7.

1992

"Merton Crosses Religious Lines": Interview with Robert E. Daggy by Michael Hirsberg. *Chicago Tribune* (May 22, 1992).

"Monastica Moderna." Comment on "Oscar Wilde and Monasticism Today: The Homosexual Question," by John Albert, OCSO, and "Thomas Merton and the Fairies," by Robert Nugent. *Cistercian Studies* 27.1 (1992) [Bulletin, 6–7].

"Merton, Thomas." *The Kentucky Encyclopedia*, ed. John E. Kleber. Lexington: University Press of Kentucky, 1992: 629.

"A Note on Thomas Merton's 'Old Uncle Tom'." *kentucky poetry review* 28.1 (Spring 1992) 93–94.

"Wandering in the Merton Dimension: A Survey of Scholarship and Publication in 1991." *The Merton Annual* 5 (1992) 357–60.

"Merton & the Feminine (Again)! (With Asides about General Meetings & Polish Poets)." *The Merton Seasonal* 17.1 (Winter 1992) 2–3.

"Merton the Writer (With Some Animadversions by the Writer Himself)." *The Merton Seasonal* 17.2 (Spring 1992) 2–3.

"Turning on the 'Lamp': More Glimpses of the Life of Thomas Merton." *The Merton Seasonal* 17.3 (Summer 1992) 2–3.

"Water, Woods, & Walnuts: Traveling (with Merton in Tow) in the Beauty of the Natural World." *The Merton Seasonal* 17.4 (Autumn 1992) 2–3.

1993

"Keeper of the Silent Lamp": Interview with Robert E. Daggy by Carl Simmons. *Burning Light: A Journal of Christian Literature* 1.1 (February 1993) 28–30.

"Choirs of Millions: A Reflection on Thomas Merton and God's Creatures." *Cistercian Studies Quarterly* 28.1 (1993) 93–107.

"Is Thomas Merton A*u Courant*?: A Reflection." *The Merton Seasonal* 18.1 (Winter 1993) 2–3.

"Merton: Christ & the Desert." *The Merton Seasonal* 18.2 (Spring 1993) 2–3.

"Thomas Merton: The Desert Call." *The Merton Seasonal* 18.2 (Spring 1993) 8–15.

"The Enduring Merton: A Survey of Recent Books." *Praying* 57 (November–December 1993) 30–31.

"Merton Montage: A Reflection on Thomas Merton Twenty-Five Years After his Death." *Spiritual Life* 39.4 (Winter 1993) 195–208.

1994

"El fuego de los dioses: una reflexion sobre el desarrollo espiritual e intelectual de Thomas Merton (Thomas Merton al filo de su siglo, con ocasion del 25 aniversario de su muerte)," trans. into Spanish by Fernando Beltrán Llavador. *Cistercium: Revista Monastica* 197 (1994) 393–404.

"Interleiding: Ideale eensaamheid: Het Alaska-dagboek van Thomas Merton," trans. into Dutch by Luc Meeusen with Jan Glorieux. *Contactblad Mertonvrienden* [Belgium] 8.2 (June 1994) 6–8.

"Discoveries and Rediscoveries Twenty-Five Years After Thomas Merton's Death." *The Merton Seasonal* 19.1 (Winter 1994) 2–3.

"Thomas Merton: Connections East & West More than Twenty-Five Years After his Death." *The Merton Seasonal* 19.2 (Spring 1994) 2–3.

"After Summer Talk of Hogs, Irises, & First Day Covers, Why Not Some More Merton Anniversaries, Books & Annuals?" *The Merton Seasonal* 19.3 (Summer 1994) 3–4.

"Anti-This & Anti-That: Thomas Merton's Experimentation & Protest." *The Merton Seasonal* 19.4 (Autumn 1994) 3.

1995

"Asian Perspectives of Thomas Merton." *Inner Directions Journal* (Fall 1995) 9–10.

"Universal Love in Mo Tzu and Thomas Merton." *Inner Directions Journal* (Fall 1995) 10-11.

"Mo Tzu and Merton: Some Associations and Reflections," trans. into Chinese by Cyrus Lee. *Harbin Shizhuan Xuebao* 6.2 (June 1995) 1–7.

"Review of *Passion for Peace: The Social Essays*, by Thomas Merton, ed. William H. Shannon." *The Merton Journal* [England] 2.2 (Advent 1995) 54–56.

"'Playing Before God': Wisdom, Freedom, and Thomas Merton." *The Merton Seasonal* 20.1 (Winter 1995) 3.

"Merton, the Movies, and 'The Image'." *The Merton Seasonal* 20.2 (Spring 1995) 3.

"Thomas Merton & the Quiz Show Scandal: 'America's Loss of Innocence?'" *The Merton Seasonal* 20.2 (Spring 1995) 4–11.

"After Bonaventure: Keeping Peace in our Hearts." *The Merton Seasonal* 20.3 (Summer 1995) 3.

"First of the Last?: The Publication of Merton's 'Personal Journals' and the Death of a Friend." *The Merton Seasonal* 20.4 (Autumn 1995) 3.

"Afterword: Mo Tzu and Thomas Merton." In *Thomas Merton and Chinese Wisdom* by Cyrus Lee. Erie, PA: Sino-American Institute, 1995: 117–31.

"Foreword." In *Thomas Merton and Chinese Wisdom* by Cyrus Lee. Erie, PA: Sino-American Institute, 1995: i–vi.

1996

"Review of *Passion for Peace: The Social Essays*, by Thomas Merton, ed. William H. Shannon." *America* 174.12 (April 13, 1996) 28–29.

"A Merton Mailbag (From Here and There)." *The Merton Seasonal* 21.1 (Spring 1996) 3.

"Creativity and a '4': Thomas Merton's Developing Style." *The Merton Seasonal* 21.2 (Summer 1996) 3.

"HurlyBurly Secrets: A Reflection on Thomas Merton's French Poems." *The Merton Seasonal* 21.2 (Summer 1996) 19–26.

"Afterword." In *Thomas Merton's Four Poems in French*, trans. Rupert E. Pickins. Lexington, KY: Anvil Press, 1996: 45–53.

"Universal Love in Mo Tzu and Thomas Merton: Some Connections and Suggestions," trans. into Chinese by Cyrus Lee. *Universitas* [Taipei] 23.11 (November 1996) 2188–97.

"Question and Revelation: Thomas Merton's Recovery of the Ground of Birth." In *Your Heart Is My Hermitage*, ed. Danny Sullivan and Ian Thomson (London: Thomas Merton Society of Great Britain and Ireland, 1996) 60–76.

1997

"Inleiding: Ideale eenzaamheid: Het Alaska dagboek van Thomas Merton (vervolg)." *Contactblad Mertonvrienden* [Belgium] 11.2 (1997) 4–14.

Editor. *Dancing in the Water of Life: Seeking Peace in the Hermitage. Journals, vol. 5: 1963–1965* by Thomas Merton (San Francisco: HarperCollins, 1997).

"Introduction." In, *Dancing in the Water of Life: Seeking Peace in the Hermitage. Journals, vol. 5: 1963–1965*, by Thomas Merton, ed. Robert E. Daggy. San Francisco: HarperCollins, 1997: xi–xviii.

1998

"Review of *Something of a Rebel: Thomas Merton, His Life and Works—An Introduction*, by William H. Shannon." *Cistercian Studies Quarterly* 33.4 (1998) 522–23.

2000

"Deep Conflict: Thomas Merton and William Carlos Williams' *In the American Grain*." *The Merton Seasonal* 25.3 (Fall 2000) 12–16.

2002

"Thomas Merton's Critique of Language." *The Merton Seasonal* 27.1 (Spring 2002) 11–15.

ENDNOTES

Foreword

1. *Monks Pond: Thomas Merton's Little Magazine*, with an Introduction by Robert E. Daggy and an Afterword by Patrick Hart, OCSO (Lexington, KY: University Press of Kentucky, 1989).
2. Thomas Merton, *The Road to Joy: Letters to New and Old Friends*, ed. with an Introduction by Robert E. Daggy (New York: Farrar, Straus, Giroux, 1989).
3. Thomas Merton, *Dancing in the Water of Life: Seeking Peace in the Hermitage. Journals, vol. 5: 1963–1965*, ed. with an Introduction by Robert E. Daggy (San Francisco: HarperCollins, 1997).

Thomas Merton and the Search for Owen Merton

1. Thomas Merton, *Learning to Love: Exploring Solitude and Freedom. Journals, vol. 6: 1966–1967*, ed. Christine M. Bochen (San Francisco: HarperCollins, 1997) 11–12; subsequent references will be cited as *"LL"* parenthetically in the text.
2. Thomas Merton, *Disputed Questions* (New York: Farrar, Straus and Cudahy, 1960) 187.
3. Clare Booth Luce on *The Seven Storey Mountain*, quoted in Michael Mott, *The Seven Mountains of Thomas Merton* (Boston: Houghton Mifflin, 1984) 243; subsequent references will be cited as "Mott" parenthetically in the text.
4. Thomas Merton, *The Road to Joy: Letters to New and Old Friends*, ed. Robert E. Daggy (New York: Farrar, Straus, Giroux, 1989) 56; subsequent references will be cited as *"RJ"* parenthetically in the text.
5. Owen Merton to Evelyn Scott, October 19, 1926 [Harry Ransom Research Center, University of Texas, Austin].
6. Owen Merton to Evelyn Scott [Winter, 1926] [Harry Ransom Research Center, University of Texas, Austin].
7. Evelyn Scott to Lola Ridge, October 1924 [Lola Ridge Collection, Smith College, Northampton, MA]; quoted in Mott 24.
8. Owen Merton to Evelyn Scott, October 19, 1926 [Harry Ransom Research Center, University of Texas, Austin].
9. Thomas Merton, *The Seven Storey Mountain* [typescript—Boston College archives] 38; subsequent references will be cited as *"SSM* (BC)" parenthetically in the text.
10. Selima Hill, "A Girl Called Owen," in *My Darling Camel* (London: Chatto and Windus, 1988) 36.

11. Thomas Merton, *The Seven Storey Mountain* (New York: Harcourt, Brace, 1948) 82; subsequent references will be cited as "*SSM*" parenthetically in the text.
12. Thomas Merton, *Collected Poems* (New York: New Directions, 1977) 615; subsequent references will be cited as "*CP*" parenthetically in the text.
13. Thomas Merton, *Witness to Freedom: Letters in Times of Crisis,* ed. William H. Shannon (New York: Farrar, Straus, Giroux, 1994) 172–73.
14. Thomas Merton, *Conjectures of a Guilty Bystander* (Garden City, NY: Doubleday, 1966) 168.
15. See letter written by John Howard Griffin to Harold Jenkins, December 1970, Thomas Merton Center, Bellarmine University, Louisville, KY.
16. Owen Merton to Evelyn Scott [April 1923] [Harry Ransom Research Center, University of Texas, Austin].
17. For a detailed discussion of this episode, see Robert E. Daggy, "Birthday Theology: A Reflection on Thomas Merton and the Bermuda Ménage," *The Kentucky Review* 7.2 (Summer 1987) 62–89.
18. Such at least is the presentation of Owen Merton's fictional analogues in Evelyn Scott's novels *Eva Gay* (New York: Smith & Haas, 1933) and *Bread and a Sword* (New York: Scribner, 1937).
19. Creighton Scott, *Confessions of an American Boy* [unpublished manuscript in the possession of Mrs. Paula Scott].
20. Evelyn Scott to Lola Ridge, October 1924 [Lola Ridge Collection, Smith College, Northampton, MA]; quoted in Mott 24.
21. Evelyn Scott to Lola Ridge, January 15, 1926 [Lola Ridge Collection, Smith College, Northampton, MA]; quoted in Mott 26.
22. Owen Merton to Lola Ridge, August 24, 1926 [Lola Ridge Collection, Smith College, Northampton, MA].
23. Owen Merton to Evelyn Scott [April 1923] [Harry Ransom Research Center, University of Texas, Austin].
24. See Evelyn Scott to Lola Ridge [1925] [Lola Ridge Collection, Smith College, Northampton, MA]: ". . . talking of me to and through the Jenkinses as if I were a whore."
25. D. A. Callard, *"Pretty Good for a Woman": The Enigmas of Evelyn Scott* (New York: Norton, 1985) 75; subsequent references will be cited as "Callard" parenthetically in the text.
26. Owen Merton to Lola Ridge, August 24, 1926 [Lola Ridge Collection, Smith College, Northampton, MA].
27. Evelyn Scott to Lola Ridge, September 18, 1925 [Lola Ridge Collection, Smith College, Northampton, MA].
28. Owen Merton to Lola Ridge, August 24, 1926 [Lola Ridge Collection, Smith College, Northampton, MA].
29. Owen Merton to Percyval Tudor-Hart [Autumn 1925] [Richard Bassett Archives, Milton, MA].
30. Owen Merton to Evelyn Scott, September 26, 1926 [Harry Ransom Research Center, University of Texas, Austin].

31. Anthony T. Padovano, *The Human Journey: Thomas Merton, Symbol of a Century* (Garden City, NY: Doubleday, 1982) 109; subsequent references will be cited as "Padovano" parenthetically in the text.
32. Owen Merton to Lola Ridge, August 24, 1926 [Lola Ridge Collection, Smith College, Northampton, MA].
33. "Sincerity in Art and Life: From a Letter of Owen Merton," *Good Work* 30:2 (Spring 1967) 58–59.

With the Eye of the Heart: Thomas Merton on Faith

1. Thomas Merton, *New Seeds of Contemplation* (New York: New Directions, 1961) 130; subsequent references will be cited as "*NSC*" parenthetically in the text.
2. Thomas Merton, "Apologies to an Unbeliever," *Faith and Violence* (Notre Dame: University of Notre Dame Press, 1968) 213; subsequent references will be cited as "*FV*" parenthetically in the text. See also Merton's letters to Dom Francis Decroix, dated August 21, 1967, and August 22, 1967, written in response to a request for input into a message from contemplatives to the world, in Thomas Merton, *The Hidden Ground of Love: Letters on Religious Experience and Social Concerns*, ed. William H. Shannon (New York: Farrar, Straus, Giroux, 1985) 154–59; subsequent references will be cited as "*HGL*" parenthetically in the text.
3. Elena Malits, *The Solitary Explorer: Thomas Merton's Transforming Journey* (San Francisco: Harper & Row, 1980) 54.
4. Thomas Merton, *The Seven Storey Mountain* (New York: Harcourt, Brace, 1948) 204; subsequent references will be cited as "*SSM*" parenthetically in the text.
5. Thomas Merton, *Seeds of Contemplation* (New York: New Direction, 1949) 77–82; subsequent references will be cited as "*SC*" parenthetically in the text.
6. *New Seeds* became the most widely read of the many Merton books on contemplation which, in addition to *Seeds*, include the early *What Is Contemplation?* (Holy Cross, IN: Saint Mary's College, 1948); *The Ascent to Truth* (New York: Harcourt, Brace, 1951) (subsequent references will be cited as "*AT*" parenthetically in the text); *The Inner Experience* (written and revised in 1959 and in 1968, but as yet unpublished as a book); *Contemplative Prayer* (New York: Herder & Herder, 1969), also published under the title *The Climate of Monastic Prayer* (Spencer, MA: Cistercian Publications, 1969) and *Contemplation in a World of Action* (Garden City, NY: Doubleday, 1971) (subsequent references will be cited as "*CWA*" parenthetically in the text). Merton wrote about contemplation elsewhere—in essays, journals, letters, poems, and books. Contemplation was *the* defining theme of his spirituality and served to frame his understanding of faith.
7. Donald Grayston has traced the development of *Seeds* and *New Seeds* in *Thomas Merton: The Development of a Spiritual Theologian* (Lewiston, NY: Edwin Mellen Press, 1985), and in a variorum edition, *Thomas Merton's Rewriting: The Five Versions of* Seeds/New Seeds of Contemplation *as a Key to the Development of his Thought* (Lewiston, NY: Edwin Mellen Press, 1985).

8. He later employs a similar strategy in speaking of contemplation in the new opening chapters of *New Seeds*.
9. Merton devotes two chapters of *NSC* (chs. 18 and 19) to the subject of faith, expanding the chapter that appeared in *SC* (126-30) and adding another chapter entitled "From Faith to Wisdom" (131-41). Additional references to faith are scattered throughout the text.
10. In *SC*, Merton had written, "Faith is first of all an intellectual assent." But, in the same paragraph, he went on to say "faith is the way to a vital contact with a God Who is alive, and not to an abstract First Principle worked out by syllogisms from the evidence of created things" (*SC*, 78).
11. Thomas Merton, *Day of a Stranger* (Salt Lake City: Gibbs M. Smith, 1981) 41.
12. Thomas Merton, *Disputed Questions* (New York: Farrar, Straus and Cudahy, 1960) 180; subsequent references will be cited as "*DQ*" parenthetically in the text.
13. Letter to Rosita and Ludovico Silva, April 10, 1965, in Thomas Merton, *The Courage for Truth: Letters to Writers*, ed. Christine M. Bochen (New York: Farrar, Straus, Giroux, 1993) 225; subsequent references will be cited as "*CT*" parenthetically in the text.
14. Thomas Merton, *A Search for Solitude: Pursuing the Monk's True Life. Journals, vol. 3: 1952–1960*, ed. Lawrence S. Cunningham (San Francisco: HarperCollins, 1996) 149 [entry for December 27, 1957].
15. Thomas Merton, *"Honorable Reader": Reflections on My Work*, ed. Robert E. Daggy (New York: Crossroad, 1989) 64.
16. Thomas Merton, *Life and Holiness* (New York: Herder & Herder, 1963) 96–97; subsequent references will be cited as "*LH*" parenthetically in the text.
17. Thomas Merton, *Dancing in the Water of Life: Seeking Peace in the Hermitage. Journals, vol. 5: 1963–1965*, ed. Robert E. Daggy (San Francisco: HarperCollins, 1997) 317 [entry dated November 15, 1965]; subsequent references will be cited as "*DWL*" parenthetically in the text.
18. Thomas Merton, *Loretto and Gethsemani* (Trappist, KY: Abbey of Gethsemani, 1962) 7; subsequent references will be cited as "*LG*" parenthetically in the text [reprinted in *Thomas Merton: Essential Writings*, ed. Christine M Bochen (Maryknoll: Orbis, 2000) 155–56].
19. Letter to Sr. J. M., dated June 17, 1968, in Thomas Merton, *The School of Charity: Letters on Religious Renewal and Spiritual Direction*, ed. Brother Patrick Hart (New York: Farrar, Straus, Giroux, 1990) 385.
20. Thomas Merton, *Witness to Freedom: Letters in Times of Crisis*, ed. William H. Shannon (New York: Farrar, Straus, Giroux, 1994) 329.
21. Thomas Merton, *Learning to Love: Exploring Solitude and Freedom. Journals, vol. 6: 1966–1967*, ed. Christine M. Bochen (San Francisco: HarperCollins, 1997) 28; subsequent references will be cited as "*LL*" parenthetically in the text.
22. In April, after he returned from the hospital, he cut and " jimmied" down the article as requested (*LL*, 42).

Interiorizing Monasticism

1. I have explicated this paradigm at great length in Lawrence S. Cunningham and Keith Egan, *Christian Spirituality: Themes from the Tradition* (New York: Paulist, 1996); the concept was inspired by Gustavo Gutierrez, *We Drink From Our Own Wells* (Maryknoll, NY: Orbis, 1983).
2. *Lumen Gentium* 2.12, in Walter Abbott, ed., *The Documents of Vatican II* (New York: Guild Press, 1966) 30; subsequent references will be cited as "Abbott" parenthetically in the text.
3. See both the Decree on the Religious Life (*Perfectae Caritatis*) #7 (Abbot, 471) and the Decree on the Missions (*Ad Gentes*) #40 (Abbott, 627–28).
4. Estevao Bettancourt, "Charism," in Karl Rahner, ed., *Sacramentum Mundi*, 6 vols. (New York: Herder & Herder, 1968) 1.284.
5. See, for example, the views expressed in Raimundo Panikkar, ed., *Blessed Simplicity: The Monk as Universal Archetype* (New York: Seabury, 1982).
6. Evdokimov discusses this theme in the recent posthumous publication *Ages of Spirituality* (Crestwood, NY: Saint Vladimir's Seminary Press, 1997). Abbot Francis Kline's recent *Lovers of the Place: Monasticism Loose in the Church* (Collegeville, MN: Liturgical Press, 1997) touches on the same issues but somewhat parenthetically, since his focus is on the monastic life traditionally understood (subsequent references will be cited as "Kline" parenthetically in the text). For a comparative study of Evdokimov and Merton, see Rowan Williams, "Bread in the Wilderness: The Monastic Ideal in Thomas Merton and Paul Evdokimov," in *One Yet Two: Monastic Traditions East & West*, ed. Basil Pennington, CS 29 (Kalamazoo, MI: Cistercian Publications, 1976) 452–73.
7. Quoted in Tomas Spidlik's *The Spirituality of the Christian East* (Kalamazoo, MI: Cistercian Publications, 1988) 284. Spidlik noted that the Greek Fathers saw a danger in too sharply distinguishing lay and monastic spirituality.
8. Thomas Merton, *The School of Charity: Letters on Religious Renewal and Spiritual Direction*, ed. Patrick Hart (New York: Farrar, Straus, Giroux, 1990).
9. Thomas Merton, *The Springs of Contemplation* (New York: Farrar, Straus, Giroux, 1992).
10. Thomas Merton, *Contemplation in a World of Action* (Garden City, NY: Doubleday, 1971).
11. This theme has been brilliantly explored in Charles Dumont's recent article "Cistercian Identity Today: Revisiting Thomas Merton," *Cistercian Studies Quarterly* 33.4 (1998) 487–98.
12. André Louf, OCSO, *The Cistercian Way* (Kalamazoo, MI: Cistercian Publications, 1989) 19.
13. Thomas Merton, *The Seven Storey Mountain* (New York: Harcourt, Brace, 1948).
14. Thomas Merton, *The Sign of Jonas* (New York: Harcourt, Brace, 1953).
15. Thomas Merton, *Conjectures of a Guilty Bystander* (Garden City, NY: Doubleday, 1966).
16. Thomas Merton, "The Quickening of John the Baptist," in *Collected Poems* (New York: New Directions, 1977) 201.
17. Thomas Merton, *Thoughts in Solitude* (New York: Farrar, Straus and Cudahy, 1958).

18. Thomas Merton, *The Asian Journal* , ed. Naomi Burton Stone, Brother Patrick Hart and James Laughlin (New York: New Directions, 1973) 309–310; subsequent references will be cited as "*AJ*" parenthetically in the text.
19. The classic study of monastic culture is Jean Leclercq's *The Love of Learning and the Desire for God* (New York: Fordham University Press, 1961); Merton would also insist in many places that monastic culture had to take account of the impulses in the world in which the monk actually lives. It was that insistence that Merton used to justify his own studies across a broad range of issues from Marxism to interreligious dialogue.
20. Merton singles out those in all religious traditions—individuals as well as communities—who do precisely that. Such persons and groups constitute analogues of monastic life.
21. In my introductory essay on Merton in the anthology *Thomas Merton: Spiritual Master* (New York: Paulist, 1992), and in *Thomas Merton & the Monastic Vision* (Grand Rapids, MI: Eerdmans, 1999), I have argued that if one does not understand Merton as a monk, one simply does not understand him at all. To call Merton a theologian, for example, only makes sense in the light of an earlier, monastic understanding of the title: see Lawrence S. Cunningham, "Thomas Merton as Theologian: An Appreciation," in *The Kentucky Review*, 7.2 (1987) 90–98.
22. From a preface to his collected works in Spanish in Thomas Merton, *"Honorable Reader": Reflections on My Work*, ed. Robert E. Daggy (New York: Crossroad, 1989) 42–43.
23. Robert Wuthnow, *After Heaven: Spirituality in America Since the 1950s* (Berkeley: University of California Press, 1998).
24. Thomas Merton, "A Letter on the Contemplative Life," in *The Monastic Journey*, ed. Patrick Hart (Kansas City: Sheed, Andrews & McMeel, 1977) 173.

"Crisis and Mystery": The Changing Quality of Thomas Merton's Later Journals

1. Thomas Merton, *The Secular Journal* (New York: Farrar, Straus & Cudahy, 1959).
2. Thomas Merton, *The Sign of Jonas* (New York: Harcourt, Brace, 1953).
3. Thomas Merton, *Run to the Mountain: The Story of a Vocation. Journals, vol. 1: 1939–1941*, ed. Patrick Hart (San Francisco: HarperCollins, 1995); Thomas Merton, *Entering the Silence: Becoming a Monk and Writer. Journals, vol. 2: 1941–1952*, ed. Jonathan Montaldo (San Francisco: HarperCollins, 1996); Thomas Merton, *A Search for Solitude: Pursuing the Monk's True Life. Journals, vol. 3: 1952–1960*, ed. Lawrence S. Cunningham (San Francisco: HarperCollins, 1996) (subsequent references will be cited as "*SS*" parenthetically in the text); Thomas Merton, *Turning toward the World: The Pivotal Years. Journals, vol. 4: 1960–1963*, ed. Victor A. Kramer (San Francisco: HarperCollins, 1996) (subsequent references will be cited as "*TTW*" parenthetically in the text); Thomas Merton, *Dancing in the Water of Life: Seeking Peace in the Hermitage. Journals, vol. 5: 1963–1965*, ed. Robert E. Daggy (San

Francisco: HarperCollins, 1997); Thomas Merton, *Learning to Love: Exploring Solitude and Freedom. Journals, vol. 6: 1966–1967*, ed. Christine M. Bochen (San Francisco: HarperCollins, 1997); Thomas Merton, *The Other Side of the Mountain: The End of the Journey. Journals, vol. 7: 1967–1968*, ed. Patrick Hart (San Francisco: HarperCollins, 1998).

4. The Thomas Merton Oral History (privately published by Deweylands Press and available at the Thomas Merton Center, Bellarmine University, Louisville, KY).
5. Ralph Waldo Emerson, "Self-Reliance," in *Selected Essays, Lectures, and Poems*, ed. Robert D. Richardson (New York: Bantam, 1990) 155.
6. Thomas Merton, *Raids on the Unspeakable* (New York: New Directions, 1966) 53–62.
7. Thomas Merton, *Conjectures of a Guilty Bystander* (Garden City, NY: Doubleday, 1966) 191–92.

Loving Winter When the Plant Says Nothing: Thomas Merton's Spirituality in His Private Journals

1. Thomas Merton, "Love Winter When the Plant Says Nothing," *Collected Poems* (New York: New Directions, 1977) 353; subsequent references will be cited as "*CP*" parenthetically in the text.
2. "When in the Soul of the Serene Disciple. . . ." (*CP*, 279–80).
3. Thomas Merton, *The Other Side of the Mountain: The End of the Journey. Journals, vol. 7: 1967–1968*, ed. Patrick Hart (San Francisco: HarperCollins, 1998) 322–24; subsequent references will be cited as "*OSM*" parenthetically in the text.
4. Thomas Merton, *The School of Charity: Letters on Religious Renewal and Spiritual Direction*, ed. Patrick Hart (New York: Farrar, Straus, Giroux, 1990) 326; subsequent references will be cited as "*SC*" parenthetically in the text.
5. See his important statement on the "work of writing" which ends, "[My] best stuff has been more straight confession and witness," in Thomas Merton, *Learning to Love: Exploring Solitude and Freedom. Journals, vol. 6: 1966–1967*, ed. Christine M. Bochen (San Francisco: HarperCollins, 1997) 371; subsequent references will be cited as "*LL*" parenthetically in the text.
6. Thomas Merton, *"Honorable Reader": Reflections on My Work*, ed. Robert E. Daggy (New York: Crossroad, 1989) 67.
7. Thomas Merton, *Run to the Mountain: The Story of a Vocation. Journals, vol. 1: 1939–1941*, ed. Patrick Hart (San Francisco: HarperCollins, 1995) 118; subsequent references will be cited as "*RM*" parenthetically in the text.
8. Thomas Merton, *Conjectures of a Guilty Bystander*. (Garden City, NY: Doubleday, 1966) 170; subsequent references will be cited as "*CGB*" parenthetically in the text.
9. Thomas Merton, *Entering the Silence: Becoming a Monk and Writer. Journals, vol. 2: 1941–1952*, ed. Jonathan Montaldo (San Francisco: HarperCollins, 1996) 154; subsequent references will be cited as "*ES*" parenthetically in the text.

10. Thomas Merton, *A Search for Solitude: Pursuing the Monk's True Life. Journals, vol. 3: 1952–1960*, ed. Lawrence S. Cunningham (San Francisco: HarperCollins, 1996) 20; subsequent references will be cited as "*SS*" parenthetically in the text.
11. Thomas Merton, *The Way of Chuang Tzu* (New York: New Directions, 1965) 115.
12. Thomas Merton, *Turning toward the World: The Pivotal Years. Journals, vol. 4: 1960–1963*, ed. Victor A. Kramer (San Francisco: HarperCollins, 1996) 87; subsequent references will be cited as "*TTW*" parenthetically in the text.
13. Karl Barth, *The Epistle to the Romans*, trans. E. C. Hoskyns (London: Oxford University Press, 1968) 33–34.
14. See the characterization by Eugraph Kovalevsky, *A Method of Prayer for Modern Times* (Newburyport, MA: Praxis Institute, 1993) 1.
15. John Cassian, quoted in Paul Evdokimov, *The Ages of the Spiritual Life* (Crestwood, NY: St. Validimir's Seminary Press, 1998) 194.
16. Gregory Nazianzen, quoted in Boniface Ramsey, *Beginning to Read the Fathers* (New York: Paulist, 1985) 77.
17. "It is in this 'hell of mercy' that, in finally relaxing our determined grasp of our empty self, we find ourselves lost and liberated in the infinite fullness of God's love. We escape from the cage of emptiness, despair, dread, and sin into the infinite space and freedom of grace and mercy. But if there remains any vestige of self that can be aware of itself as 'having arrived' and as having 'attained possession,' then we can be sure of the return of the old dread, the old night, the old nothingness, until all self-sufficiency and self-complacency are destroyed." *The Climate of Monastic Prayer* (Kalamazoo, MI: Cistercian Publications, 1969) 138; subsequent references will be cited as "*CMP*" parenthetically in the text.
18. A classic insight into St. Benedict's Prologue which has been restated in M. Basil Pennington, OCSO, "Returning to the Prologue," *Cistercian Studies Quarterly* 32.3 (1997) 289.
19. "Mother wanted me to be independent, and not to run with the herd. I was to be original, individual. I was to have a definite character and ideals of my own. I was not to be an article thrown together, on the common bourgeois pattern, on everybody else's assembly line." *The Seven Storey Mountain* (New York: Harcourt, Brace, 1948) 11.
20. From the *Salve Regina*, a hymn at Compline, the last office of psalms in the monastic day.
21. Thomas Merton, *Dancing in the Water of Life: Seeking Peace in the Hermitage. Journals, vol. 5: 1963–1965*, ed. Robert E. Daggy (San Francisco: HarperCollins, 1997) 167–68; subsequent references will be cited as "*DWL*" parenthetically in the text.
22. See his dream of and letters to "Proverb" (*SS*, 175–77, 182).
23. See "Hagia Sophia" (*CP*, 363–71).
24. Daniel Carrere, OCSO, "Review of *Turning toward the World*," *The Merton Annual* 10 (1997) 337.
25. See the seminal and rich study of *kenosis* in the Merton literature and of his "sapiential theology of experience" in George A. Kilcourse, *Ace of Freedoms: Thomas Merton's Christ* (Notre Dame: University of Notre Dame Press, 1993).

26. See his famous prayer "My Lord God, I have no idea where I am going," in Thomas Merton, *Thoughts in Solitude* (New York: Farrar, Straus and Cudahy, 1958) 83; subsequent references will be cited as "*TS*" parenthetically in the text.
27. See *The Asian Journal of Thomas Merton*, ed. Naomi Burton Stone, Brother Patrick Hart and James Laughlin (New York: New Directions, 1973) 296.
28. "But for me, the vow of stability has been the belly of the whale," in Thomas Merton, *The Sign of Jonas* (New York: Harcourt, Brace, 1953) 10; subsequent references will be cited as "*SJ*" parenthetically in the text.
29. Thomas Merton, *The Courage for Truth: Letters to Writers*, ed. Christine M. Bochen (New York: Farrar, Straus, Giroux, 1993) 29; subsequent references will be cited as "*CT*" parenthetically in the text.
30. "Perhaps I am afraid of being absorbed in the *public anonymity* of the priest, of becoming one of those masks behind whom Christ hides and acts. I think of so many priests I know in their strange, sensitive isolation, innocent, hearty men, decent and *unoriginal* and generally *unperplexed*, too; but all of them lost in a public privacy" [emphasis added] (*ES*, 164–65); "Sometimes I am terrified at the thought of being incorporated into a caste full of spiritual limitations and rigidity" (*ES*, 209).
31. "A going clear out of the midst of all that is transitory and inconclusive. The return to the Immense, the Primordial, the Unknown, to Him who loves, to the Silent, to the Holy, to the Merciful, to Him Who is All" (*TTW*, 101).
32. "Prayer is all I have left—and patient, humble (if possible) obedience to God's will" (*DWL*, 348).
33. "To go beyond everything, to leave everything, and press forward to the End and to the Beginning, to the ever new Beginning that is without End" (*TTW* 101).

On Mind, Matter, and Knowing: Thomas Merton and Quantum Physics

1. Thomas Merton, *Turning toward the World: The Pivotal Years. Journals, vol. 4: 1960–1963*, ed. Victor A. Kramer (San Francisco: HarperCollins, 1996) 322; subsequent references will be cited as "*TTW*" parenthetically in the text. See Werner Heisenberg, *Physics and Philosophy: The Revolution in Modern Science* (New York: Harper & Row, 1962); subsequent references will be cited as "Heisenberg" parenthetically in the text.
2. Thomas Merton, "Working Notebook, 1963" (Thomas Merton Center, Bellarmine University, Louisville, KY).
3. Thomas Merton, *Learning to Love: Exploring Solitude and Freedom. Journals, vol. 6: 1966–1967*, ed. Christine M. Bochen (San Francisco: HarperCollins, 1997) 237–38, 243–44; subsequent references will be cited as "*LL*" parenthetically in the text. See George Gamow, *Biography of Physics* (New York: Harper & Row, 1961); subsequent references will be cited as "Gamow" parenthetically in the text. Ruth Moore, *Niels Bohr: The Man, His Science, & the World They Changed* (Cambridge, MA: MIT Press, 1985), originally published by Alfred A. Knopf,

Inc., 1966; subsequent references will be cited as "Moore" parenthetically in the text. Merton mentions that he is reading the biography by Moore explicitly in a letter to Guy Davenport, dated June 11, 1967; see Thomas Merton, *The Courage for Truth: Letters to Writers*, ed. Christine M. Bochen (New York: Farrar, Straus, Giroux, 1993) 252; subsequent references will be cited as "*CT*" parenthetically in the text.

4. Thomas Merton, *Thomas Merton on St. Bernard* (Kalamazoo, MI: Cistercian Publications, 1980) 130; subsequent references will be cited as "*TMSB*" parenthetically in the text.
5. I am grateful to colleague and physicist S. Leslie Blatt for his patience in explaining some of the basic ideas of quantum physics, and for checking my rendering of them.
6. Heisenberg discusses the implications of quantum physics for Cartesian philosophy in *Physics and Philosophy*, undoubtedly influencing Merton's subsequent thinking about and reference to the false Cartesian duality of self and world; see especially pp. 78–81.
7. For a discussion of the degeneration of Cartesian philosophy into an infatuation with technique, see William Barrett, *The Illusion of Technique: A Search for Meaning in a Technological Civilization* (Garden City, NY: Doubleday Anchor, 1978); for a more psychological view, see Robert Jay Lifton and Eric Markusen, *The Genocidal Mentality: Nazi Holocaust and Nuclear Threat* (New York: Basic Books, 1990).
8. Thomas Merton, *The Other Side of the Mountain: The End of the Journey. Journals, vol. 7: 1967–1968*, ed. Patrick Hart (San Francisco: HarperCollins, 1998) 323.
9. For an example of Merton's thinking on this point, see Thomas Merton, *Dancing in the Water of Life: Seeking Peace in the Hermitage. Journals, vol. 5: 1963–1965*, ed. Robert E. Daggy (San Francisco: HarperCollins, 1997) 259.
10. Thomas Merton, "Herakleitos: A Study," in *The Behavior of Titans* (New York: New Directions, 1961) 79; subsequent references will be cited as "*BT*" parenthetically in the text.
11. Thomas Merton, *New Seeds of Contemplation* (New York: New Directions, 1961) 5.
12. Thomas Merton, "Community and the Christian Life," Conference Tape AA2456 (Kansas City: Credence Cassettes, 1988); subsequent references will be cited as "'CCL' tape" parenthetically in the text. See also Thomas Merton, *Zen and the Birds of Appetite* (New York: New Directions, 1968) 23–26; subsequent references will be cited as "*ZBA*" parenthetically in the text.
13. In this respect, one wonders how Merton might have compared Chuang Tzu's thought to Bohr's concept of complementarity or to the Herakleitean notion of "harmony-in-conflict." The idea of "complementarity of opposites" was key to the thought of this Chinese philosopher in the fourth century B.C.E according to Merton. See Thomas Merton, *The Way of Chuang Tzu* (New York: New Directions, 1965) 30.
14. See Merton's similar statement in *Conjectures of a Guilty Bystander* (Garden City, NY: Doubleday, 1966): "How absolutely central is the truth that we are

first of all *part of nature*, though we are a very special part, that which is conscious of God" (268).

15. Thomas Merton, *Love and Living*, ed. Naomi Burton Stone and Brother Patrick Hart (New York; Farrar, Straus, Giroux, 1979) 120; subsequent references will be cited as "*L&L*" parenthetically in the text.
16. Thomas Merton, *A Search for Solitude: Pursuing the Monk's True Life. Journals, vol. 3: 1952-1960*, ed. Lawrence S. Cunningham (San Francisco: HarperCollins, 1996) 190; subsequent references will be cited as "*SS*" parenthetically in the text.
17. Thomas Merton, "The Need for a New Education," in *Contemplation in a World of Action*, ed. Naomi Burton Stone (Garden City, NY: Doubleday, 1971) 201; subsequent references will be cited as "*CWA*" parenthetically in the text.
18. See Evelyn Fox Keller, *A Feeling for the Organism: The Life and Work of Barbara McClintock* (San Francisco: W. H. Freeman, 1983).
19. Edward O. Wilson, *Naturalist* (Washington, DC: Island Press, 1994) 191.
20. Heisenberg's controversial role in the German atomic bomb project and its impact on his relationship with Bohr has recently received a great deal of attention as the subject of Michael Frayn's critically acclaimed play about the 1941 meeting of the two men, *Copenhagen* (New York: Alfred A. Knopf, 2000). See also Thomas Powers' book *Heisenberg's War: The Secret History of the German Bomb* (New York: Alfred A. Knopf, 1993), as well as his articles on the play in *The New York Review of Books*, "The Unanswered Question" 47.9 (May 25, 2000) 4, 6–7 and "What Bohr Remembered" 49.5 (March 28, 2002) 25–26, along with Frayn's article "'Copenhagen' Revisited" in the latter issue (22–24).

Dancing with the Raven: Thomas Merton's Evolving View of Nature

1. Robert E. Daggy, Introduction to Thomas Merton, *Dancing in the Water of Life: Seeking Peace in the Hermitage. Journals, vol. 5: 1963-1965*, ed. Robert E. Daggy (San Francisco: HarperCollins, 1997) xi-xii; subsequent references will be cited as "*DWL*" parenthetically in the text.
2. Ruth Jenkins Merton, "Tom's Book" (1916), unpublished ms. in Thomas Merton Center Collection, Bellarmine University, Louisville, KY; subsequent references will be cited as "*TB*" parenthetically in the text.
3. Several dissertations on file at the Thomas Merton Center, Bellarmine University, Louisville, KY, offer useful insights into Merton's poetry. See especially Alan Altany, "Transformation of the Idea of the Sacred in the Poetry of Thomas Merton" [Diss. University of Pittsburgh, 1987]; Bonnie L Bowman, "Flowers of Contemplation: The Later Poetry of Thomas Merton" [Diss. University of Virginia, 1979]; Michael W. Higgins, "Thomas Merton, the Silent Speaking Visionary: A Study of His Poetry" [Diss. York University, 1979]; George A. Kilcourse, Jr., "Incarnation as the Integrating Principle in Thomas Merton's Poetry and Spirituality" [Diss. Fordham University, 1974]; Gail Ramshaw Schmidt, "The Poetry of Thomas Merton: An Introduction" [Diss. University of Wisconsin-Madison, 1976].

4. Thomas Merton, *The Seven Storey Mountain* (New York: Harcourt, Brace, 1948) 72.
5. Thomas Merton, *Run to the Mountain: The Story of a Vocation. Journals, vol. 1: 1939-1941*, ed. Patrick Hart, OCSO (San Fransciso: HarperCollins, 1996) 399; subsequent references will be cited as "*RM*" parenthetically in the text.
6. Thomas Merton, *Day of a Stranger* (Salt Lake City: Gibbs M. Smith, 1981) 33; subsequent references will be cited as "*DS*" parenthetically in the text.
7. Thomas Merton, *The Asian Journal*, ed. Naomi Burton Stone, Brother Patrick Hart and James Laughlin (New York: New Directions, 1963) 233, 235–36.
8. Thomas Merton, *Entering the Silence: Becoming a Monk and Writer. Journals, vol. 2: 1941-1952*, ed. Jonathan Montaldo (San Fransciso: HarperCollins, 1996) 216; subsequent references will be cited as "*ES*" parenthetically in the text.
9. See my article on the influence of William Wordsworth on Thomas Merton: "Beyond the Shadow and the Disguise: 'Spots of Time' in Thomas Merton's Spiritual Development," *The Merton Seasonal* 23:1 (Spring 1998) 21–27.
10. Thomas Merton, *Turning toward the World: The Pivotal Years. Journals, vol. 4: 1960-1963*, ed. Victor A. Kramer (San Francisco: HarperCollins, 1996) 229; subsequent references will be cited as "*TTW*" parenthetically in the text.
11. For a discussion of how landscape influences being, see Belden C. Lane, *The Solace of Fierce Landscapes: Exploring Desert and Mountain Spirituality* (New York: Oxford University Press, 1998); subsequent references will be cited as "Lane" parenthetically in the text.
12. Thomas Merton, *A Search for Solitude: Pursuing the Monk's True Life. Journals, vol. 3: 1952–1960*, ed. Lawrence S. Cunningham (San Francisco: HarperCollins, 1996) 22; subsequent references will be cited as "*SS*" parenthetically in the text.
13. Thomas Merton, *Striving towards Being: The Letters of Thomas Merton and Czeslaw Milosz*, ed. Robert Faggen (New York: Farrar, Straus & Giroux, 1997) 64; subsequent references will be cited as "*STB*" parenthetically in the text.
14. Wendell Berry, "Work Song," *Clearing* (New York: Harcourt, Brace, Jovanovich, 1977) 31–36.
15. John Elder, *Reading the Mountains of Home* (Cambridge: Harvard University Press, 1998) 21.
16. Patrick Hart, *Thomas Merton: First and Last Memories* (Bardstown, KY: Necessity Press, 1986) 4.
17. Thomas Merton, *Witness to Freedom: Letters in Times of Crisis*, ed. William H. Shannon (New York: Farrar, Straus, Giroux, 1994) 70; subsequent references will be cited as "*WF*" parenthetically in the text.
18. George H. Williams, *Wilderness and Paradise in Christian Thought* (New York: Harper, 1962).
19. Thomas Merton, *Learning to Love: Exploring Solitude and Freedom. Journals, vol. 6: 1966–1967*, ed. Christine M. Bochen (San Francisco: HarperCollins, 1997) 161; subsequent references will be cited as "*LL*" parenthetically in the text.
20. Ulrich W. Mauser, *Christ in the Wilderness* (Naperville, IL: A. R. Allenson, 1963).
21. Reprinted in Thomas Merton, *The Monastic Journey*, ed. Brother Patrick Hart (Kansas City: Sheed, Andrews & McMeel, 1977) 144–50; subsequent references will be cited as "*MJ*" parenthetically in the text.

22. Roderick Nash, *Wilderness and the American Mind* (New Haven: Yale University Press, 1967).
23. Thomas Merton, *Preview of the Asian Journey*, ed. Walter H. Capps (New York: Crossroad, 1989) 104; subsequent references will be cited as "*PAJ*" parenthetically in the text.
24. Thomas Merton, *Conjectures of a Guilty Bystander* (Garden City, NY: Doubleday, 1966) 268.
25. Thomas Merton, *Thoughts in Solitude* (New York: Farrar, Straus & Cudahy, 1958) 94.
26. St. Bernard of Clairvaux, Epistle 106.

Sacrament and Sacramentality in Thomas Merton's *Thirty Poems*

1. Thomas Merton, *Thirty Poems* (Norfolk, CT: New Directions, 1944); subsequent references will be cited as "*TP*" parenthetically in the text. In *The Seven Storey Mountain* (New York: Harcourt, Brace, 1948), Merton writes: "The exceedingly tidy little volume, *Thirty Poems*, reached me at the end of November, just before we began the annual retreat, in 1944" (410); subsequent references will be cited as "*SSM*" parenthetically in the text.
2. See Appendix 2 of Thomas Merton, *"Honorable Reader": Reflections on My Work*, ed. Robert E. Daggy (New York: Crossroad, 1989) 150–51.
3. All but six of the poems in this collection date from before Merton entered the monastery. For a chronology of the early poetry, see Ross Labrie, "The Ordering of Thomas Merton's Early Poems," *Resources for American Literary Study* 8 (1979) 115–17, which draws on a 1951 letter, written by Merton's secretary, providing the year of composition for almost all the poems in Merton's first three collections; subsequent references will be cited as "Labrie" parenthetically in the text. For *Thirty Poems* and *A Man in the Divided Sea*, the information in the letter is evidently based on dates written in Merton's personal copy of *A Man in the Divided Sea*, now at the Thomas Merton Center, Bellarmine University, Louisville, KY.
4. The poems included in *A Man in the Divided Sea* were written between 1939 and 1946 (see Labrie); see also the sixteen poems published posthumously in *Early Poems: 1940–1942* (Lexington, KY: Anvil Press, 1971), all but two of which date from before Merton's entrance into the monastery; despite the title, at least one of the poems was written as early as 1939, and one of the monastic poems may date from as late as 1944 or 1945. Six poems from 1939 and one from 1942 are found in the "Uncollected Poems" section of Thomas Merton, *Collected Poems* (New York: New Directions, 1977). About a dozen premonastic and early monastic poems not included in the *Collected Poems* have also been discovered subsequently and published in *The Merton Seasonal* (see 21.1 [Spring 1996] 8; 25.1 [Spring 2000] 6–8; 25.2 [Summer 2000] 5–8; 25.3 [Fall 2000] 7–9; 25.4 [Winter 2000] 12–18), 28.2 [Spring 2003] 9–10.
5. Thomas Merton, *A Man in the Divided Sea* (New York: New Directions, 1946) 11; subsequent references will be cited as "*MDS*" parenthetically in the text. This statement is actually more accurate for the original *Thirty Poems* than for this

volume, in which five of the poems are reordered, evidently for thematic reasons (e.g., "Evening" is moved to follow "The Trappist Abbey: Matins"). There are also slight textual changes in the reprinting; the text of *A Man in the Divided Sea* will be followed here, with any changes from *Thirty Poems* noted. The text and ordering in the *Collected Poems* generally follows that in *Thirty Poems;* two poems (as well as six poems from *A Man in the Divided Sea*) incorporate alterations found in Merton's personal copy of *A Man in the Divided Sea.*

6. See, for example, Thomas Merton, "The Inner Experience," *Cistercian Studies,* 18.4 (1983) 298.
7. Chronologically, however, "The Holy Sacrament of the Altar" is one of the latest pieces included in *Thirty Poems,* dating from 1943 (see Labrie, 116).
8. All versions of the text read "Your" at the beginning of 1. 7, but "You" makes better sense.
9. *TP* reads "monstrance, for" in 1. 21; it also separates the following four verses (ll. 24–27) as a distinct stanza, whereas there is no break between ll. 23 and 24 in *MDS.*
10. *TP* reads "apostles," in 1. 30.
11. See *SSM,* 329, and especially Thomas Merton, *The Secular Journal* (New York: Farrar, Straus & Cudahy, 1959) 199: "There the monks washed the feet of some poor men, put money in their hands, kissed their hands and feet, gave them a dinner. . . . I saw Christ washing the feet of Peter. The monks had heard Christ and were doing what He had told them to do" (subsequent references will be cited as "*SJ*" parenthetically in the text). For a slightly different version of this same material, see Thomas Merton, *Run to the Mountain: The Story of A Vocation. Journals, vol. 1: 1939-1941,* ed. Patrick Hart (San Francisco: HarperCollins, 1995) 348; subsequent references will be cited as "*RM*" parenthetically in the text.
12. See discussion below.
13. William Blake, *The Poetry and Prose,* ed. David V. Erdman (Garden City, NY: Anchor, 1965) 12–13; subsequent references will be cited as "Blake" parenthetically in the text.
14. This poem dates from 1941 (see Labrie, 116).
15. *TP* reads "lightenings" in 1. 2.
16. The *Spiritual Exercises of St. Ignatius,* Anthony Mottola, trans. (Garden City, NY: Doubleday Image, 1964) 54, 72; for Merton's personal experience with the *Spiritual Exercises* see *SSM,* 268–73.
17. Only Matthew's version includes the mention of gall; Mark's parallel passage mentions myrrh, a mild narcotic (Mk 15:23); the Revised Standard translation retains the term "vinegar" where a number of other contemporary translations use "common wine."
18. There seems to be no association with the Zhar-ptitsa, the firebird of Russian folklore and of Stravinsky's ballet of that name.
19. *TP* reads "thundercracks of massbells," in l. 10.
20. Gerard Manley Hopkins, *Poems and Prose,* ed. W. H. Gardner (Baltimore: Penguin, 1963) 62.
21. John Donne, *The Complete Poetry,* ed. John T. Shawcross (Garden City, NY:

Doubleday Anchor, 1967) 115.

22. This poem dates from 1941 (see Labrie 116); it is moved in *MDS* from immediately before to immediately after "The Communion."
23. See *SSM*, 344–49; *SJ*, 234–38; *RM*, 384–86, 464–65.
24. All versions omit the quotation marks at the end of l. 4, which should be included as the speaker changes at this point.
25. *TP* reads "massbells" in 1. 11.
26. In addition to the poems to be discussed, see "The Communion," ll. 3–4, 8, 15–17, 19; "The Vine," ll. 1–4, 17–19, 23–27; "The Holy Child's Song," ll. 9, 27.
27. This poem dates from 1941 (see Labrie, 116). In *TP*, "Evening" follows "The Communion" (the eighteenth position); in *MDS*, it follows "The Trappist Abbey: Matins" (the twenty-second position).
28. This image may be borrowed from Henry Vaughan's "Ascension-day," l. 45: "When Heav'n above them shin'd like molten glass" (*The Complete Poetry*, ed. French Fogle [Garden City, NY: Doubleday Anchor, 1964] 268).
29. This image may be borrowed from George Herbert's "Vertue," 1.2: "The bridal of the earth and skie" (*The Works of George Herbert*, ed. F. E. Hutchinson [Oxford: Clarendon Press, 1941] 87).
30. While Merton later dates this poem as being written in 1941 (see Labrie, 116), at least a preliminary draft was written in connection with Merton's hitchhiking trip from Olean to Cleveland in the summer of 1940: see Jim Knight, "The Merton I Knew," *The Merton Seasonal* 27.3 (Fall 2002) 14–16. The poem follows "Poem: Watching, among the rifled branches . . ." in *TP*, and precedes it in *MDS*.
31. See Yeats' poem "A Dialogue of Self and Soul," in *The Collected Poems* (New York: Macmillan, 1956) 230–32, as well as Marvell's "A Dialogue of the Soul and Body," in *Complete Poetry*, ed. George de F. Lord, ed. (New York: Modern Library, 1968) 17–18.
32. See, for example, Thomas Merton, *New Seeds of Contemplation* (New York: New Directions, 1961) 38.
33. Thomas Merton, "Poetry and Contemplation: A Reappraisal," in *The Literary Essays of Thomas Merton*, ed. Patrick Hart, OCSO (New York: New Directions, 1981) 345; for a comparison of this essay with "Poetry and the Contemplative Life," a version published twelve years earlier, see Patrick F. O'Connell, "Poetry and Contemplation: The Evolution of Thomas Merton's Aesthetic." *The Merton Journal* [England] 8:1 (Easter 2001) 2–11.

Wrestling with Angels: Some Mature Poems of Thomas Merton

1. See Bonnie Bowman, "Flowers of Contemplation: The Later Poetry of Thomas Merton," Diss. University of Virginia, 1979.
2. "In Silence" and "Stranger" both appeared in *The Strange Islands* (New York: New Directions, 1957).
3. Thomas Merton, *Emblems of a Season of Fury* (New York: New Directions, 1963).
4. See George Woodcock, *Thomas Merton, Monk and Poet* (New York: Farrar,

Straus, Giroux, 1978) 51 ff.

5. For studies on Merton and contemporary nature writers, see the work of Monica Weis, SSJ, for example "Living Beings Call Us to Reflective Living: Mary Austin, Thomas Merton, and Contemporary Nature Writers," *The Merton Seasonal* 17.4 (1992) 4–9.
6. George Kilcourse, "'A Shy Wild Deer': The 'True Self' in Thomas Merton's Poetry," *The Merton Annual* 4 (1991) 103; subsequent references will be cited as "Kilcourse" parenthetically in the text.
7. See Thomas Merton, "Is the World a Problem?" in *Contemplation in a World of Action* (New York: Doubleday, 1973) 143–44: "Due to a book I wrote thirty years ago, I have myself become a sort of stereotype of the world-denying contemplative—the man who spurned New York, spat on Chicago, and tromped on Louisville, heading for the woods with Thoreau in one pocket, John of the Cross in another, and holding the Bible open at the Apocalypse. This personal stereotype is probably my own fault."
8. Unless otherwise noted, Biblical citations are from the Revised Standard Version of the Bible.
9. Thomas Merton, *Conjectures of a Guilty Bystander* (Garden City, NY: Doubleday, 1966) 268–69; subsequent references will be cited as "*CGB*" parenthetically in the text.
10. Thomas Merton, *Collected Poems* (New York: New Directions, 1978) 351–52; subsequent references will be cited as "*CP*" parenthetically in the text.
11. Thomas Merton, *Thoughts in Solitude* (New York: Farrar, Straus & Cudahy, 1958) 81; subsequent references will be cited as "*TS*" parenthetically in the text.
12. See chapters 5–7 of *New Seeds of Contemplation* (New York: New Directions, 1961) (subsequent references will be cited as "*NSC*" parenthetically in the text) and William Shannon's commentary in *Thomas Merton's Dark Path: The Inner Experience of a Contemplative* (New York: Farrar, Straus, Giroux, 1982) 39–50, 80–86, 155–60.
13. See, for example, "Mystics and Zen Masters" in *Mystics and Zen Masters* (New York: Farrar, Straus, Giroux, 1967) and *Zen and the Birds of Appetite* (New York: New Directions, 1968).
14. For the sake of accuracy of quotation, I have retained Merton's exclusive language.
15. For further discussion of this idea, see *NSC*, chapter 5, "Things in Their Identity."
16. For the genesis of this poem, see the entry of July 27, 1956, in Thomas Merton, *A Search for Solitude: Pursuing the Monk's True Life. Journals, vol. 3: 1952–1960*, ed. Lawrence S. Cunningham (San Francisco: HarperCollins, 1996) 56–57; subsequent references will be cited as "*SS*" parenthetically in the text.
17. See Rudolf Otto's classic work *The Idea of the Holy* (1923; New York: Galaxy Books, 1958).
18. Thomas Merton, *"Honorable Reader": Reflections on My Work*, ed. Robert E. Daggy (New York: Crossroad, 1989) 116.
19. This is an intriguing remark. Did Merton think we cannot expose or exhibit

our "true selves" in ordinary, day-to-day life, in the "light of day"?

20. Certainly this is born out in the lives of St. Paul, St. Francis of Assisi, Dame Julian of Norwich, Blaise Pascal, and in Merton himself, whether we think of that experience as hearing Gethsemani's bells at St. Bonaventure, the "Fourth and Walnut" experience or the visit to Polonnaruwa.
21. I have argued elsewhere that Merton's departure from Cartesian dualism was a result of his studies in Zen Buddhism and that his changed cosmology radically altered his poetic voice. See "Zen in the Eye of Thomas Merton's Poetry," *Buddhist-Christian Studies* 4 (1984) 103–17.
22. Sheila M. Hempstead, "Emblems of Birds: Birds as Symbols of Grace in Three Poems of Thomas Merton," *The Merton Seasonal* 18.1 (1993) 23 (subsequent references will be cited as "Hempstead" parenthetically in the text). Merton's journal entry for October 5, 1957, has a long paragraph on warblers and contains this interesting statement: "Seeing this beautiful thing which people do not usually see, looking into this world of birds, which is not concerned with us or with our problems. I felt very close to God or felt religious awe anyway. Watching those birds was as food for meditation or as mystical reading. Perhaps better" (*SS*, 123–124).
23. John F. Teahan, "Solitude: A Central Motif in Thomas Merton's Life and Writings," *Journal of the American Academy of Religion* 50.4 (1982) 521.

Thomas Merton and Ananda Coomaraswamy

1. Letter to N. Chatterji, October 29, 1965, in Thomas Merton, *Witness to Freedom: Letters in Times of Crisis*, ed. William H. Shannon (New York : Farrar, Straus, Giroux, 1994) 173; subsequent references will be cited as "*WF*" parenthetically in the text.
2. Letter to M. R. Chandler, July 19, 1963 (*WF*, 165).
3. Letter to Dona Luisa Coomaraswamy, January 13, 1961, in Thomas Merton, *The Hidden Ground of Love of Love: Letters on Religious Experience and Social Concerns*, ed. William H. Shannon (New York: Farrar, Straus, Giroux, 1985) 126–27; subsequent references will be cited as "*HGL*" parenthetically in the text.
4. Thomas Merton, *The Seven Storey Mountain* (New York: Harcourt Brace, 1948) 85–88.
5. Roger Lipsey, *Coomaraswamy*, 3 vols. (Princeton: Princeton University Press, 1977) 3.107–108, 96–97, 103–104; subsequent references will be cited as "Lipsey" parenthetically in the text. The first two volumes of this set consist in selected essays of Coomaraswamy edited by Lipsey; the third is a biography of Coomaraswamy by Lipsey.
6. Thomas Merton, "Nature and Art in William Blake. An Essay in Interpretation" (1939), in *The Literary Essays of Thomas Merton* (New York: New Directions, 1981) 414–19; subsequent references will be cited as "*LE*" parenthetically in the text. See also William Blake's *A Descriptive Catalogue 1809* (Oxford: Woodstock Books, 1990) 59; and John Adlard's article "Blake and the 'Geeta'," *English Studies* 45 (1964) 460–62.
7. Ananda Coomaraswamy, *The Transformation of Nature in Art* (Cambridge,

MA: Harvard University Press, 1935) 5–6; subsequent references will be cited as "Coomaraswamy" parenthetically in the text.

8. Meister Eckhart, *The Essential Sermons, Commentaries, Treatises, and Defense.* Trans. and Ed. Bernard McGinn and Edmund Colledge (New York: Paulist, 1981) 253-54; subsequent references will be cited as "Eckhart" parenthetically in the text.
9. Thomas Merton, *The Way of Chuang Tzu* (New York: New Directions, 1965) 110–11.
10. Thomas Merton, *The Asian Journal*, ed. Naomi Burton Stone, Brother Patrick Hart, and James Laughlin (New York: New Directions, 1973) 204; subsequent references will be cited as "*AJ*" parenthetically in the text.
11. Thomas Merton, *New Seeds of Contemplation* (New York: New Directions, 1961) 290–97.
12. Thomas Merton, *Raids on the Unspeakable* (New York: New Directions, 1966) 155–61; subsequent references will be cited as "*RU*" parenthetically in the text.
13. Ananda Coomaraswamy, *The Dance of Shiva* (New York: Noonday Press, 1957) 67–77.

Thomas Merton in Dialogue with Eastern Religions

1. *L'Express*, 20–26 March, 1997, quoted in *The* (*London*) *Tablet*, March 29–April 5, 1997.
2. Quoted in a letter to the editor in *The* (*London*) *Tablet*, April 12, 1997.
3. Declaration on the Relationship of the Church to Non-Christian Religions (*Nostra Aetate*), par. 2, in Norman P. Tanner, ed., *Decrees of the Ecumenical Councils*, vol. 2 (Washington, DC: Georgetown University Press, 1990) 968; subsequent references will be cited as "Tanner" parenthetically in the text.
4. Thomas Merton, *Conjectures of a Guilty Bystander* (Garden City, NY: Doubleday, 1966) vii (italics added); subsequent references will be cited as "*CGB*" parenthetically in the text.
5. The title of a book by Tillich published in 1948.
6. William H. Shannon, *Silent Lamp: The Thomas Merton Story* (New York: Crossroad, 1992) 279.
7. See Thomas Merton, *The Hidden Ground of Love: Letters on Religious Experience and Social Concern*, ed. William H. Shannon (New York: Farrar, Straus, Giroux, 1985) 115; subsequent references will be cited as "*HGL*" parenthetically in the text.
8. Thomas Merton, *Zen and the Birds of Appetite*, (New York: New Directions, 1968) 39; subsequent references will be cited as "*ZBA*" parenthetically in the text.
9. Thomas Merton, *The Ascent to Truth* (New York: Harcourt Brace, 1951) 106; subsequent references will be cited as "*AT*" parenthetically in the text.
10. Abbot Zenkei Shibayama, *A Flower Does Not Talk* (Rutland, VT: Tuttle, 1970) 23.
11. Meister Eckhart, Sermon 57, in *German Sermons and Treatises*, trans. M. O'C. Walshe, 3 vols. (London: Watkins, 1979–87) 2.87.
12. William H. Shannon, *Silence on Fire: The Prayer of Awareness* (New York: Crossroad, 1991) 28–29.
13. Thomas Merton, *The Asian Journal*, ed. Naomi Burton Stone, Brother Patrick

Hart and James Laughlin (New York: New Directions, 1973) 308; subsequent references will be cited as "*AJ*" parenthetically in the text.

14. Thomas Merton, *Mystics and Zen Masters* (New York: Farrar, Straus and Giroux, 1967) 18.
15. Thomas Merton, *The Way of Chuang Tzu* (New York: New Directions, 1965).
16. Herbert A. Giles, *Chuang Tzu, Mystic, Moralist and Social Reformer* (Shanghai: Kelley & Walsh, 1926) ch. 2.
17. Thomas Merton, *New Seeds of Contemplation* (New York: New Directions, 1961) 3; subsequent references will be cited as "*NSC*" parenthetically in the text.
18. John of the Cross, *The Ascent of Mount Carmel*, bk. I, c. 13, no. 11, quoted in *AT* 52–53.
19. Tenzin Gyatso, *Freedom in Exile: The Autobiography of the Dalai Lama* (New York: Harper Collins, 1990) 189; subsequent references will be cited as "Dalai Lama" parenthetically in the text.
20. This visit was videotaped at the Abbey of Gethsemani.

Notes on Contributors

Christine M. Bochen, professor of theology at Nazareth College, Rochester, NY, served as seventh president of the International Thomas Merton Society; she is co-author of *The Thomas Merton Encyclopedia* and has edited both *The Courage for Truth*, the fourth volume of Merton's letters, and *Learning to Love*, the sixth volume of Merton's journals.

Lawrence S. Cunningham, the John A. O'Brien Professor of Theology at the University of Notre Dame, is the author of numerous books, including *Thomas Merton & the Monastic Vision*, and has edited *Thomas Merton: Spiritual Master* and *A Search for Solitude*, the third volume of Merton's journals.

Thomas Del Prete, professor and chair of education at Clark University, Worcester, MA, served as sixth president of the International Thomas Merton Society as well as program chair for the ITMS seventh General Meeting, and is the author of *Thomas Merton and the Education of the Whole Person*.

Patrick Hart, OCSO, a monk of the Abbey of Gethsemani, was Thomas Merton's last secretary; he has edited numerous Merton works, including *The School of Charity*, the third volume of Merton's letters, and both *Run to the Mountain* and *The Other Side of the Mountain*, the first and last volumes of the Complete Journals of Thomas Merton, for which he served as general editor.

Victor A. Kramer is professor emeritus of English at Georgia State University and director of the Aquinas Center of Theology at Emory University, Atlanta; he is author of *Thomas Merton, Monk and Artist*, the founding editor of *The Merton Annual*, and editor of *Turning toward the World*, the fourth volume of Merton's journals.

Jonathan Montaldo, former director of the Thomas Merton Center at Bellarmine University, Louisville, is the eighth president of the International Thomas Merton Society and editor of *Entering the Silence*, the second volume of Merton's journals, as well as of Merton's *Dialogues with Silence: Prayers & Drawings*.

Thomasine (Tommie) O'Callaghan was a close friend of both Thomas Merton and Robert Daggy, and has served as a member of the Thomas Merton Legacy Trust since its inception in 1967. She has been a featured speaker at Merton conferences both in the United States and in Great Britain.

Patrick F. O'Connell, associate professor of English and Theology at Gannon University, Erie, PA, served as fifth president of the International Thomas Merton Society and has been editor of *The Merton Seasonal* since 1998; he is co-author of *The Thomas Merton Encyclopedia* and has edited the forthcoming *Cassian and the Fathers*, the first volume of Merton's Novitiate Conferences.

Erlinda G. Paguio, a development officer at the University of Louisville, is former treasurer and current vice president of the International Thomas Merton Society; she has written and spoken widely on Merton's spiritual roots and Merton and Eastern wisdom. She becomes the ninth president of the Merton Society in June 2003.

William H. Shannon, professor emeritus of theology at Nazareth College, Rochester, NY, and a priest of the Diocese of Rochester, served as founding president of the International Thomas Merton Society; he has written numerous books on Merton and on spirituality, is co-author of *The Thomas Merton Encyclopedia*, and edited *The Hidden Ground of Love* and *Witness to Freedom*, the first and last volumes of Merton's collected letters, for which he served as general editor.

Bonnie Thurston, an ordained minister of the Christian Church (Disciples of Christ) and formerly professor of New Testament at Pittsburgh Theological Seminary, served as third president of the International Thomas Merton Society; she is author of numerous books on scripture and on spirituality, including *Women in the New Testament* and *The Spirituality of the Early Church*.

Monica Weis, SSJ, professor of English at Nazareth College, Rochester, NY, is former vice president and current Board member of the International Thomas Merton Society and served as program chair for the ITMS fourth General Meeting. She has written and spoken widely on the theme of Merton and nature and is currently researching a book-length study of the topic.